Gustavo Gutiérrez

Gustavo Gutiérrez

An Introduction to Liberation Theology

Robert McAfee Brown

ORBIS BOOKS

Maryknoll, New York 10545

Second Printing, July 1990

The Catholic Foreign Mission Society of America (Maryknoll) recruits and trains people for overseas missionary service. Through Orbis Books, Maryknoll aims to foster the international dialogue that is essential to mission. The books published, however, reflect the opinions of their authors and are not meant to represent the official position of the society.

Manuscript editor and indexer: William E. Jerman

Library of Congress Cataloging-in-Publication Data

Brown, Robert McAfee, 1920-
    Gustavo Gutiérrez: an introduction to liberation theology /
Robert McAfee Brown.
      p. cm.
    Includes bibliographical references.
    ISBN 0-88344-597-2
    1. Gutiérrez, Gustavo, 1928-   . 2. Liberation theology.
I. Title.
BT83.57.B76   1990
230'.2'092 — dc20
                                   90-30881
                                    CIP

For
Colin, Akiyoshi, Jordan, and Caitlin
that their liberation
and the liberation of all children
may create a vision
for the rest of us

*". . . y los únicos privilegiados serán los niños"**

*". . . and the only privileged ones will be the children"

There is a little man in Peru, a man without any power, who lives in a barrio with poor people and who wrote a book. In this book he simply reclaimed the basic Christian truth that God became human to bring good news to the poor, new light to the blind, and liberty to the captives.

Ten years later this book and the movement it started is considered a danger by [the United States of America], the greatest power on earth.

When I look at this little man, Gustavo, and think about the tall Ronald Reagan, I see David standing before Goliath, again with no more weapon than a little stone, a stone called *A Theology of Liberation*.

—Henri Nouwen, *¡Gracias!*,
Harper and Row, New York, 1983
pp. 174–75

Contents

Acknowledgments

This book is a labor of love on the part of many people, even though only one name appears on the title page as author. I have despaired of trying to name them all—the list grows each day—and some must remain anonymous for their own safety's sake. I trust all of them know the extent of my gratitude, which is measureless.

Three books, however, must be mentioned. They were not available during the writing of the text, but have been invaluable in compiling the documentation, and readers who find the footnotes useful will know whom to thank. The first of these is Alfred Hennelly, ed., *Liberation Theology: A Documentary History*, Orbis, 1990. This includes all the basic primary sources, many of which have never before been available in English, along with helpful introductions and interpretations. The second is Arthur McGovern, *Liberation Theology and Its Critics*, Orbis, 1990. The author gives a detailed treatment of the development of liberation theology, interwoven with the critical assessments of its friends and foes. The book combines judicious assessment and massive documentation. The third book is Marc Ellis and Otto Maduro, eds., *The Future of Liberation Theology: Essays in Honor of Gustavo Gutiérrez*, Orbis, 1989, the *Festschrift* presented to Gustavo on his sixtieth birthday. Almost every one of the fifty essays adds to one's understanding of Gustavo and theology, as my numerous references to it will make clear. Another book, Curt Cadorette, *From the Heart of the People: The Theology of Gustavo Gutiérrez*, Meyer-Stone, Oak Park, 1988, was useful throughout the writing, giving me a feel for Gustavo in the Peruvian setting that I could not have gotten otherwise.

Over a decade ago I wrote a small paperback, *Gustavo Gutiérrez*, John Knox Press, Atlanta, 1980, published in a series called "Makers of Contemporary Theology." The book is long out of print and out of date. While the present work incorporates occasional paragraphs from the earlier one, and further elaborates the drama-imagery initially found in it, the present book is in every sense a new book, both in size and scope. Since I own the copyright on the now defunct volume, it has not seemed necessary to identify brief excerpts from it in the present text. Similarly, I have made use of material from numerous articles I have written about liberation theology in the past decade, and rather than clutter the notes with references to each of these, I have collected the various sources here, with thanks to the various publishers for permission to reprint brief passages from them:

"A Preface and a Conclusion," in Torres and Eagleson, eds., *Theology in the Americas*, Orbis, 1976; pp. ix–xxvii.

"Why Puebla Matters," *Christianity and Crisis*, September 18, 1978, pp. 207–11.

"The Significance of Puebla for the Protestant Churches in North America," in Eagleson and Scharper, eds., *Puebla and Beyond*, 1979, Orbis, pp. 330–46.

Gustavo Gutiérrez (Makers of Contemporary Theology), John Knox Press, Atlanta, 1980.

"After Ten Years," introduction to Gutiérrez, *The Power of the Poor in History*, Orbis, 1983, pp. vi–xvi.

Preface to Cabestrero, *Ministers of God, Ministers of the People: Testimonies of Faith from Nicaragua*, Orbis, 1983, pp. iv–xiv.

"Drinking from Our Own Wells," *Christian Century*, May 9, 1984, pp. 483–86.

"Espiritualidad y liberación: en favor de Gustavo Gutiérrez," *Páginas*, Separata, no. 65–66, November-December 1984, pp. 1–6 (also published as "Spirituality and Liberation: The Case for Gustavo Gutiérrez," in *Worship*, vol. 58, no. 5, September 1984, pp. 395–404).

"Liberation Theology and the Vatican: A Drama in Five Acts," *Harvard Divinity Bulletin*, April-June 1985, pp. 4–6, 10 (the Dudleian Lecture at Harvard University for 1984).

"The 'Preferential Option for the Poor' and the Renewal of Faith," in Tabb, ed., *Churches in Struggle: Liberation Theologies and Social Change in North America*, Monthly Review Press, New York, 1986, pp. 7–17.

"Recent Titles in Liberation Theology," *Quarterly Review*, vol. 6, no. 4, Winter 1986, pp. 31–42.

"The Roman Curia and Liberation Theology: The Second (and Final?) Round," *Christian Century*, June 4–11, 1986, pp. 552–54.

"Leonardo Boff: Theologian for All Christians," *Christian Century*, July 2–9, 1986, pp. 615–17.

"Liberation as Bogeyman," *Christianity and Crisis*, April 6, 1987, pp. 124–25.

"Global Realities, Local Theologies," *Christianity and Crisis*, February 13, 1988, pp. 45–46.

Spirituality and Liberation: Overcoming the Great Fallacy, Westminster Press, Philadelphia, 1988.

"How Vatican II Discovered the Bible," *National Catholic Reporter*, October 21, 1988, pp. 12–13.

"El futuro de la teología de la liberación: reflexiones de un norteamericano," *Páginas*, 93, October 1988, pp. 25–39 (also published as "The Future of Liberation Theology: Reflections of a North American," in *The Future of Liberation Theology: Essays in Honor of Gustavo Gutiérrez*, Orbis, 1989, pp. 491–501).

"Correspondence," *Commonweal*, January 27, 1989, pp. 34, 62.

Foreword to Schipani, ed., *Freedom and Discipleship: Liberation Theology in an Anabaptist Perspective*, Orbis, 1989, pp. vii–viii.

It is my intention that this book serve as an introduction *both* to Gustavo Gutiérrez and to liberation theology as a whole. I have tried to design it so that the text can stand on its own in relation to either subject, quite apart from documentation. But I have also tried to supply sufficient documentation in the back so that those who wish to pursue any of the matters discussed in more detail will have the materials at hand to do so.

Robert McAfee Brown
Palo Alto, California
Heath, Massachusetts
September 1989

Key to Abbreviations

Books by Gustavo

TheoLib	*A Theology of Liberation**
LibChange	*Liberation and Change* (with Richard Shaull)
PP	*The Power of the Poor in History*
Wells	*We Drink from Our Own Wells*
Job	*On Job: God-Talk and the Suffering of the Innocent*
Truth	*The Truth Shall Make You Free*

Other Books

Cadorette	Curt Cadorette, *From the Heart of the People*
Emergent	Sergio Torres and Virginia Fabella, eds., *The Emergent Gospel*
Festschrift	Marc Ellis and Otto Maduro, eds., *The Future of Liberation Theology*
Frontiers	Rosino Gibellini, *Frontiers of Theology in Latin America*
Geffré	Claude Geffré and Gutiérrez, eds., *The Mystical and Political Dimension of the Christian Faith*
Hennelly	Alfred T. Hennelly, *Liberation Theology: A Documentary History*
McGovern	Arthur McGovern, *Liberation Theology and Its Critics*
Puebla	John Eagleson and Philip Scharper, eds., *Puebla and Beyond*

---

*The initial page reference is always to the fifteenth anniversary edition (1988), the second to the original 1973 edition.

A Personal Note

My initial exposure to liberation theology was cerebral. I was asked by Philip Scharper of Orbis Books to do a dust jacket blurb for a book by a theologian of whom I had never heard, Gustavo Gutiérrez, on a topic of which I was totally innocent, *A Theology of Liberation*. As I turned over page after page of galley sheets in the summer of 1972, I thought, "If this is right, I have to start my theological life all over again."

The cerebral exposure took on flesh and blood a year later when our daughter Alison, fresh out of high school, began a year in Chile just three months after the bloody coup that established Pinochet in power. She shared with us what she was experiencing of both the brutality of the dictatorship and the extraordinary courage of "ordinary" Christians who were living and dying for the liberation of all oppressed peoples.

Shortly after that I attended the first "Theology in the Americas" conference at Detroit in 1975, when theologians from Latin America and North America met face to face for the first time. My conscienticizing took a quantum leap after a comment by Gonzalo Arroyo, a Chilean Jesuit, who asked the North Americans, "Tell me, why is it that when you speak of *our* theology you call it 'Latin American theology' but when you speak of *your* theology you call it 'theology'?" I realized, uncomfortably, that with the best will in the world we North Americans were identifying *our* point of view as the norm, and *their* point of view as culturally conditioned and thus in need of correction by reference to the norm. Another decade of theological existence down the drain.

But liberation theology cannot truly be communicated through books, or second-hand experiences, or conferences. It can be communicated only through human lives; a subsequent trip to South America after the above events, two later trips to Cuba, and four still later trips to Nicaragua, have provided whatever inklings I now have of its power. I see it as a "theology of the people," rather than of professional theologians; rising out of the cries of the oppressed; refined in the experience of those who may not even be able to read or write; clarified in thousands of base communities; embodied in lives that risk everything to be faithful to the good news that God hears their cry, sides with them in their distress, and works with them for liberation—a liberation in which they play a central role even while recognizing that the ultimate attainment of liberation will be God's gift.

It is out of gratitude to all of them, and to one in particular, that this book has been written.

INTRODUCTION

Arranging the Program Notes

Using the imagery of a drama to tell the interwoven story of Gustavo Gutiérrez and liberation theology is not a device imposed from the outside, but imagery consistently employed by Gutiérrez himself in describing theology as "the second act." It is not presumptuous to assume from this that a second act necessitates a first act and presupposes a third act as well. A drama also implies a script, a plot, actors and actresses, heroes, heroines and villains — all of which we shall find in abundance. It even suggests program notes that can be studied ahead of time.

Even as we employ the imagery Gutiérrez provides us, we should be clear that it is no ordinary drama we are investigating. Our conventional questions do not elicit the kinds of answers we expect.

Who is the author? The drama does not have a single author. There are many authors. The authors are actors and the actors are authors.

Where can we get a version of the script? There is no final version. The script is always being revised by those on stage, for the authors are the actors, and vice versa. See above.

In what theater is the drama being staged? It is not being staged in a theater at all, save as the entire world is a theater. It is closest of all to what we call "street theatre," and the action takes place wherever there is a combination of human need and human caring. It is an "off-Broadway" production all the way.

Who are the wealthy donors who advance the capital to underwrite the rehearsal and production costs? There are no wealthy donors. Next question.

What is the size of the advertising budget? Either nonexistent or infinite, depending on who is talking. Nobody has the resources to buy ads in the newspapers or on TV, so there is no advertising budget at all. The word gets around through the human authenticity of the actors and actresses, and their authenticity is infinite.

What do the actors and actresses do when they are not on stage? They are always "on stage." They do not play "roles," they play themselves. Anyone playing the part of a hungry person is hungry; a woman shown mourning the death of a child is mourning the death of her own child. When the militia fires bullets at demonstrators, the bullets are real. Those who are hit do not just pretend to die. They die.

Is there an intermission during the drama? Three answers. First answer: *no,* for the reason just explained—that is, the drama is unceasing. Second answer: *yes.* Just when things are toughest, somebody throws a party. Maybe the only food is rice and beans, or, alternately, beans and rice, but there is joy all over the place. Sometimes there is bread and wine that mysteriously empowers people far beyond the minimal physical nourishment provided. Third answer: *no.* Such events are not really "intermissions" at all. They are the joyful side of life that can never (so the actors and actresses affirm) be fully destroyed by the terror. Hope is greater than despair. Which, incidentally, is the theme of the drama.

So is the drama comedy or tragedy? Such categories do not mean much in this kind of theater. If we used them, we would have to say that most of the time the drama seems to be tragedy—children terrorized, women raped, lives destroyed. Nobody, watching scene after scene of such unrelieved exploitation, has the moral luxury of calling it comedy. But, quite unexpectedly, given their circumstances, those on stage claim that now and then there are real signs of hope: an evil regime finally topples, a victim refuses to exercise revenge against an enemy but offers love instead; the face of God, so often hidden, is seen for just a moment in the face of an elderly woman or a young child; hope and joy inexplicably enter at such moments, and leave all subsequent moments open to the possibility of their return.

Who are the critics? They are legion. The wealthy, who are clever enough to know which way the wind is blowing; the secure, who do not want their security challenged; armchair theologians (often "neoconservatives"), who transform the life and death struggles of others into an intellectual exercise; church people, who want the church to remain "neutral"; defenders of tradition (either politicians or church authorities) who cannot endure the risk of change; and, on a very different level, the people on stage themselves, whose capacity for *self*-criticism keeps the drama honest.

What about the audience? A curious thing happens. The members of the audience, detached and watching the action from afar, as they believe, discover that the stage is always encircling them, and whether they like it or not a moment comes when they find themselves on stage, part of the action as well, with no choice but to play the parts they play best, themselves (which is what chapter 7 is all about). That is when things begin to get interesting, for they can help to shape the outcome.

So where does the curtain rise on a stage that includes the whole world?

It does not rise first on a library where a scholar is checking references (though the scholar we will be considering does check references in libraries).

It does not rise first on a classroom where a teacher is giving a lecture (though the teacher we will be considering does give lectures in classrooms).

It does not even rise first on a church where a priest is celebrating Mass (though the priest we will be considering does celebrate Mass in church).

It rises on Ayacucho.[1]

Ayacucho is a city in Peru about two hundred miles southeast of Lima, a city, as Gutiérrez describes it, that "has been buffeted by poverty and violence." Like most of those who live in Peru, the inhabitants of the Ayacucho region are not only desperately poor to begin with, they are also victims of ongoing economic and military repression. Between 1980 and 1985, over eight thousand people died in guerilla attacks and military counterinsurgency, a reality that continues to the present day. Ayacucho is an area of corpse-filled common graves, a reality that the local dialect captures with fearful descriptive accuracy: in Quechuan it means "the corner of the dead."

All that Ayacucho is and symbolizes is at the heart of Gustavo Gutiérrez's concerns:

> How are we to do theology *while Ayacucho lasts?* How are we to speak of the God of life when cruel murder on a massive scale goes on in "the corner of the dead"? How are we to preach the love of God amid such profound contempt for human life? How are we to proclaim the resurrection of the Lord where death reigns, and especially the death of children, women, the poor, indigenes, and the "unimportant" members of our society?

Such questions are the charter of Gustavo Gutiérrez's concerns as a theologian. In all that he is and does, the people of Ayacucho are close at hand. His book, *On Job: God-Talk and the Suffering of the Innocent,* which wrestles with these questions, is dedicated first to his parents, and then

> To the people of Ayacucho who,
> like Job,
> suffer unjustly and cry out
> to the God of life.

But Ayacucho is more than just an impoverished city in the Andes. It is also a vivid symbol of the plight of the poor and exploited on every continent—replicated in Soweto, Sri Lanka, Calcutta, Manila, Haiti, Tegucigalpa, the Bronx. The common thread that unites them all beyond their differences is precisely that they are "the poor and exploited," and that in their unwelcome enslavement they cry out for liberation. A drama is being staged in the world today, and the stakes are high.

The initiators of the drama are the ones Frantz Fanon has called "the wretched of the earth." But they have made a precious discovery. They have learned that they do not need to remain that way. God did not ordain their wretchedness, despite what some of God's emissaries have told them. There are goods enough to go around, but the rich have most of them. The poor are now demanding their fair share. The rich are not willing to comply. The drama is a struggle for life. The alternative is death. The stakes are high indeed.

The struggle is increasingly referred to as the liberation struggle. It is initiated by victims of oppression who want liberation not as a theoretical concept, but as a condition of physical survival and full humanity.

The churches have a long track record of opposing liberation struggles. They tend to side with the upholders of the status quo who are enemies of liberation, those whom the oppressed call the oppressors. But in a few parts of the world, certain people within the churches are entering the drama on the side of those seeking liberation. Where this happens, theologies emerge that are called, appropriately enough, "theologies of liberation."

This book is an introduction to one such theology of liberation as it has been articulated in Latin America by Gustavo Gutiérrez. He is liberation theology's servant rather than its master. When it comes to theology, it is from the servants rather than the masters that we learn.

In the liberation struggle, neutrality is not possible. Not to support the liberation struggle of oppressed people is to contribute, by default, to their ongoing oppression. In the drama that is being waged we must take sides. With the best will in the world, many of us are on the wrong side. In the imagery of the paradigm liberation story—the exodus from Egypt—we are servants in the pharaoh's court rather than subversive agents working for the liberation of the slaves.

This is an uncomfortable discovery, and part of this book's purpose is to spread the discomfort to other servants in the pharaoh's court so that we can rethink our allegiances and priorities. Discomfort is not the last word of the gospel, but it can be an important first word, in response to which we might begin to disengage from our roles as the pharaoh's partisans. And then we could begin to hear the last word, which (in however different an accent) is the good news of liberation for us as well.

I taught on the same theological faculty with Gustavo Gutiérrez for two semesters in New York City, and we have subsequently team-taught summer courses at the Graduate Theological Union in Berkeley, California. My wife and I got to know him, both in the classroom and in our home, and later spent some days with him in Lima. These and other ongoing personal encounters—culminating in the magnificent "celebration" of his sixtieth birthday at Maryknoll School of Theology in the summer of 1988—have been important realities in my ongoing theological journey, whose direction he has drastically rerouted. For the rest of this book I will refer to him as "Gustavo," simply because everyone who knows him does so. Nothing would be less authentic in writing about this unprepossessing and humble man than to give him a title like "professor" or "doctor" or "father," or to formalize him as "Gutiérrez." He is "Gustavo," plain and simple, to all who know him.

Come along and get to know him too.

CHAPTER 1

A Collective Biography
of the Authors
of Liberation Theology

From the depths of the countries that make up Latin America a cry is rising to heaven, growing louder and more alarming all the time. It is the cry of a suffering people who demand justice, freedom, and respect for the basic rights of human beings and peoples.

A little more than ten years ago, the Medellín Conference noted this fact when it pointed out: "A muted cry wells up from millions of human beings, pleading with their pastors for a liberation that is nowhere to be found in their case."

The cry might well have seemed mute back then. Today it is loud and clear.

       —the Roman Catholic bishops at the Puebla Conference, 1979

All liberation theology originates among the world's anonymous, whoever may write the books or the declarations articulating it.

       —Gustavo, in *The Emergent Gospel,* p. 250.

Among those described today as "liberation theologians," Gustavo's name would probably head the list. There are even some who call him "the father of liberation theology." And if one were to seek a quantitative assessment—whose name appears most frequently, whose books are most widely read, who has the greatest impact—such a description might gain in plausibility. But it would falsify the reality. For even though he has written many of "the books or declarations articulating [liberation theology]," it is not his creation. He did not return from a European theological education and decide to create a "theology for the masses." He found, instead, that the new stirrings in Latin America were coming not from the professors and professional theologians and church leaders, but from those whom Gustavo refers to above as "the world's anonymous." In the midst of their anonymity,

1

they have given birth to a new way of seeing the world, and a new way of acting within the world, for the purpose of changing it.

To oversimplify, Gustavo and others like him live with "the world's anonymous," share in their perplexities, participate in their discussions and actions, and then, because of their training, are able to record and transmit accounts of what is going on, accounts that reach us in the form of books or articles. And it is out of this kind of mix of everyday people and special circumstances that liberation theology is born and reborn.

Consequently, if one wants to write about Gustavo and liberation theology, one can do so authentically only by writing also about those who preceded him and those with whom he presently lives and works. To isolate him, to put him in an academic setting, to present him as a detached thinker, would be to falsify from the start.[1]

A Basic Conflict: *Los Conquistadores* vs. Las Casas[2]

In response to the received wisdom that "Columbus discovered America in 1492," Enrique Dussel, one of the foremost historians of the church in Latin America, has commented that Latin America was "discovered" about 20,000 years earlier when certain Asians ventured across the Bering Straits to a new landmass and started working their way south. About 19,500 years later, they were invaded by the Spaniards. . . .

Whether said tongue-in-cheek or not, the comment tells us something important: life and culture did not begin in Latin America when so-called Western civilization first appeared in the Andes and along the Amazon. There were already many long-established cultures, and in order to gain possession of the land, the Spaniards and Portuguese (and later the North Americans and Europeans) had to fight and decimate an indigenous population that had been there for millennia.

The sixteenth-century Spanish conquistadores were just that, "conquerors" rather than explorers or neighbors. They pillaged, raped, shot, and subjugated whatever indigenes stood between them and the gold they wanted to take back to Spain. To them, the Amerindians were subhuman, objects who could be swindled in trading, manipulated as cheap labor, and killed if recalcitrant. They might have gotten away with it and completed a continental genocide, if there had not been another Spaniard, Bartolomé de Las Casas (1474-1566), a Dominican priest active in Latin America. With mounting conviction, Las Casas began to oppose his fellow countrymen and take the side of the Amerindians. It would be fair to describe him as "the first liberation theologian," unless that honor should be reserved for Jesús de Nazarét.

Gustavo has been instrumental in the contemporary rediscovery of Las Casas. Some of the reasons for Las Casas's importance today can be indicated by a brief summary of convictions he argued against the conquistadores and the Spanish royal court, in an effort to stop the ravages of the Spaniards against the Amerindians:

1. Las Casas affirmed that there was a close link between salvation and social justice, asserting that to the degree that the Spaniards exploited the Amerindians, their own salvation was jeopardized. "It is impossible for someone to be saved, if he does not observe justice."

2. Instead of seeing the Amerindians as "infidels," Las Casas saw them as "the poor" about whom the gospel speaks so centrally. They should not be threatened with death if they do not convert—a necessary warning, for the Spaniards felt justified in killing Amerindians who remained "infidels." In the face of this widespread injustice, Las Casas made a devastating response: it is better to be "a live Indian, even though infidel" than "a dead Indian, even though Christian."

3. Las Casas judged the theologies of his opponents by their political consequences; theologies that lead to murder and enslavement invalidate their claim to be Christian.

4. Las Casas's own method of theological reflection began with the specific case of exploited Amerindians, rather than with abstract principles from which "applications" could be deduced. (Sepúlveda, his chief theological opponent in Spain, began with an Aristotelian principle that Amerindians were "naturally inferior" to whites and could therefore be enslaved.)

5. Las Casas theologized as a participant in the struggle between the conquistadores and the Amerindians, rather than as an outside spectator who could deal with their fate in purely intellectual terms.

6. In the midst of the Amerindian plight, Las Casas heard Jesus Christ speaking directly to him. "In the Indies I left behind Jesus Christ, our God, suffering affliction, scourging, and crucifixion, not once but a million times over." It was Las Casas's view, Gustavo concludes, that "in and through the 'scourged Christ of the Indies,' Jesus is denouncing exploitation, denying the Christianity of the exploiters, and calling people to understand and heed his gospel message."

All six concerns have their counterparts in contemporary liberation theology.

Varieties of Colonialism and "a Rich Church"

Because there were not enough emulators of Bartolomé de Las Casas in the sixteenth century, the dominant control of Latin America in succeeding centuries remained firmly in the hands of Spaniards and other Europeans, rather than Amerindians. Colonialism became the order of the day as the invaders appropriated the land, the wealth, and the power. The various countries were looked upon as "colonies"—that is, outposts of empires far away, rather than nations able to rule themselves. This domination was initially exercised as *political colonialism*: all power—most notably the deployment of the economic resources and riches that the colonies produced—was taken over regardless of the interests of local populations.

By the nineteenth century, however, the indigenous and mixed populations of Latin America had acquired enough sense of their own identity to begin to wage wars of independence from European rule. These uprisings and revolutions were widespread enough and successful enough that political colonialism, in the sense of *overt* control from outside, was overcome.

But the victories turned out to be more apparent than real, for the overthrow of political colonialism did not secure real freedom; what came to be called *economic colonialism* took its place. The shift was from overt to *covert* control from outside; the real hold of Europe over Latin America was economic, and this persisted just below the facade of apparent political disengagement. Economic manipulators from abroad joined forces with indigenous manipulators at home, to continue the exploitation of the many by the few. The ostensible leaders in the Latin American countries were, to be sure, Argentinians, Paraguayans, Peruvians, Brazilians, but they were more beholden to outside forces than to their own citizenry. The indigenous leaders themselves did very well under this arrangement, and created alliances with military forces that enabled both groups to prosper and stay in power.

The net result was a society in which a few were very rich and powerful (their riches and power guaranteed by guns supplied from overseas), while the rest were very poor and powerless (their plight seeming hopeless and without possibility of change). To protest this state of affairs was to ensure one's own annihilation.

During these developments, the church became increasingly identified with the rich and powerful, who saw that religion was a good thing, useful in keeping the masses submissive through promises of an eternal reward in heaven if they made no trouble on earth. And it went hand in glove with a theory of the divine right of rulers over subjects—a European legacy that also brooked no uprisings from below and assured divine sanction for the status quo.

It was a good arrangement for the rich, and a good arrangement for the church, which became not only a church of the rich, but a rich church as well. It was a bad arrangement for the poor.

Transition: Two Views of the Crucifix

The omnipresent Christian symbol in Latin America is the crucifix—the bleeding and dying Christ nailed to a cross. It is found in virtually every home, every village square, every church and chapel, every cemetery, every crossroads, and on almost every hairy chest. What is its message? Beyond the individualistic and "religious" message that Jesus is atoning for the sin of the world and that belief in him can help the sinner secure eternal redemption, there has been a "political" message as well. It goes like this:

"You see the resignation and acceptance on the face of the Son of God in his moment of greatest suffering? He knows that it is the Father's will that he die this way, and so he gives himself, uncomplaining, in utter trust and love, assured that after these brief moments of suffering he will be in paradise forever. Is he complaining to God? Is he challenging Herod and Pilate who put him there? Is he trying to change society? Is he agitating among the poor for a redistribution of wealth or a new social order? Is he wishing he had a gun so that he could destroy his oppressors?

"Of course not! He knows that God knows best. So instead of turning aside from God's plan, he accepts it and plays his assigned role.

"This is a picture of how we are to bear *our* suffering, accepting it without complaint as God's will, just as Jesus did. Who are we to know more than God, or to challenge what God decrees? If it is God's will for us to be poor, we are to accept it without complaint. Who are we, whose pain is so small by comparison, to refuse to bear whatever pain God sends us while we live on earth? The joys of paradise will be so great that nothing we endure here below is too much to bear for the sake of what we will know on high, when God calls us back to our reward."

For centuries, the church taught such acquiescence, passivity, and resignation in the face of poverty and injustice — a political message that the rulers and the rich found ideally suited for keeping the masses docile.

But that is by no means the universally received opinion today. New voices are being heard as they, too, reflect on the meaning of Jesus' death, and as they, too, propound a message that has "political" import, but of a very different sort:

"You see the terrible thing that is happening to Jesus? He who came to teach us to love one another, and who always acted toward us in love, is being killed for thinking such thoughts and doing such deeds. What a terrible thing that this should happen! What a terrible thing that Jesus should continue to be crucified in his brothers and sisters today! If we love Jesus, we must find out who is doing this to him and put a stop to it, for people will continue to kill Jesus every time they kill those who try to follow him today by loving their neighbors and working to create a better world. We must work to see that torture and death of this sort are not the lot of *any* persons in God's world. We must create a society in which no one is crucified or harmed as Jesus was. That will be one way we can thank him for his great love for us."

Here is a different "religious" message that carries a very different "political" message, and suggests that the two cannot be separated. It speaks of outrage rather than acquiescence, commitment to change rather than acceptance of the unchanging, engagement rather than detachment.

Changes Sparked from Inside: The "Situation" and the Bible

How did such a change begin to come about? We can distinguish a few threads involved in weaving a new pattern.

One reason for change is that life becomes so intolerable that people will no longer accept it passively, regardless of the odds against bringing about change for the better. Outrage can no longer be contained, particularly when those being victimized are ones' families and friends. It needs little arguing that the situation for the great majority of those in Latin America had been intolerable for centuries.

We have already noted that the church, by its complicity with the ruling and corrupt powers, was on the side of injustice. And because the church is a hierarchical institution, changes "from below" were not likely. Even so, however, there began to be an increasing number of priests and religious, along with "the world's anonymous" and even an occasional bishop, who started moving in new directions.

Many became dissatisfied at serving in conventional parishes, administering just enough "charity" to defuse whatever revolutionary zeal the poor might otherwise have developed, and began to identify more directly with the poor. For some this represented a literal "conversion"—that is, being "turned around" to identify no longer with the rich but with the poor. As they read their Bibles alongside the poor (new experiences for many of them), they concluded that it was by and for just such people that the Bible had originally been written. Read from that perspective, the clear biblical message was "good news *to the poor,*" as Jesus had said in the first public setting out of his agenda in a synagogue in Nazareth. (Luke 4:16-30 contains the whole subversive account.)

Until the second half of the twentieth century, the Bible was not an important or even accessible book for most Latin American Catholics. Many of them could not read anyhow, and the rest had a carefully selected handful of scriptural rationalizations for the status quo ("the poor you have always with you" was a favorite) and felt no qualms about the poverty just beyond their doorsteps. Christian instruction came through the Mass and private devotional exercises, and concern for the poor was not high in such activities. But when the Bible began to be available, partly through a resurgence of Catholic biblical scholarship, and when people began to study it together, surprise followed surprise. Who had ever thought that religion, instead of just being about heaven, was also about earth? Who had envisioned an earth where there would be "liberation for the oppressed," and "freedom for captives"—to cite two further portions of Jesus' agenda. Such a message, from the very lips of the Son of God himself, had revolutionary implications never before entertained.[3]

It was soon apparent that "good news to the poor" could only, initially at least, be "bad news to the rich," who could be held accountable for thwarting, subverting, and denying the message. Moreover, current social structures that benefitted the rich (such as ownership of huge landed estates, the practice of paying starvation wages or less, not to mention active liquidation of "labor organizers") were continuing to destroy the poor. So part of the "good news to the poor" meant opposing structures that benefitted only the rich. Which meant "taking sides." Which meant politics. Which meant organizing. Which might mean, not too far down the road, revolution. . . .

The rich responded that this was dirty pool. The church was "taking sides," and that was not fair. The church was supposed to be above such mundane squabbles, preaching eternal verities and offering access to heaven for those who knew their place on earth. Not so, responded the gradually growing handful captured by the new vision. The church was not suddenly "taking sides," it was only in process of "changing sides." It had always been on the side of the rich, with no noticeable complaints from the rich. Now it was going to be on the side of the poor, for that was the mandate of the newly discovered gospel.

Changes Sparked from Outside: The "Social Encyclicals" and the Vatican Council

The unacceptability of the present situation, and the discovery of a biblical message challenging that situation, became potential catalysts for change. But were these anything more than subjective impressions, powerful in emotional appeal, but lacking direct authority? Biblical materials are notoriously susceptible to being twisted in ways that do not reflect official church teaching.

At this juncture, a new resource appeared, or rather an "old" resource that had been overlooked. This resource was a series of "social encyclicals," beginning in 1891, that demonstrated an increasing convergence between papal teaching and the concerns now being openly discussed in Latin America. Although the story of the encyclicals is too long to tell here, the substance is that through these papal letters the church began inching its way into the modern world, more and more seen from the point of view of the oppressed.[4]

Early on, there were routine condemnations of "atheistic communism" and criticisms of Catholics who were soft on socialism. But even in the first social encyclical, *Rerum Novarum* (1891), there are condemnations of the inhuman conditions under which workers earn their daily bread, attacks on the callousness of employers, and warnings about "the greed of unrestrained competition." The few, Leo XIII concludes, have too much power over the many. Yet more: "workers must share in the benefits they create." *Quadragesimo Anno* (1931), issued by Piux XI, is critical of "the right of private property," which cannot be deemed absolute. The pope includes harsh admonitions against capitalists who make excessive profits and provide minimum subsistence or less for their workers. Criteria for a "just wage" are introduced, for it is too important to be left solely to the discretion of owners. While strictures against socialism are still strong, a new position, "mitigated socialism," is described as having some affinity with Christian principles.

In John XXIII's two encyclicals, *Mater et Magistra* (1961) and *Pacem in Terris* (1963), and even more in Paul VI's *Populorum Progressio* (1967), the trend toward openness, especially toward socialism, continues. By 1971 the mood has become so open that Paul VI, in an "apostolic letter" to Cardinal Roy, *Octogesima Adveniens,* urges that if Christians are going to be socialists, there are some considerations they should ponder. The blanket condemnations have disappeared.

Another resource for those seeking change in Latin America was the whole ethos, and some of the specific documents, of the Second Vatican Council, convened in Rome from 1962 through 1965, and attended by all the bishops of the Roman Catholic world.[5] The very calling of the council was an indication by Pope John XXIII of the need for the church to enter the modern world, and an acknowledgment that "change" was in the air. And although most of the council documents dealt with internal matters in the church's life, the longest of them, *Gaudium et Spes* (The Church and the World Today), grapples directly with problems of social injustice that had been high on the Latin American list for years. Criticism of certain socialist and communist practices is linked with equally powerful criticism of abuses of capitalism, such as "excessive desire for profit." Full support is given to the right to form labor unions and to strike, and the traditional right of private ownership is balanced by attention to "the *right* inherent in various forms of *public* ownership."

The spirit of the document—and of the council—can best be communicated by one extended quotation rather than further paraphrase:

Persons should regard their lawful possessions not merely as their own but also as common property in the sense that they should accrue to the benefit not only of themselves but of others.

For the rest, the right to have a share of earthly goods sufficient for oneself and one's family belongs to everyone. The Fathers and Doctors of the Church held this view, teaching that persons are obliged to come to the relief of the poor, and to do so not merely out of their superfluous goods. If a person is in extreme necessity, such a one has the right to take from the riches of others what he or she needs. . . .

According to their ability, let all individuals and governments undertake a genuine sharing of their goods. Let them use these goods especially to provide individuals and nations with the means for helping and developing themselves [*The Church and the World Today,* § 69].

New winds are blowing.

Storm Clouds: The "National Security State" and the Witness of Martyrs

To those within these new movements, the "new winds" were clearly the breath of the Holy Spirit. But to others they represented more evidence that the privileges and power of the wealthy were under assault. Inasmuch as those with power will do whatever is necessary to retain it, another force emerged in Latin America, identified by the term *seguridad nacional,* the philosophy of "national security."[6] The more the churches began to side with the poor, the more they charted a collision course with the philosophy of "national security." Its chief characteristics are these:

1. The state is *an end in itself,* and its triumph over other states — all of which potentially threaten it — is the reason for its existence. The state does not exist for the welfare of the people; the people exist for the welfare of the state.

2. The human condition is one of *perpetual warfare.* "Peace" is only an interlude to regroup for further conflict, a temporary waging of war by other means. The vigilance of the state against inner challenge and criticism must be especially strong in times of "peace."

3. Because the survival of the state is the absolute goal, *any means can be employed to ensure survival.* It is an act of good citizenship to "inform" on friends or neighbors whose motives or actions appear suspect. The "secret police" naturally keep a file on all such persons, and those who think or act in strange ways can be tortured to extract information.

4. Enforcement of the law in the national security state is entrusted to *the military.* The military is either overtly in charge or covertly behind civilian politicians whose tenure in office is directly proportional to their subservience to the military's wishes.

5. The universal enemy is *communism,* which means any idea or movement that threatens the power of the national security state. Any challenge, internal or external, is "communistic," and any opponent of the state is automatically a "communist."

6. Because *the church* has a direct stake in the survival of the national security state as a condition of its own survival, the church must be uncritically pro-state and anti-communist.

This is as blatant a challenge to individual and collective freedom as one could imagine, and the widespread adoption of this perspective in Latin America has meant dark days and fearful nights for the church and for individuals. Here we note the consequences for individuals, and will explore the response of the church in chapter 5.

For individuals who oppose it, the consequence of the philosophy of the "national security state" is *martyrdom.*

And here the mood must change. How can one write dispassionately or analytically about martyrdom? To do so is to betray the martyred and reduce them to statistics. Even to write about "martyrdom" is misleading, for a reality is reduced to a concept. One must write about "martyrs," persons in their own right, not examples of a concept.

But how, on the other hand, can one write passionately about martyrs? To do so is to make a futile attempt to reduce the distance between the dying person and the printed page. That distance remains so vast that the very effort to bridge it trivializes the sacrifices of the dead.

There is a roll call of the martyred in Latin America, and it is very long. The names themselves may mean little to readers thousands of miles from the scenes of the killings, but they can at least remind us that the names have infinite meaning for those near at hand: Raoul was a brother, a son, a husband, who founded an agricultural cooperative and thus showed himself to be a communist; María was a mother, a daughter, an aunt, who worked at a clinic and thus showed herself to be a communist; Rutilio was a priest, a son, an uncle, a trusted leader of the poor who thus showed himself to be a communist; Anna, childless, was head of the infant care center, surrogate mother to sixty orphans, who thus showed herself to be a communist.

And there are those whose names we do not know and will never know, those who simply "disappeared" and have never been found or heard from; or those known in tiny villages but not elsewhere, for whom there will never be a public record of their sacrifice, and whose only private record will be the ache in the hearts of those who have no way to share the story.

These martyrs—thousands of them over the last two decades—whatever the differences in their stories, share one thing in common: they all committed the same crime. They were killed because *they dared to challenge the system.* They dared to argue that starving children should have food; that peasants should be able to farm their own land; that the gospel should mean education and uncontaminated drinking water here and now, and not only bliss and purity in heaven; that workers should be able to organize in order to receive their fair share of the world's goods.

Such claims—which threaten the system to its core—are dealt with appropriately in the national security state: their proponents are simply denounced by the authorities as "communists." To the interlocking board of directors that maintains the system, "communists" are fair game for *civilian* authorities to imprison and torture, natural targets for *military* authorities to shoot on sight, and "godless agitators" for *church* authorities to impugn.

But all the authorities have made one massive miscalculation. They have forgotten that the creation of martyrs does not extinguish the resolve of those dedicated to the liberation struggle. On the contrary, it stiffens it. Liberation logic does not go, "Pablo has been shot, therefore I must give up the struggle or I will be shot too." It goes, "Pablo has been shot, therefore I must take his place."

It was said many centuries ago that "the blood of martyrs is the seed of the church." That is not a slogan in Latin America today. It is a statement of plain fact.

The Breakthrough: Medellín 1968[7]

In 1955 there was founded CELAM, the Consejo Episcopal Latinoamericano (the Episcopal Council of Latin America). A gathering of all the bishops of Latin America was held that year under the leadership of the enterprising Cardinal Larraín of Chile. Not a great deal of consequence emerged from the meetings, but a structure was in place; when the time was ripe, there was to be another series of meetings out of which a great deal of consequence emerged. For after Vatican II it was mandated that regional conferences of bishops be held to relate the council to problems in their own areas.

Medellín, Colombia, became the scene for a second convening of CELAM in 1968 to discuss "The Church in the Present-Day Transformation of Latin America in the Light of the Council." In the course of the meetings the title was de facto reversed: the real agenda became "The Present-Day Transformation of the Council in the Light of Latin America." That is to say, the council, viewed through Latin American eyes, had a different message than the one originally perceived in Rome when the council adjourned. For the council's "universal" themes were couched in very European terms—a fact not lost on the Latin American bishops, who proceeded at Medellín to build on the council's statements in such a way that the Latin American scene would itself be subject to transformation. "Medellín" has become a symbol of these new directions. And while the city itself is chiefly known today for its coffee and orchids and cocaine traffic, its enduring claim may well be that it was the site of the conference that initiated a revolution in Latin American church life that will finally mean a revolution in Latin American history.

Medellín and Vatican II each produced sixteen documents. Some of the documents are eminently forgettable, but a few deserve to be memorized. The Medellín documents "Peace," "Justice," "Poverty," and "Education" are the most enduring (four out of sixteen is a very high batting average for corporate episcopal prose), and we will use the document "Peace" to sample the bishops' concerns, not only because it is typical of the rest but because the fine hand of Gustavo, who was at Medellín as a "theological expert," can be detected within it.

The very structure of the document (and, indeed, of all the Medellín documents) presages a new theological method to be examined in chapter 4. The sequence is (a) an analysis of the actual situation in Latin America, followed (b) by doctrinal reflection, and completed (c) by pastoral conclusions.

1. The *analysis* of the situation describes "an unjust situation that promotes tensions that conspire against peace." There are *class tensions,* the

result of "internal colonialism," based on the marginalization of many groups and the radical disparity and inequality between rich and poor. All "rising expectations" of the disadvantaged are blocked by those with power. Not only are the powerful insensitive to the misery of others, but they make "use of force to repress drastically any attempt at opposition." The usual ways of keeping things from changing are crusades against "communism" and in defense of "order."

The inner class tensions are exacerbated by *international tensions*. Because Latin American nations are dependent on foreign powers for their economic survival, this leads to the economic domination called "economic colonialism," which is alive and well throughout the continent. It is a characterization of the system that "the countries that produce raw materials ... always remain poor, while the industrialized countries enrich themselves," imbalances that are only made worse by the rapid flight of capital overseas.

2. In the light of this unjust situation, the document then deals with *doctrinal reflection*, centering, not unnaturally, on "peace" and the presence of violence. Peace is linked with justice and the creation of a society in which persons will not be objects but can be subjects, creating their own history rather than being pawns in someone else's hands. Peace "is not the simple absence of violence and bloodshed." The maintenance of law and order may give the illusion of peace, but what is really present is (in the words of Paul VI), the "continuous and inevitable seed of rebellion and war."

This lays the groundwork for an important discussion of violence. After necessary cautions about not glorifying violence and always preferring peace to war, the bishops (drawing again on Paul VI) develop the notion of "institutionalized violence":

> Because of a structural deficiency of industry and agriculture, of national and international economy, of cultural and political life, "whole towns lack necessities, live in such dependence as hinders all initiative and responsibility as well as every possibility for cultural promotion and participation in social and political life," thus violating fundamental rights [Medellín, "Peace," § 16].

The new realization is that the situation is *already violent*, even when there is no overt conflict. Social injustice is ongoing violence against its victims.

The bishops press their analysis to ask who is responsible for ongoing "institutional violence" against the powerless. They do not mince words: it is "those who have a greater share of wealth, culture, and power," who are the real perpetrators of violence. Not only that, "if they jealously retain their privileges, and defend them through violence, they are responsible to history for provoking 'explosive revolutions of despair.'" Furthermore, those who remain on the sidelines as spectators are also culpable for ongoing violence.

3. Out of this hard-hitting analysis and series of doctrinal reflections, a number of *pastoral conclusions* are offered, including a call (a) to defend the rights of the oppressed, (b) to achieve "a healthy critical sense of the social situation," (c) to develop "grass-roots organizations" [base communities], (d) to demand "just prices for our raw materials," and (e) "to denounce the unjust action of world powers that works against the self-determination of weaker nations."

Here, then, is a new way of looking at the world, reflecting on what is seen, and offering specific suggestions for dealing with an accumulation of wrongs. Medellín has become known as the conference in which the church chose to stand with the oppressed, attacked the political and economic structures of Latin America as purveyors of injustice, pointed out the unjust dependency of Latin America on outside powers, and called for radical change across the continent. Medellín saw clearly that the present order guarantees that the rich will grow richer at the expense of the poor, with the inevitable result that the poor will grow poorer in relation to the rich. And the bishops refused any longer to bless such an order. A breakthrough, indeed.

Three further realities beginning to appear before Medellín convened were stronger when it adjourned. Each will be treated in detail in later chapters.

One reality was the extraordinary growth of the *comunidades de base,* the base communities that were surfacing before Medellín and got sufficient support at Medellín to sweep like a prairie fire across the continent afterward. There may be as many as 100,000 such communities today. The late Penny Lernoux, one of the best reporters on the Latin American church, suggested there may be as many as 300,000. Gustavo is more cautious. For him, "100,000" translates into "many, many groups, how many we do not know." Numbers aside, they have become the lifeblood of the Latin American church, Penny Lernoux commented on their spread in Brazil:

> As the early base communities were organized, the Brazilian bishops had seen them as a means of converting the poor. By the end of the seventies, the poor had converted the Brazilian church ["Transforming Latin America," *Maryknoll,* July 1988, p. 16].

A *second* reality just beginning to emerge before Medellín and energized by it was *liberation theology.* As we will see in chapter 2, it was at a conference just a few weeks before Medellín that Gustavo first spoke of a comprehensive new viewpoint he called "a theology of liberation." Thanks to his presence at Medellín, many of the concerns of a liberation perspective made their way into the documents. In addition, liberation theology and the base communities had a symbiotic effect on one another; each was strengthened by the other.

A *third* reality was *flak,* what the dictionary calls "strong, clamorous criticism and opposition." Waive the question of whether the bishops really knew the far-reaching consequences of the documents they signed. The fact is that the documents were signed, sealed, and delivered by CELAM, and large throngs were waiting to run with them. As a result, the decade following Medellín was not only a time of exciting advance in the liberation struggle, but a time of frantic regrouping by conservatives determined to reverse the direction Medellín had given the church.

More Storm Clouds: Opposition at Home and Abroad

So a funny thing was happening to the church on its way to the people, but the leaders were not amused. It was time to close ranks.

No one who surveys the history of the church between CELAM II (Medellín 1968) and CELAM III (Puebla 1979) will ever be tempted to claim that church life is dull. Medellín had come as a surprise, and its concerns were broadcast to a church and continent not yet attuned to them. But as the base communities flourished, the conservative forces had to marshal their resources to confront a patent challenge to old patterns of authority and placid acquiesence to the status quo. And the growth of a more self-conscious movement known as liberation theology—with its stress on empowering the poor and advocating militant involvement in the body politic—served notice that new forces were on the scene that must be immediately contained if they were not to undo all the received patterns of Latin American life. The conservatives swung into action.

The new general secretary of CELAM, Archbishop Alfonso López Trujillo, and his assistant, Belgian Jesuit Roger Vekemans, both conservatives, not only sponsored conferences and issued communiqués attacking liberation theology, but began to lay groundwork for a subsequent meeting of CELAM that would reverse the consequences of Medellín. The tone of these activities can be surmised from a figure of speech employed by Vekemans: "The actual expansion [of liberation theology] occurs like the spread of a contagious disease, through which the carriers of the bacillus are multiplied."

An example of the alternative to liberation theology that López commended to the church can be gathered from his book *Liberation or Revolution?*, terms that he considered mutually exclusive.[8] Instead of a priest exploring socialist options, radical change, or politicization, "the church wants the priest . . . to renounce all this in order to teach profound values." By teaching "profound values," priests will enable people to approach them "in confidence, secure in the knowledge that they are not going to receive new burdens brought about by divergences in political systems, models, and programs."

López acknowledges that liberation has become "a fashionable issue," "a new fad," appealing to those who are "easy prey of vindictive men of violent inclinations." What he calls "true liberation," however, can have permanent value, if salvaged from politics. The key is to distinguish absolutely between a Christian and a Marxist viewpoint. An "authentic theology of liberation" must be separated from one that is merely "an emotional pretext for plotting a social revolution," replacing the evangelical vision with a political one, substituting Marx for Christ, appealing to the use of violence "without discrimination," and leading people to "intoxication with the struggle." (The degree of López's own sensitivity to the struggle can be gauged by his description of Martin Luther King, Jr., as "the black man with a white soul.")

About half the book is rebuttal of a document produced by priests in Lima. López fears that those who wrote it were infected by exposure to "the troubled waters of the universities" and influenced by "Christians for Socialism" documents produced in Chile. López does not believe "the Church today should abandon its neutrality and become a promoter of new systems." On the contrary, he believes that *"the political neutrality of the church* is a mandatory condition for protecting pastoral independence" (italics added). The church is a "mother," not a "midwife for revolution"; it is a "mansion for dialogue," where all are welcome (torturers, apparently, as well as the tortured).

López rejects the notion that one can accept a Marxist analysis of society without accepting the whole Marxist worldview. He feels that liberation theologians have fallen into this trap. Although he avers that "strictly speaking, we cannot claim that these priest leaders are Marxist," he goes on to insist that the real danger confronting the church today is "Marxist penetration."

López's program is clear and speaks for itself. He resists any commitment to the poor that would threaten existing structures, challenge existing governments, or involve the church in "taking sides." Only by remaining "neutral"—the unchallenged home of dictator and dispossessed, executioner and victim, exploiter and exploited, well-fed and starving—can the church fulfill its mission.

As the preparations for CELAM III proceeded, the Costa Rican Ecumenical Council, among others, charged that López was guilty of "the manipulation of CELAM." The charge was based on the abusive literature being disseminated, the filling of high leadership posts with conservatives, the deliberate exclusion from planning sessions of any theologians tarred with the brush of liberation concerns, and a decision that "theological advisors" would have no official access to the bishops' meetings.

The major attempt by López and his associates to predetermine the agenda for Puebla was a long "Preliminary Document" purporting to define the appropriate issues for episcopal discussions and the appropriate conclusions to reach. It was circulated throughout Latin America for comment and response, as a gesture toward "involving the grassroots." The gesture backfired spectacularly, for the Preliminary Document was universally repudiated. Reasons: It had not arisen out of the Latin American experience. It was an "academic" European-style document, which is not surprising for López had drafted Europeans and European-trained theologians to supervise its creation. It "spiritualized" the reality of poverty so that steps to confront it were not needed. It dealt with "national security" in abstract terms, and hardly mentioned the reality of martyrdom. After giving multinational corporations a polite slap on the wrist, it thanked them for having improved wages and working conditions.[9]

Alternative drafts for consideration flooded the CELAM office. The continent had been alerted. Now the bishops were being alerted.

Concurrently, a Roman Catholic international theological commission issued a report on liberation theology that was expected to be negative, but which, while it did not wildly embrace liberation theology, certainly did not anathematize it. This added fuel to the polemical flames on both sides.

As the time for Puebla neared, López, sensing a possible loss of control, asked Rome to appoint supplementary bishops (with vote), and the request was granted. His fear was that Medellín, rather than being repudiated, might be reaffirmed, a consequence he wanted at whatever cost to forestall.

The conference, originally scheduled for 1978, had to be postponed due to the death of Paul VI, and his successor, John Paul I, who died after only thirty-three days in office. But under John Paul II the conference was rescheduled for January 1979. The stage was set for a showdown.

Reinforcing the Breakthrough: Puebla 1979[10]

The attempts at what the Costa Ricans called "manipulation" did not cease once the conference began. The bishops were housed in a seminary, Palifoxiano, to which the liberation theologians could not gain access. Thus insulated from what Roger Vekemans had called the "contagious disease," the bishops were presumably to follow the script created in advance by López.

But although the theologians could not get into Palifoxiano, the bishops could get out, and those of a more liberal bent found their way to a rented house where the excluded liberation theologians had set up shop for the duration. The bishops were thus able to take into the official meetings proposed drafts for many portions of the final document, many of which were actually adopted.

The major event as far as the outside world was concerned was the presence of the newly-elected pope, who received a tumultuous welcome from the people of Mexico. His opening address was a carefully crafted papal utterance, giving encouragement to most and suggestions to all, but without a strong polemical bent. The *New York Times* reported the speech as a condemnation of liberation theology, which it was not. (In the ethos of Puebla, partisans of liberation concerns soon realized that "not to be condemned" was a victory.)

Far more important than his inaugural address were later speeches given by the pope in other parts of Mexico. Particularly notable was a speech to the Indians of Oaxaca and Chiapas, a speech interlaced with concern for the poor:

> [The poor] have a right to effective help, which is neither a handout nor a few crumbs of justice, so that they may have access to the development that their dignity as human beings and as children of God merits. . . . *There is always a social mortgage on all private property,* so that goods may serve the general assignment that God has given them. And if the common good demands it, there is no need to hesitate at expropriation itself, done in the right way [in *Puebla and Beyond,* p. 82, italics added].

The pope went on to speak directly to the "responsible officials of the people," describing them as:

> power-holding classes who sometimes keep your lands unproductive when they conceal the food that so many families are doing without. The human conscience, the conscience of the peoples, the cry of the destitute, and above all the voice of God and the Church join me in reiterating to you that it is not just, it is not human, it is not Christian, to continue certain situations that are clearly unjust. You must implement real, effective measures on the political, national, and international levels [ibid, p. 83].

The papal track record on such matters is far from consistent, but on this occasion, at least, the concerns of those struggling for liberation were given papal reinforcement.

The final document of Puebla is long and diffuse, and its reflections on the social scene, its doctrinal portions, and its pastoral admonitions (following the Medellín methodology) often contain internal contradictions. But as always in such situations, the "meaning" of the document is not measured by the text itself but by the subsequent *use* of the text. While it is regrettable that the reality of martyrdom is not more significantly highlighted, there are new recognitions of the gravity of the political and economic situation, and there are new emphases, such as recognition of the rights of indigenous peoples and the rights of women, who are described as those "doubly oppressed."

Despite the ambiguities, some important themes are highlighted, which reinforce Medellín at crucial points. Their presence is a tribute to the fact that liberation concerns were not, as López and his coterie had hoped, repudiated, but gained new prominence by the very fact that pressures to repudiate them failed. Three emphases (all to be developed more fully in later chapters) deserve brief mention here:

1. The conservatives wanted very much to clip the wings of the *base communities,* which they perceived not only as hotbeds of radical thought and action, but as threats to the authority structure of the church. Cardinal Baggio in Rome had been entrusted with trying to bring about condemnations. He did not succeed. While there were some strictures on the activities of the communities apart from participation of priests and the oversight of bishops, support for the communities is overwhelming in the document. Whereas at Medellín the base communities were just beginning, "they now are one of the causes for joy and hope in the church" (§ 96). "The multiplication of small communities [is] an important ecclesial event that is peculiarly ours, and [is] the 'hope of the church'" (§ 629). In a few places there is apprehension that the communities will succumb to a "secularized milieu" or "the loss of an authentic ecclesial sense" (§ 627) but these are notes of warning in otherwise supportive texts.

2. The rise of the philosophy of *national security* has already been noted. And although the Preliminary Document tried to soft-pedal this menace, the final document was relentless in condemning it. The bishops refused to accept the role the church was supposed to play: "don't rock the boat, don't question, don't complain, teach the people to be passive, accept military authority." The bishops rose to significant new heights in the reports of three different commissions. One example:

> [National Security] enrolls the individual in unlimited service in the alleged total war against cultural, social, political, and economic strife – and thereby against the threat of communism. In the face of this permanent danger, be it real or merely possible, individual freedoms are restricted as they are in any emergency situation, and the will of the State is confused with the will of the nation. Economic development and the potential to wage war are given priority over the dire needs of the neglected masses. Now National Security is certainly necessary to any political organization. But when framed in these terms, it presents itself as an Absolute holding sway over persons; in its name the insecurity of the individual becomes institutionalized [§ 314].

3. The theme that unifies the Puebla document (the "core" of the declaration, as Jon Sobrino and others have pointed out) is the attention given to *the preferential option for the poor.* The document recognizes that the situation of the poor is much worse than it was ten years ago, when the bishops last met, and gives attention to the plight of women in a way the church had not previously done. The new fact, of which the church must take account, is that the poor, rather than remaining passive, "have begun to organize themselves to live their faith in an integral way, and hence to

reclaim their rights" (§ 1137). The church has not been supportive enough in the past and must identify more clearly with the poor in the future.

A pivotal (and frequently overlooked) statement from Vatican II is invoked so that "concern for the poor" will not be understood as charity from the haves to the have-nots:

> The demands of justice should first be satisfied, lest the giving of what is due in justice be represented as the offering of a charitable gift. Not only the effects but also the causes of various ills must be removed. Help should be given in such a way that the recipients may gradually be freed from dependence on others and become self-sufficient [quoted in § 1146].

The bishops have some clear proposals for moving in this direction: the church must reexamine its structures, affirm an austere life style, and be present in "the image of being authentically poor." But it must also "understand and denounce the mechanisms that generate this poverty" (§ 1160). This is an adoption of the view of "systemic evil" originally voiced at Medellín, and means that the poor must themselves be involved in decisions that affect their own futures. A stern call lurks behind these proposals: the church, rather than being simply "the church of the poor," must become "the poor church." Whether such words come to define the church in actuality, only the future can determine.

The above materials are culled from a very long document, overburdened with so much conventional material that new insights can be lost amid the verbiage, unless those within the church keep pointing to discrepancies between word and deed. Those with liberation concerns have made that one of their tasks.

Still More Storm Clouds: The Costs Increase

When the bishops returned from Puebla, it was clear that, however gingerly, they had ratified a revolution in the life of the church. Within six months another revolution had been ratified, not gingerly at all—the triumph of the Sandinista forces over the dictatorship of the Somoza family that (thanks to U.S. backing) had held power in Nicaragua for forty years. July 19, 1979, marked the beginning of new possibilities not only for Nicaragua but for the whole of Latin America: if liberation from a ruthless dictator could succeed in one Latin American country, perhaps it could succeed in others.

But the euphoria did not last long. Within a few months the United States had a new president, whose fear was identical with the Latin American hope: if a revolution could succeed in one Latin American country, perhaps it could succeed in others. And because such an eventuality could only threaten United States power, Ronald Reagan gave himself unstintingly over the next eight years to the task of destroying the Nicaraguan government, determined that the Sandinistas should "say uncle" to Uncle Sam, just as Uncle Sam has forced Nicaraguans to say for the preceding hundred years.

Mr. Reagan did not succeed in destroying the Nicaraguan government, but he did succeed in causing extraordinary suffering for Nicaraguans, both by (a) creating and funding the Contras, a military group of erstwhile Somoza supporters who engaged in terrorist attacks on their countrymen, and (b) imposing a trade embargo that helped to bring the Nicaraguan economy to virtual collapse.

The story is important not only because the possibility of liberation from evil structures became a reality instead of a dream, even though the costs continue to be high, but also because much of the church was involved in the struggle long before victory was assured. Usually when the institutional church is involved in such a struggle, it sides with the forces of reaction, seeking to maintain "a preferential option for the rich," but in Nicaragua the reverse was true, and after the successful overthrow of Somoza's forces, three priests became part of the new government: Miguel d'Escoto, a Maryknoll Missioner, became minister of state; Ernesto Cardenal, a diocesan priest, became minister of culture; and Fernando Cardenal, a Jesuit, became minister of education and supervised the highly successful literacy campaign that began within weeks of the Sandinista victory.

But the notion of priests being directly involved in politics was more than the Vatican would countenance, and the three were repeatedly ordered to resign their positions. They refused, citing not only the need for their presence in the government, but affirming that their involvement was an authentic exercise of priesthood: being "ministers of the people" was their way of being "ministers of God." Rome responded by suspending their priestly "faculties," forbidding them to say Mass or hear confession. And although the personal costs to them have been high, they have continued to be "ministers of the people" rather than abandoning the people to a technicality of canon law."[11]

Only fifteen months after Puebla, one of its most active participants, Archbishop Oscar Romero of San Salvador, was murdered by a "death squad." We will look at this event in more detail in chapter 2, but mention of it prompts mention also of the raping and killing of three U.S. Catholic sisters and a lay missionary in El Salvador in 1980. Terrible in themselves, the killings are a further reminder that for every archbishop or sister whose name we know, thousands of "the world's anonymous," whose names we do not know, continue to die, often with the connivance of our own government.

It is costly for church members in Latin America to challenge their governments. But the stakes are high as well in challenging the internal life of the church. The most celebrated contretemps has been between Rome and the Brazilian Franciscan, Leonardo Boff. After being summoned to

Rome for a hearing on his presumably controversial writings, Boff was "silenced" indefinitely, forbidden to write or speak in public. His particular troubles stemmed not so much from accusations of Marxist leanings, the conventional charge in such situations, but because the strong emphasis on the Holy Spirit in his writings, and his involvement in Brazil's base communities, seemed to threaten orderly hierarchical patterns within the church. The gesture backfired, for not only was Boff given worldwide public support, but he used the enforced leisure to continue writing, even though forbidden to publish. When Rome lifted the ban eleven months later, Boff already had an arsenal of new materials to share with the world.[12]

Gustavo endured similar inquisitorial pressure (the adjective is not too strong) during this period—a story we will examine in chapters 2 and 6.[13] Indeed, so close are the convergences between the wider story and Gustavo's story that it is time to turn directly to him and reassess from his perspective some of the events reported above.

CHAPTER 2

An Individual Biography
of One Author
# of Liberation Theology

Gustavo Gutiérrez has lucidly described his own experience, recounting how, from the common Christian and Catholic injunction to help the poor, he was led to understand Christian commitment as solidarity with the struggle of the poor for their salvation.
> —José Míguez Bonino, *Doing Theology in a Revolutionary Situation*, p. 157

I was a Christian long before liberation theology and I will be a Christian long after liberation theology.
> —Gustavo, in conversation

By northern hemisphere standards, biographical information is relatively easy to assemble. Within a few lines we can gather the important "facts" about a person: birth, education, professional appointments, publications, membership in organizations, honors received, and so forth. *Who's Who* is a model of such compact reporting. In that style, Gustavo can be described as follows:

Gutiérrez Merino, Gustavo, theologian, writer, priest; b. June 8, 1928, Monserrat barrio, Lima, Peru; educ: San Marcos Univ., Lima, 1947-50, BSc; Catholic Univ. Lima, philosophy; Santiago de Chile, theology; Catholic Univ., Louvain, Belgium, 1951-55, master's degree in philosophy and psychology, thesis topic, "The Psychic Conflict in Freud" (1955); theological faculty of the Univ. of Lyons, France, 1955-59, master's degree in theology, thesis on "Religious Liberty" (1959), doctorate in theology *summa cum laude,* 1986, on the corpus of his writings; Gregorian Univ., Rome, Italy, 1959-60, Institut Catholique de Paris, 1962-63. hon. degrees: Univ. of Nijmegen, Holland, doc.

theol. *honoris causa,* 1979; doc. degree, Univ. of Tübingen, Germany, 1985.

Teaching positions: prof. Cath. Pontifical Univ., Lima, theol. and soc. sciences (1960-65); visiting prof. Union Theol. Sem., New York; Pacific School of Religion, Grad. Theol. Union, Berkeley, CA; Univ. of Michigan, Ann Arbor; Boston Coll., Boston; Maryknoll Sch. of Theol, Maryknoll, N.Y.; Mexican-American Cultural Center, San Antonio, Texas, etc., etc.

Ecclesiastical activities: ordained priest, Rom. Cath. church, Jan. 6, 1959; advisor, National Union of Cath. Students, Lima; advisor, numerous pastoral and theological reflection groups, Peru; founding member ONIS (Oficina Nacional de Investigación); theological advisor, CELAM II (Latin American Bishops' Conference), Medellín, Colombia, 1968; member, editorial board *Concilium,* intnl. Cath. publishing program, and *Páginas,* pastoral review in Lima; participant, conf. on "Christians for Socialism," Santiago de Chile, 1973; speaker, SODEPAX conf. Cartigny, Switzerland, 1969, and Lambeth Conf. of Anglican Bishops, Canterbury, England, 1988; participant EATWOT (Ecumenical Assn. of Third World Theologians) conferences, Dar-es-Salaam, Accra, São Paolo, Sri Lanka, New Delhi.

Books (in English): *A Theology of Liberation: History, Politics and Salvation* (1973; 15th anniv. ed. 1988); (w. Richard Shaull), *Liberation and Change* (1977); *The Power of the Poor in History: Selected Writings* (1983); *We Drink from Our Own Wells: The Spiritual Journey of a People* (1984); *On Job: God-Talk and the Suffering of the Innocent* (1987); *The Truth Shall Make You Free* (1990).

Books in Spanish: all of the above; *Líneas pastorales de la Iglesia en América latina* (1976); *El Dios de la vida* (1982, in process of expansion for new edition); *Dios o el oro en las Indias* (Siglo XVI), the first of four volumes of historical research on Bartolomé de Las Casas.

Present occupation: parish priest, Rímac, Lima; founder and director, Centro Bartolomé de Las Casas, Rímac, Lima.

Such compilations help us understand certain kinds of lives, but they do not help much to understand Gustavo's life. He must be seen on his own terms in relation to his own culture, rather than through imposing our criteria of what is "important." So let us try to fill in the spaces between all those semicolons.

A Tension: Upbringing in Peru vs. The Theological Grand Tour[1]

Gustavo was born on Arco Street in "old Lima," Peru, on June 8, 1928. His birth did not make the social pages of Lima's daily press, for his family was not part of the aristocracy, and did not live in a "desirable" part of town. He is a mestizo, sometimes condescendingly referred to as a "half-breed," part Hispanic and part Indian — a Quechuan. He is thus positioned by birth among the oppressed of his nation.

There were two sisters in the family as well as the one son, and of his early years Gustavo says, "I remember that I received a great deal of affection and love from my parents and family." He also remembers that the family had "certain economic difficulties," but that they lasted "only for relatively short periods of time." The family moved to Rímac, a poor barrio, and later to Barranco, an area just outside metropolitan Lima.

Although all the children were in school, more was expected from young men in a male-oriented culture than from young women, and higher hopes for education were placed on the son than on the daughters. Gustavo's fondness for reading turned out to be a blessing, for between the ages of twelve and eighteen he was first bedridden and then confined to a wheel-chair because of a severe case of osteomyelitis. This left him with a permanent limp but had no effect on the lightning quality of his mind — a trait clearly evident when he converses in Spanish, French, German, English, or Quechua. "There was physical pain," he recalls, "although I must say that the strong bonds of friendship that I formed in those years compensated greatly for my physical limitations." "During the years I was sick," he continues, "my house became a regular center for meetings, conversations, games. I developed a real passion for chess and one of my frustrations as an adult is not having time to play."

The illness inclined him toward a degree in medicine, and as an undergraduate he took medical studies in anticipation of becoming a psychiatrist, an interest still present in his later theological training, when he wrote a master's dissertation at Louvain, "The Psychic Conflict in Freud." The years at San Marcos University included political activity as well, but midstream Gustavo decided instead to become a priest, and moved from the study of medicine at the university to begin his study of philosophy at the seminary in Santiago de Chile. The influence of two of his teachers, César Arrospide and Geraldo Alarco, was an important factor in this decision.

The received wisdom in Latin America was that a promising young candidate for ordination should be sent to Europe for graduate study and final formation, and so Gustavo, having given evidence of being "a promising young candidate," was sent on The Theological Grand Tour, which in his case included study in Belgium, France, and Rome, culminating in ordination in 1959.

The theological credentials thus attained were vintage theology. Certain friendships had significant effect as well on his final "formation." While at Louvain, he was a friend of François Houtart, who became one of the leading theological sociologists of the contemporary Catholic Church. Houtart recalls Gustavo as an excellent student, not at that time overpolitical, and hazards the guess that the most formative influence of all was the presence of *seminaristas* from all parts of the world, who gave each other a global perspective and sensitivity that went far beyond their formal curricular studies. One of the enduring friendships was with another Latin American ordinand, Camilo Torres. Although Torres came from a "bourgeois" background very different from that of Gustavo, the two of them shared many social concerns that were important when they returned to South America.

After Louvain, the time at Lyons exposed Gustavo to what was known as *la nouvelle théologie,* an attempt by certain French Catholic scholars to relate their faith more clearly to the twentieth-century world. The venture got some of them in trouble in the post-World War II years, and there was a proscription of sorts in a papal encyclical, *Humani Generis* (1950), which, however, turned out to be so general that none of the advocates of *la nouvelle théologie* felt threatened by it. The most prominent names were Henri de Lubac, Jean Daniélou, and Yves Congar. Gustavo's ongoing debt to Congar is evidenced by frequent references to him in Gustavo's later writings. Others who impacted him during this period were Karl Rahner, Maurice Blondel, and the Old Testament scholar Gerhard von Rad.

After being away from his native country for almost a decade, Gustavo returned in 1960 to begin teaching part-time at the Catholic University in Lima. Believing that theology must enter into dialogue with daily life and culture, Gustavo reflects on those years:

> It seemed important to me to take up themes in my classes that would allow an examination of the meaning of human existence and the presence of God in the world in which my students lived. This led me to confront Christian faith with thinkers like Albert Camus, Karl Marx, and others, as well as film directors like Luis Buñuel and Ingmar Bergman, and writers like José María Arguedas or poets like our César Vallejo.
>
> I believe that the dialogue of faith with contemporary thought, especially with thought that is critical of Christianity, is necessary and lifegiving. I remember with great affection those years I spent at the university and the conversation with students such topics brought about.

But in addition to the classroom, there was a world outside, and there were also students who were concerned about that world outside. As he carried on his activities with student groups, saw what was happening to the poor, and directly confronted the ongoing and unremitting reality of poverty, hopelessness and misery, the "professional career" that church leaders must have privately mapped out for Gustavo began to take some unexpected directions.

Not to put too fine a point on it, the summation of wisdom accumulated on The Theological Grand Tour simply did not fit the South American reality. So the next stage in Gustavo's education consisted of unlearning much of his hard-won education, rereading the history of his own continent, rereading the Bible, rereading theology, and discovering that rereading meant a remaking of the situation of the poor and oppressed, and a refashioning of the theological tools he was continually honing to use more directly in that situation.

The Break with "Dominant Theology" and the Beginnings of Rebuilding

In chapter 5 we will examine characteristics of the "dominant theology" Gustavo gradually disavows, and the new alternative, "liberation theology," that takes its place. Such changes come slowly and indeed never cease, for Gustavo recognizes that a living theology is always growing and deepening; the moment it has become firmly entrenched, decay has set in. So there is no dateable "Damascus Road" experience to mark the moment of definitive shift. ("As the years pass," Gustavo ruminates, "I have learned that there is nothing less exact than dates.")

Before looking at events that mark the readjustment, we must take account of three thinkers who were influential during these years and have remained central throughout Gustavo's subsequent theological reflection.

Bartolomé de Las Casas

We have already encountered the extraordinary bishop, Bartolomé de Las Casas, one of the few Spaniards during the colonizing of Latin America to take the side of the oppressed Amerindians and struggle for them against the oppressive acts of the conquistadores. The roots of liberation theology are discernible not only in the content of Las Casas's faith, but in the methodology he espoused, and the personal involvement he risked in response to his convictions. It is a telling tribute to his ongoing influence that Gustavo has devoted years to research and preparation for a definitive study of Las Casas that will surely be his largest written contribution to the theological world and possibly his most enduring.

José Carlos Mariátegui[2]

In terms of the political-economic maturing of Gustavo's thought, the Peruvian sociologist José Carlos Mariátegui (whom Cadorette describes as "one of Peru's foremost social theorists") plays a significant role. Mariátegui was a thinker who, instead of being content with generalities, applied Marxist insights specifically to Peru, editing a Peruvian journal and helping to found both the Socialist Party of Peru and the General Confederation of Workers. He saw that class stratification in Peru was reinforced by racism, so that Peru was "a country in which Indians and foreign conquerors live side by side but do not mingle or even understand one another." A mestizo like Gustavo, Mariátegui was a socialist who was not only brought up in a Catholic home but retained a significant religious perspective throughout his life, even though he left the institutional church because of its ties to structures of injustice. Gustavo taught a course on his writings for several years, and appreciated particularly that Mariátegui's "action and thought arise from his experience of the popular classes."

Mariátegui saw myth as an important vehicle for social revolution; the power of revolutionaries, he believed, resides in "faith, passion, and will," rather than science. When focused on earth rather than a distant heaven, religion has the power to engender change.

As Michael Candelaria points out, Mariátegui makes three particular contributions to Gustavo's thought:

(a) *The search for an indigenous socialism.* Mariátegui attempted to reinterpret life from the perspectives of the mestizos, using their cultural values and popular religion, rather than imposing an alien framework upon them—an impulse clearly related to Gustavo's increasing restiveness at imposing European theology on Latin America.

(b) *"Class struggle" as an interpretive key.* Gustavo accepts "class struggle" as a description of Latin American reality, though he nuances the discussion carefully in the 15th anniversary edition of *A Theology of Liberation.* But he acknowledges Mariátegui's importance in bringing this to the attention of theologians (*PP,* p. 217). The patent reality of social conflict makes neutrality impossible, and forces one to take sides with the oppressed. There are connections here with "a preferential option for the poor" that Gustavo helped incorporate in the documents of Medellín and Puebla.

(c) *The unity of theory and praxis* was another concept Mariátegui "indigenized" for the Peruvian situation. Praxis must lead to reflection and reflection must be verified in praxis. In *A Theology of Liberation* Gustavo notes that Mariátegui had predicted that "only a sufficiently broad, rich, and intense revolutionary praxis, with the participation of people of different viewpoints, can create the conditions of fruitful theory" (pp. 56 [90]). It is not far from this insight to one of Gustavo's strongest insistences: that theology is the "second act," following the initial act of commitment.

José María Arguedas[3]

Mariátegui died when Gustavo was two years old, so his acquaintance was only through the printed page, although Mariátegui's son and Gustavo were classmates at the university. But in the case of Arguedas there was a brief though close personal relationship that enriched them both.

Arguedas grew up in the Andes, where his father was a circuit judge. When the judge remarried after the death of his first wife, the hostility of the stepmother toward the stepson was so great that, when her husband was away on long trips, she forced the young boy to live in the servants' quarters with the Amerindians. Fortunately, they were kind, and as Arguedas puts it, "my childhood went by singed between fire and love." Throughout his life Arguedas felt closer to the oppressed of his culture than to the "oppressor" class to which he ostensibly belonged.

Arguedas became deeply aware of the plight of the Amerindians, an interest further deepened by his own exposure to the social analyses of Mariátegui. For a while he was a member of the communist party, and he and a number of friends were imprisoned for denouncing Franco during the Spanish Civil War. With much struggle he completed a university education and taught ethnic studies at the University of San Marcos and later ethnology in the Escuela de Agricultura.

During these professional years, Arguedas continued to write fiction. His finest novel, *Deep Rivers,* was a thinly-veiled autobiographical account of his upbringing, illustrating the tremendous tension under which he lived, of trying to relate the two radically different cultures of Peru—the Amerindian of the Andes and the Hispanic of the cities. It was Arguedas's great gift—and the source of his inner malaise—that he could so accurately portray the world of the oppressed from the "inside," even though he did not fully dwell there.

A later novel, *Todas las sangres,* had a deep impact on Gustavo, and an episode from it is included as a frontispiece in the 15th anniversary edition of *A Theology of Liberation*, a book dedicated to Arguedas and to Henrico Pereira Neto, a black Brazilian priest. In his last novel, *El zorro de ariba e el zorro de abaja,* finished after he had come to know Gustavo, Arguedas included a priest who is modeled on Gustavo. This represents an astonishing breakthrough, for Arguedas had long felt that Catholicism in Peru was part of the problem rather than part of the solution, a cause of human suffering rather than an alleviator of it, and that the church as an institution "lived off suffering." Many of the autobiographical episodes in *Deep Rivers* illustrate the charge.

Arguedas and Gustavo did not meet until 1968, about a year and a half before Arguedas, unable to hold together the conflicting forces that tore him apart, took his own life. Gustavo had just given the lecture at Chimbote that represented his first full-dress presentation of liberation theology. Arguedas got a copy of the speech and was deeply impressed; here was a kind of faith to which he might be able to relate. A mutual friend arranged a meeting, and deep bonds were immediately established. Gustavo recalls the evening:

> It was a very interesting meal in which Arguedas told me that in the dialogue of the sacristan and the curate in *Todas las sangres* [the passage Gustavo later included in *A Theology of Liberation*] there was anticipated a "theology of liberation"; later he called the curate of that dialogue "curate of the inquisitor god" [cited in Grider, *Crossing Deep Rivers,* p. 181].

Arguedas wrote to Gustavo after a subsequent get-together:

Your visit did me a great deal of good. Reading the words you wrote in Chimbote and having had a chance to be with you strengthened my faith in a future which cannot fail me. How marvelous that we understand each other, together enjoying a light that no one can extinguish [cited in Cadorette, p. 72].

These two men, coming from very different starting points—one an agnostic, the other a priest—discovered unexpected points of convergence because they shared a common commitment: "to understand the poor and give voice to the voiceless" (Cadorette, p. 71).

Examples:

Arguedas wrote about "the fraternity of the miserable," about the violence done to the poor and the conflicts inherent in the very structure of Peruvian society, and this meshed clearly with Gustavo's increasing emphasis on identification with the poor as the starting point for Christian living.

Arguedas peopled his novels with "anonymous" heroes and heroines, those whose names the world will never know, which parallels Gustavo's stress on the importance of the "absent ones" in history, and the nature of the base communities springing up "from below."

Arguedas, the agnostic, has to deal with the role of God in the lives of the oppressed; in the face of so much injustice, and the church's complicity in that injustice, he is harsh in his condemnation of God's role. Gustavo affirms him: "I believe that José María was right. ... The God of the oppressors, of those who pillage and kill people, is not the God of the poor, not the same God at all" (Cadorette, p. 75). This distinction is the main point of the passage from *Todas las sangres* that Gustavo discusses in *A Theology of Liberation*: a priest who has been blandly assuring his sacristan that "God is everywhere" is responded to by the sacristan (who, as Gustavo reminds us, "knows no metaphysics but is well acquainted with injustice and oppression"):

Was God in the heart of those who broke the body of the innocent teacher Bellido? Is God in the bodies of the eye-witnesses who are killing "La Esmeralda"? in the official who took the cornfields away from their owners? [*TheoLib*, pp. 111 (195)].

The answer, of course, is no. Gustavo was able to introduce the author of these tortured lines to a God who is not the God of the predators but the God of the poor, the God who is identified with justice rather than with injustice. This alternative, he feels, is not simply a theological quirk of his own, but can be found in the teaching of the church as well. He immediately cites Medellín:

Where this social peace does not exist there we will find social, political, economic, and cultural inequities, there we will find the rejection of the peace of the Lord, *and a rejection of the Lord himself* [*TheoLib*, pp. 111 (195), italics added, from Medellín, "Peace," §14].

The tension with which Arguedas struggled throughout his life is clarified in Gustavo's long essay on Arguedas's writings, "Entre las calandrias." A *calandria* is a South American species of lark, called a "calander lark." As Stephen Judd notes:

> Arguedas saw himself as a lark whose song has a consoling tone [*calandria consoladora*]. But later he came to regard himself as a *calandria de fuego,* a lark consumed by fire, passion, and uneasiness about the Peruvian conditions. According to Arguedas, both kinds of lark are metaphors for Peru [Stephen Judd, M.M., in correspondence with the author].

A terminological clarification: in this context, "consoling" is not understood as an act of healing or renewal, but an enjoiner to passivity, to accepting without question whatever comes. Later on, Arguedas suggests a more positive meaning, as we will see below.

Gustavo insists that the tension "between the two larks" be maintained:

> The tone of [Arguedas's] voice cannot be heard unless it is accompanied by the unequal chorus of voices—in Quechuan or Spanish— of joy and pain, of liberation and oppression, of life and death, which is part of this country. . . . In Arguedas, there is a coherent, painfully urgent and, for that reason, hope-giving vision of Peru without which his writing is incomprehensible [cited in Cadorette, p. 71].

Gustavo's essay distinguishes six themes in Arguedas's writings that he finds theologically significant: (1) mythic time, (2) cleansing the soul, (3) subversive memory, (4) the universal humanity of the poor, (5) liberative consolation, and (6) idolatry as complicity with oppressors.

Without summarizing these points individually, we can extract certain themes that show further affinities between the two men.

The only kind of God in whom Arguedas could believe would be a God who "rejoins the poor," and makes common cause with them, a God who suffers with them. In terms of the imagery of the two larks, the "consoling" lark represents the God of the whiplashings, funeral processions and ongoing exploitation—a fearful God removed from the plight of the people, the God of the oppressors, in short, the "inquisitorial" God. The lark symbolized by "fire," passion, and uneasiness about the state of things is comparable to the "liberator" God, who brings hope, who "rejoins" or "reincorporates" with the people, who bears the marks of the poor, and enters into their struggles for liberation.

Arguedas's novels are also reminders of the importance of memory, for nothing would better suit those in power than to wipe past indignities out of the minds of the poor, so that future indignities could continue to be heaped upon them. On this level, all of Arguedas's novels are "acts of recollection" to forestall such a likelihood. Elsewhere Gustavo writes about the need for "a therapy for historical amnesia" (*PP*, pp. 7ff.), and in the essay on Arguedas he comments, "The memory of the poor is *subversive* because it creates historical identity—reason enough for the powerful to insist on wiping it out" ("Entre las calandrias," p. 256, my translation). Such memory "lends force and sustenance to our positions, refuses to compromise or equivocate, learns from failures and knows (by experience) that it has the capability of overcoming every obstacle, even repression itself" (*PP*, p. 80).

Perhaps, then, even consolation can be redeemed. If, for Arguedas, consolation is more often a means of prolonging rather than alleviating suffering, the reverse can also be true. There can be "a consolation that liberates." In *Deep Rivers*, Ernesto (a fictionalized version of the youthful Arguedas) finds consolation, in the sense of *strengthening*, in the power of nature, and in certain human beings. The memory of the Amerindian reality, and the power latent in it, also consoles. This is a kind of consolation that involves solidarity with the poor, by resisting, rather than succumbing to, the inquisitor God, and exposes the worship of that God as idolatry, for it leads to complicity with the oppressor rather than identification with the oppressed.

References to Arguedas are found throughout Gustavo's writings, but the most concentrated example comes at the beginning of *On Job*, where Gustavo is struggling with the problem of how it is possible to talk about God in the context of the suffering of the innocent. He recalls the young Ernesto's discovery in *Deep Rivers*: "I found that people everywhere suffered." And in staying with the hostile Old Man who treated his servants, the *pongos,* shamefully, Ernesto further discovered that none suffered more "than the Old Man's *pongo.*" In the town of Abacan there was a bell, called María Angola, that tolled in the cathedral tower, which housed a painting of the Lord of the Earthquakes, whose face was like the faces of the most despised servants. "The face of the crucified Christ was dark and gaunt, like that of the *pongo*" (*Job*, pp. xv-xvi).

For Gustavo, this connection is a reminder of Bartolomé de Las Casas's conviction that Jesus Christ is present in the scourging of the Amerindians, so that those who exploit and destroy them are doing the same thing to Christ, "not once but thousands of times." To this somber scene, however, Arguedas brings a note of hope. The bells can bring cheer as well as gloom; there is a hope that "the voice of the bells can rise up to heaven and return to earth with the song of the angel." But this can be true only for the one who has taken with utmost seriousness the weary, broken, frame of the *pongo*. If the message cannot be true for him, it cannot be true for anyone else.

El Escorial and New Discoveries

During a meeting of liberation theologians in Spain in 1972, Gustavo talked about some of the things that had been most important in forming his new perspective.[4]

Having begun by working with the poor in traditional fashion, Gustavo discovered that in order truly to do so, he had to enter a new world, the world of the "other," the world of the poor. He could not look upon "poverty" as an abstract bit of sociological data. Love of neighbor remained an essential component of Christian existence, but how was he to actualize that love in a new situation? If he simply continued to view the neighbor as someone "nearby," part of his own world and situation, his own world remained unchanged. What was required was to see the neighbor as someone "far off," whom he must seek out, and whose world he must enter — whether it was the world of the streets, marginated neighborhoods, farms, mines, or factories. When he did this, his own world was changed. The neighbor was found not by waiting for the neighbor to come to him, but by *seeing the neighbor as the one to whom he must go rather than the one for whom he must wait.* This, he discovered, was the axis on which a new way of being a Christian must turn. Within that 180° shift, Gustavo made three discoveries:

1. He discovered that *poverty is destructive,* something to be fought against and destroyed, not something to be accepted or condoned by occasional acts of charity, or justified on the basis of biblical passages like "the poor you have always with you."

2. He discovered that *poverty is not accidental but structural.* This is why occasional handouts from the rich to the poor are not sufficient. The poor do not exist by a decree of fate, nor can their condition be dealt with by political neutrality or ethical indifference. On the contrary, the poor are the result of the system within which the rest of us live and for which we are responsible. The poor live on the margins of *our* social and cultural world, where they are oppressed, exploited, and have the fruits of their labor snatched away, so that their very humanity is degraded. That many are poor is not a matter of chance, but the inevitable result of sinful structures. For these reasons, the "poverty of the poor" is not a call to intermittent generous actions to alleviate need temporarily, but a challenge to construct a new social order.

3. He discovered that *the poor are a social class.* The poor belong to those levels of culture that are not respected by others, to races against whom discrimination is practiced, and to a social class that, either subtly or openly, is exploited. Consequently, to opt for the poor is to opt for one social class and against other social classes, to become aware of the reality of "class struggle," and to side with the dispossessed, identifying with their concerns and their struggles.

As a result of these three discoveries, Gustavo concluded that in order to serve the poor one must move into political action. When he did this, he says, "I discovered the nature of political action, its rationality, and all-encompassing character."

Such discoveries began to push Gustavo in new directions, and at the conclusion of the speech at El Escorial, he gave a brief summary of what these discoveries meant for his theological reconstruction:

> Commitment to the process of liberation introduces Christians into a world quite unfamiliar to them and forces them to make what we have called a qualitative leap — the radical challenging of a social order and of its ideology, and the breaking with old ways of knowing. . . .
>
> But simultaneously, the buds of a new type of understanding of the faith are emerging within these same experiences. In them we have learned how to link knowing and transforming, theory and practice. A re-reading of the gospel forces itself upon us [*Mission Trends,* No. 3, p. 65].

The most important consequence of this rereading is a rediscovery of the biblical claim that truth is something to be *done.* The fourth Gospel speaks consistently about "doing the truth." "To believe in God," Gustavo concludes, "is not to limit ourselves to affirming [God's] existence; to believe in God is to commit our lives to [God] and to all people" (ibid., p. 65).

Faith becomes a "liberating praxis," and it does battle with sin, which is now understood to refer not only to individual shortcomings but to "oppressive structures created for the benefit of the few and for the exploitation of peoples, races, and social classes" (ibid., p. 66). So Christian liberation will include political liberation as well. As the bishops said at Medellín (no doubt after prompting from Gustavo), the liberation Christ brings to the entire human family is liberation "from the slavery to which sin has subjected them — hunger, misery, oppression, and ignorance, in a word, injustice and hatred, which have their origins in human selfishness" (Medellín, "Justice," §3). At the same time, Gustavo insists, "Christ's liberation is not reduced to political liberation, but Christ's liberation occurs in liberating historical events...in the concrete historical and political circumstances of today" (ibid. p. 68). The charge of "reduction," so often leveled at Gustavo, is wide of the mark.

Two important reminders are offered in conclusion:

1. Our praxis involves an *identification with persons,* specifically the interests and conflicts of those social classes that suffer "misery and exploitation," and Christ's liberating praxis must be announced "from within that process."

2. The crucial factor, however, will not be "our" identification with "them." It will be the liberation of previously subjected groups who can "freely and creatively express themselves in society and among the people

of God," so that they can become "the artisans of their own liberation" (ibid., p. 69).

Camilo Torres[5]

Gustavo began to share his new concerns with others. As early as August 1962 he had been one of a dozen younger theologians and lay Catholics invited by Bishop Larraín of Chile to a conference in Buenos Aires to reflect together on how to relate the church's message more relevantly to the particular circumstances of Latin America. This was only weeks before the convening of the Second Vatican Council, and Bishop Larraín undoubtedly wanted to take as many fresh ideas to Rome as possible.

There were varieties of opinions within the group, ranging from those who wanted to go the "Christian Democrat" route—that is, working through electoral channels—to the most radical priest present, Gustavo's old friend from Louvain, Camilo Torres. Although Camilo and Gustavo were convinced that the various national oligarchies were calling the tune and that profound change was needed, the group did not emerge from the meetings with a mutually agreed-upon plan of action. Gustavo wanted to explore "a specifically Christian form of radicalism that did not simply follow the Marxist current," while Camilo felt that this was an abstraction and that since Marxists were the ones who were fighting for a new society, Christians should work openly with them. As far as their own involvements were concerned, Gustavo drew some distinctions between the roles of clergy and laity, but Camilo felt that in critical times the priest should simply take on the secular role himself.

The two met on later occasions after Camilo had left the priesthood and was contemplating joining guerilla forces. Gustavo urged him not to do so, for both human and political reasons. However, as is well known, Camilo disregarded this advice, and after only a few weeks in the jungle he was shot—as Gustavo had almost predicted he would be. Louvain had not been a good training ground for guerilla warfare. When he left the priesthood, Camilo said that he was not going to celebrate the eucharist again until there was justice in the world. Gustavo is reported to have commented, "If we can't celebrate the eucharist until we have attained a perfect society, then we will have to wait until we get to heaven, in which case the eucharist will be superfluous."

The Gradual Emergence of a "Theology of Liberation"

A similar gathering of theologians took place at Petrópolis, Brazil, two years later, in 1964. The motivation that brought Gustavo into such discussions was the search for a new *pastoral* focus in communicating the word of God. Dissatisfaction with the church's position was evident in his presentation, and he raised the specific issue of the relationship of the growing revolutionary struggle in Latin America to the gospel stress on self-emptying (*kenosis*), as well as urging further thinking about such issues as violence and birth control.[6]

The material presented at Petrópolis was refined on a number of subsequent occasions, including a conference of leaders of Catholic University student groups in Montevideo in 1967, and finally published in 1968 as *Líneas pastorales de la Iglesia en América latina* (CEP, Lima, 1968; revised and expanded edition 1976).

A further exploration of new perspectives was contained in a course given at Montreal in 1967, "The Church and Poverty," the substance of which is included as the last chapter in *A Theology of Liberation,* and will be discussed here in chapter 3.

These tentative soundings came to fruition in 1968, the year when Gustavo feels that "theology of liberation" came to birth. The occasion was a conference at Chimbote, Peru, sponsored by ONIS (Oficina Nacional de Investigación), a group of priests working for social change that Gustavo had earlier helped to organize. Here he presented the fundamental outlines of what for the first time he called "a theology of liberation."[7]

The Medellín Conference of Latin American bishops occurred shortly after this meeting, and a considerable number of the themes the priests discussed at Chimbote found their way into the Medellín documents, a process aided by the fact that Gustavo and a number of other members of ONIS were at Medellín as "consultants" to bishops.

A similar presentation was made the following year at an ecumenical gathering in Cartigny, Switzerland, of SODEPAX (Commission on Society, Development, and Peace, jointly sponsored by the Pontifical Commission on Justice and Peace and the World Council of Churches). A basic outline of what became the text of *A Theology of Liberation* is included in the report of this meeting, and it is typical of the single-mindedness of Gustavo that although the Cartigny conference was convened to explore a "theology of development," he unabashedly presented a "theology of liberation"—a distinction we will clarify in chapter 3.

A theological symposium at Bogotá in 1970 provided a final reworking of the material before its publication in Spanish the following year. The book immediately attracted wide attention and was translated into nine other languages within a short time.

No longer was Gustavo's audience a small group of Catholics in Latin America. From now on he would be affirmed—and defamed—on a world scale.

In the Spotlight and behind the Scenes

How did Gustavo begin to get into trouble? Perhaps if he had settled into the quiet "academic" career the leaders of the church had projected for him, he could have written scholarly books for his peers that would have attracted little public attention, and taught courses that (even though they might have raised an occasional eyebrow in the chancery office) would never have been occasions for public ecclesiastical debate.

A Theology of Liberation

Not only did Gustavo not fit the mold, as we have seen, but with the publication of *A Theology of Liberation* in 1971, he immediately became a public figure. Concerns in Rome about his orthodoxy could not be avoided, and began to be more widely discussed whenever anxious conservatives gathered to bemoan the attention being accorded liberation theology as a result of his book.

On one level, it is hard to see what the fuss was all about. The book is a solid piece of scholarship, copiously and even extravagantly documented, surveying history, tradition, and scripture with utmost deference (albeit with critical eyes as well), reviewing earlier theologians, popes, and councils with meticulous care, and remaining church-centered throughout.

But the book is less benign than such a description would warrant. Earlier theological and ecclesial models are treated respectfully, but are then respectfully set aside as inadequate for a new day. There is more economic and political analysis than would have been expected even in a book of theology subtitled, *History, Politics, and Salvation*. The theme of salvation itself is repositioned by moving from a "quantitative" mode (estimating how many will make it to heaven) to a "qualitative" mode (suggesting that God may finally intend salvation for all). Knowledge of God is inexorably linked to the doing of justice, and such a theme, though indisputably present in the book of Jeremiah and elsewhere (as Gustavo shows), challenges so many established theological shibboleths that the only appropriate conclusion to draw seemed to be that Gustavo was reading things into the book of Jeremiah that did not belong there.

The section "Christian Brotherhood and Class Struggle," instead of following the received wisdom that the two are mutually exclusive, seems to imply that they should be exercised together. (This is the one section Gustavo rewrote for the 15th anniversary edition, and the changes will be discussed here in chapter 4.) Even the treatment of poverty, usually a "safe" subject ("blessed are the poor," "the poor you have always with you," "poverty is an evangelical virtue"), asserts that since poverty is "a scandalous condition," one must engage in "solidarity with the poor as a protest against poverty," and do so considerably before the eschaton, which, it had previously been assumed, would be God's way of bailing us out of the whole messy situation.

It seems to have been the insistence that theology is not just an academic exercise but a way of reflecting about activity *in the world* that rankled most. Such a concern, it was ominously charged, sounded "Marxist," and once the code word had been uttered, not even four hundred biblical references in three hundred pages of text could save the author from the charge of "reducing" the gospel to a social theory, and an unacceptable one at that.

Christians for Socialism[8]

The "Marxist" charge, or at least the "socialist" charge, was given added impetus when Gustavo participated in a conference at Santiago de Chile in 1972, sponsored by a group known as Christians for Socialism. Chile was a good location for the meetings: a socialist government had come into power in 1970, making Chile the only socialist state on the subcontinent. About four hundred delegates from all over the world attended.

The distance in theological and social climate between even Medellín and the Santiago conference was considerable:

> Medellín was in tune with Vatican II, even if beginning to move beyond it, whereas Santiago is more self-consciously "postconciliar." Medellín usually leans toward a "third way" between capitalism and Marxism, whereas Santiago sees no "Christian solution" as such, denounces the collapse into a "third way," and insists that Christians be involved in the liberation process in socialist terms. With a few important exceptions (such as the document on "Peace"), Medellín speaks of inequality between persons, whereas Santiago consistently links inequality to class struggle and to exploitation of the poor by the rich. Medellín presses strongly for basic reform, whereas Santiago sees no solution without revolution, not necessarily violent. Medellín hopes that love, working for justice, can provide solutions, while Santiago argues that love is not a historical force apart from engagement in the class struggle. Medellín offers a theoretical analysis of Marxism, while Santiago calls upon Christians to "form a strategic alliance with Marxists." At Medellín the theologians were summoned by the bishops, at Santiago they were summoned by the militant [Brown, *Theology in a New Key,* pp. 55-56].

The final document of the Santiago meetings was a hard-hitting one, drafted by Giulio Girardi, Hugo Assmann, Gustavo, and a few others. The task of the delegates, the document states, is "the task of fashioning socialism [as] the only effective way to combat imperialism and to break away from our situation of dependence" (Eagleson, ed., *Christians and Socialism,* p. 163). The analysis rejects the possibility of a "middle way" between capitalism and socialism, and exhorts Christians to take "a definite stand on the side of the exploited in order to break this alliance" [between Christianity and the ruling class] (ibid., p. 173). Revolutionary praxis can lead to a new reading of the Bible and the Christian tradition, so that by deep involvement in the struggle the church can shed the wraps of "respectability" with which timid Christians in the past have tried to smother it.

These hopeful words were rudely challenged the following year when the bloody coup of General Pinochet (aided by the U.S. government) toppled the fledgling socialist experiment in Chile and replaced it with a ruthless tyranny of the right. Many Chilean Christians who had "surfaced" during the Allende years were hunted down and destroyed. Until the triumph of the Sandinistas in Nicaragua in 1979, actual socialist options disappeared in Latin America.

The Puebla Conference[9]

We have seen that in the interval between the episcopal conferences of Medellín and Puebla, the conservatives in CELAM made determined efforts to neutralize the gains of Medellín by a barrage of pamphlets, books, and conferences. The relative ease with which Gustavo and his friends had official access at Medellín, and the degree to which their concerns were included in the Medellín documents, undoubtedly contributed to the decision of the general secretary of CELAM, Archbishop López Trujillo, to avoid a repetition of such catastrophes at Puebla. As a result, those officially excluded from participation at Puebla represented a veritable *Who's Who in Latin American Liberation Theology*. In addition to Gustavo, the officially unwelcome included people of the stature of Juan Luis Segundo, Hugo Assmann, Jon Sobrino, Ignacio Ellacuría, Raúl Vidales, Enrique Dussel, Segundo Galilea, Pablo Richard, and José Comblin. Anybody who was somebody was not there.

However, as Moises Sandoval reports in his spritely account of these events, "Denied the opportunity to bring their own experts [Rome selected all the theologians to be admitted], the progressive bishops in many instances asked their theologians and social scientists to come along anyway" (Eagleson and Scharper, eds., *Puebla and Beyond*, Orbis, 1979, p. 35). As a result, about forty theologians and social scientists agreed to try to support the progressive bishops. They rented a house nearby and, though they could not get to the bishops inside the enclosed seminary grounds, the bishops could leave their "enclosure" and get to the theologians. The group prepared eighty-four position papers for the twenty-one commissions while the documents were going through four drafts. Sandoval's estimate is that as much as twenty-five percent of the final document was written by these uninvited assistants, in texts that were taken through the checkpoint by sympathetic bishops. "At one point," he reports, "Gustavo Gutiérrez went twenty-four hours with only one hour of sleep" (ibid., p. 36).

The crowds at Puebla, while giving the pope an enthusiastic welcome, were not predisposed to support the "liberation" forces whom they perceived as betraying the church. In one public demonstration, a well-dressed group of entrepreneurs carried a banner that read LIBERATION THEOLOGY IS BAD FOR BIG BUSINESS. Commented Gustavo, "Is very true."

In addition to the twenty-five percent of the final document referred to above, there is considerable chaff amid the wheat in the lengthy and almost unmanageable Puebla text. But those "on the outside" made an important tactical decision: instead of attacking the deficiencies of Puebla, they agreed to affirm its strengths and claim it as a charter for the future. The result is that Puebla has gotten more attention and across-the-board support than would otherwise have been anticipated, and is consistently quoted in subsequent literature. A few months later, one of the "outsiders" (not Gustavo) said in my hearing at another conference, with an exultant ring in his voice, "There are fifty phrases we can use!"

Not bad for a group of outsiders.

The Murder of Archbishop Romero[10]

One of the "progressive" bishops at Puebla was Oscar Romero, archbishop of San Salvador. Initially chosen to head the Salvadoran bishops on the grounds that he had a clear track record as a conservative, Romero was rapidly radicalized upon assuming office, the most significant catalyst being the brutal murder of a priest, Rutilio Grande, only a few days after Romero's elevation. Grande's "crime" had been to help organize rural cooperatives. As the days stretched into weeks and the weeks into months, the killing of priests, sisters, Delegates of the Word, and thousands of "anonymous" lay people, remained not exceptions to life in El Salvador but the ongoing daily reality, as they had been for the preceding decade. Romero continually escalated his protests against the repression, and publicly urged President Carter to stop sending military aid to El Salvador, for it was used chiefly to finance the "death squads" — an appeal the Carter administration chose to ignore. In his last broadcast homily from the radio station of the archdiocese, Romero urged young men in the Salvadoran army to refuse to obey orders to kill their countrymen.

This was the straw that broke the back of a very militaristic camel, and the next day Romero was summarily disposed of by an assassin's bullet while saying Mass. His funeral drew supporters from over Latin America, and, like many other friends of Romero, Gustavo was among those present. As they were leaving the cathedral after Mass and going into the public square outside, members of the right-wing National Guard began firing indiscriminately on the crowd. In the panic that ensued, those nearest Gustavo were swept back into the church as people retreated for safety. Because he is so short, Gustavo expected to be knocked over and trampled to death. He made it safely into the cathedral and administered the last rites of the church to a woman who had been shot and was bleeding to death.

Romero's death, and the repression it exemplified, were worldwide news. The attention to his death left some with the impression that it was exceptional. It was not. But it did serve to give new meaning to the deaths of thousands in "the communion of saints" who had been killed for their faith without benefit of press coverage. Commenting on this fact three years later, Gustavo said:

> The most important event since the Puebla conference was the assassination of Archbishop Oscar Romero of San Salvador. I think that

his martyrdom—because his death can be called that in a broad sense—has greatly enriched the Latin American church overall. . . . For some years now something has been happening in Latin America that some people refuse to recognize: the fact that many Christians are giving their lives, witnessing unto death to the gospel, to the God of love and the God of the poor. . . . I see [Romero's death] as illuminating other instances, deaths of lay people, of nuns, and of priests, that have occurred recently in Latin America. It gives them value. It makes plain their meaning [interview with Brockmann, *Christian Century*, p. 931].

Shortly before his assassination, Archbishop Romero had prophesied, "If they kill me, I will rise in the hearts of the Salvadoran people." The prophecy is daily fulfilled.

Behind the Scenes

We have been noting the activities of an individual on whom the spotlight of public attention has increasingly focused, particularly since the publication of *A Theology of Liberation* in 1971 made his name a theological household word. But it would leave an erroneous impression if we did not recognize that all the public acclaim (and notoriety) are set against the backdrop of a day-to-day existence for which public events are an intrusion at best, and never the core of Gustavo's own personal commitments and activity. The core remains the poor of the parish he continues to serve. Born and raised in Rímac, Gustavo has not aspired to move to the other side of the tracks.

The brief trips away to teach, however, serve a number of important ends. First, they provide time for a secondary part of his calling, the research and writing that could never be accomplished in the pressure of being on 24-hour call as a parish priest. The whole world is the beneficiary of the resultant books and articles. (The assumption is a bit unrealistic, however, for wherever Gustavo goes there are journalists who want a scoop or at least an interview, TV cameramen looking for a sensational news bite, and graduate students doing dissertations on Gustavo who would each like about four hours of uninterrupted time to ask questions.)

Second, doing short stints of teaching away from home enables Gustavo to acquaint First World students with theological perspectives they need in order to understand the world in which they live. The whole church is the beneficiary. Third, the traffic goes both ways on this street, for the trips enable him to listen as well as speak. By Gustavo's own admission, his sensitivity to womens' issues (from the start greater than that of most of his colleagues) has been stretched and deepened by classroom contacts with First World feminists. Fourth, the honoraria, lavish by Peruvian standards, can be ploughed back into the work of the Bartolomé de Las Casas

Center in Rímac, and into other projects that need funding not otherwise available.

This cosmopolitan flavor, however, is not without its drawbacks, and the most significant one was initiated by his lengthy student foray in Europe. In talking about "identifying with the poor," Gustavo is honest in acknowledging that even for him this is no longer fully possible. The fact that he is educated, has traveled widely, has a certain influence and even fame, and is the subject of charged discussions on Peruvian radio and television, inevitably "distances" him from those among whom he lives. He who can speak five languages fluently and has written many books, can no longer fully share the mind-set of a parishioner who knows only a native dialect, a smattering of Spanish, and can neither read nor write. It has even meant, Gustavo acknowledges, learning a new way to preach. "Is not possible to have three points," he says, ruefully abandoning the hallmark of his lecture method when he enters the pulpit. "The people shrug and say, 'Three points. . . . So?' " So . . . the sermons have become more centered on the retelling of biblical narratives, which may, in fact, represent gain all around.

When he is not preaching or celebrating Mass or traveling or leading a retreat or participating in a base community or defending himself against attack, Gustavo is involved in the activities of the Bartolomé de Las Casas Center in Rímac, which he established as a place for research on various aspects of life in the church today. Aided by such competent workers as Raúl Vidales, Diego Irarrázaval, and Tokihiro Kudo, Gustavo has initiated projects on such topics as "Popular Religion and Liberating Evangelism." This particular title is highlighted to indicate that the concerns at the center are not elitist ("The Influence of the Third Volume of Thomas Aquinas's *Summa Contra Gentiles* on 14th-Century Piety in the Lucarno Region of Northern Italy"), but very practical and down-to-earth. As we will see in chapter 3, "popular religion" is the religion of people who are usually uneducated, a curious amalgam of folklore, superstition, biblical imagery, and magic, which tends to be scorned by the educated. But Gustavo and his team believe there is much in popular religion that can be utilized to provide people with tools from their own religious heritage to fashion their own liberation.

So, much of Gustavo's life goes on behind the scenes, and it is at least as important as what goes on in the spotlight. Probably more so.

"High-Intensity Conflict" — The Clash with Rome

If there is any series of encounters Gustavo would prefer to have experienced "behind the scenes" rather than "in the spotlight" it is surely the encounter to which we now turn.

For several years, the clash with Rome was low-key and relatively private — what in military circles is called "low-intensity conflict" — waged quietly in order to draw minimal attention from elsewhere. If all goes well, any initiator of low-intensity conflict prefers to keep it that way and win a secure but unpublicized victory. But if all does not go well, the ante is raised, covert attacks become overt, public rather than private, and victory is pursued by whatever high-intensity means are necessary. We will explore the baleful consequences of both kinds of military conflict in chapter 6. Here we will explore the equally baleful consequences of both kinds of ecclesiastical conflict when targeted on liberation theology in general and Gustavo in particular.

The shift from low-intensity to high-intensity conflict was gradual. We have already noted the earlier stages—restiveness after Medellín at the inroads that liberation themes had made into the final document, the subsequent appearance of unfavorable reviews here, harsh comments there, increasingly strident attacks elsewhere, culminating in a successful maneuver to exclude liberation theologians from the interior dynamics of the Puebla meetings. But the attempt to exclude liberation *ideas* from the Puebla meetings was unsuccessful, and as a result Rome (and conservative Latin American bishops) moved the struggle from behind the scenes into the spotlight.

The attacks, the substantive contents of which will concern us in chapter 6, were of various sorts:

1. For a number of years after Puebla, especially from about 1980 to 1985, Gustavo was under direct investigation by the Congregation for the Doctrine of the Faith (formerly the Holy Office of the Inquisition) headed by Joseph Cardinal Ratzinger. The Sacred Congregation, an arm of the Curia, is charged with maintaining purity of doctrine and has engaged in similar explorations of the possible heretical leanings of such Catholic theologians as Edward Schillebeeckx, Hans Küng, Leonardo Boff, Bishop Casaldáliga, and Charles Curran. Gustavo was at least in good company.

Long lists of charges, usually centering around alleged reductionism of faith to politics, or dangerous enchantment with Marxist ideology, were submitted to Gustavo, in response to which he had to offer detailed rebuttal from his writings. (It was during this period that Gustavo commented wryly, "They have devised a new form of torture for me. They have forced me to ready many times my books.") Some of these rebuttals involved lengthy written responses, while other necessitated trips to Rome (at his own expense) to defend himself in person. At least two years were occupied almost exclusively with such activity.

2. Cardinal Ratzinger himself made a trip to Lima to bring personal pressure on the Peruvian hierarchy to issue a condemnation of liberation theology in general and Gustavo in particular. The Vatican apparently felt that a domestic repudiation would be more palatable to the church at large than a denunciation handed down unilaterally from Rome. But at the time, the Peruvian bishops were split virtually down the middle into pro- and contra-Gustavo factions, and the president of the episcopal conference,

Cardinal Landázuri Ricketts, was supportive of Gustavo. Ratzinger's bid for a Peruvian condemnation failed.

3. Following this, the entire Peruvian episcopate was summoned to Rome to engage in a week-long "conference" on liberation theology. It was apparently felt that the atmosphere of Rome might be more conducive to a condemnation than the atmosphere in Lima had been, for condemnation was clearly the hoped-for, if not absolutely mandated, outcome of the deliberations. But once again, the dynamics within the Peruvian hierarchy were sufficiently strong to avert a repudiation of Gustavo. A document on liberation theology was created that contained some critique, but it did not include a condemnation, and it was simultaneously supportive enough so that Gustavo and his friends realized that they would have no trouble living with it.

4. And then came a curious episode. Cardinal Ratzinger, an eminent theologian in his own right, accustomed to doing things through the appropriate ecclesiastical channels, chose to turn to the mass media. He agreed to a series of interviews with an Italian journalist that were published in a popular format and created a sensation. Entitled *The Ratzinger Report: An Exclusive Interview on the State of the Church* (with Victorio Messori, Ignatius Press, San Francisco, 1985), the book is chatty, superficial, highly opinionated, sensationalistic, and often dead wrong. Ratzinger read Messori's transcript of the interviews and stated that "he has approved them by declaring that he recognizes himself in the texts" (p. 15). Discussions with the journalist range over a wide variety of topics — Vatican II (which, when all is said and done, Ratzinger appears to deplore), heresy, scripture, sexual permissiveness, liturgy, feminism, eschatology, ecumenism, and "A Certain 'Liberation.'" The latter chapter produces in toto a "private" document on liberation theology earlier written by Ratzinger that became public by a "journalistic indiscretion" not further defined. The theme of the article is clearly indicated by its second paragraph:

> An analysis of the phenomenon of liberation theology reveals that it constitutes *a fundamental threat to the faith of the church.* At the same time it must be borne in mind that no error could persist unless it contained a grain of truth. Indeed, an error is all the more dangerous, the greater the grain of truth is, for then the temptation it exerts is all the greater [p. 175, emphasis added].

The essay then recounts the familiar charges we will examine in chapter 6, that liberation theology is reductionistic, Marxist, humanistic, destructive of faith, and the like. One characterization of liberation theology, however, that is absolutely new is Cardinal Ratzinger's conviction that liberation theology is somehow the fault of Rudolf Bultmann, a Protestant exegete who would have been astonished at the charge had he still been alive to hear it.

Ratzinger also asserts, earlier in the report, that the moral conviction of many liberation theologies "becomes the moral norm that justifies violence, homicide, mendacity" (p. 91). If one desires a moment when low-intensity conflict escalated uncontrollably into high-intensity conflict, the moment when that statement was first uttered provides the occasion.

5. In a more serious vein, the Congregation for the Doctrine of the Faith issued two "Instructions on Liberation Theology" on August 6, 1984, and April 5, 1986, the substantive contents of which will concern us in chapter 6. The first "Instruction" was stern, despite some concessions to "authentic" liberation themes, but the second was surprisingly supportive in overall tone, leading one to wonder if Rome had not decided to put the destruction of liberation theology on hold, at least for the time being.

It is always risky, however, for anyone (particularly a Protestant) to second-guess Rome, but even if the vigor of its attack on Gustavo has temporarily abated, there is no assurance of his survival back home, for the exquisite balance within the Peruvian hierarchy between pro- and contra-Gustavo forces is changing. There are two reasons for this: (1) as older bishops retire, Rome consistently replaces them with conservatives opposed to liberation theology, and (2) Cardinal Landázuri's successor, who wields great internal power, is Ricardo Durand, a longtime foe of liberation theology who, before being elevated to his new position, wrote two books attacking Gustavo. Perhaps Rome, always adept at reading certain "signs of the times," will achieve its initial aim without itself firing the shot.

These years of conflict with Rome have been difficult for Gustavo. He has been the target of official attack at the very heart of the church he loves and serves, as well as being castigated by many self-appointed critics (including some from North America) who, however different their perspectives, share in common at least that they have usually not taken the trouble to study Gustavo's thought carefully, but have moved almost immediately into ideological and often ad hominem warfare.

On the other hand, the plight of this tiny David, who has not only been attacked by the "Goliath of the north," but by his own church as well, has drawn people from all over the world to his defense, some of whose affirmations will be reported later. Two supportive events can be described to complete this portion of the story:

In May 1985, when Gustavo most needed expressions of support and solidarity, the theological faculty in Lyons, where Gustavo had earlier studied, agreed to examine him formally on the corpus of his writings, for the possible bestowal of a doctoral degree. The event consisted of a lecture by Gustavo in the morning on "Theology and Spirituality," and a four-hour interrogation by eight professors in the afternoon.

While the morning lecture contains no surprises, it is a helpful summary of central themes in Gustavo's thought, particularly during this period when he was under such intense attack. He begins with concerns about theological language (fully articulated in the book *On Job* published shortly there-after), stressing the need for both contemplative and prophetic language. "Our methodology," he insists, "is our spiritually. ... Reflection on the mystery of God can be undertaken only by following in the footsteps of Jesus" (*Truth,* p. 5). Theology must start with the questions of nonpersons, and acknowledge the "irruption of the poor" from "the underside of history." But this emphasis cannot be allowed to reduce Christianity either to a "discarnate spiritualism" or to an exclusively political orientation.

To deal with the world of the poor means "to analyze and denounce the structural causes of the injustice and oppression in which the poor of Latin America are living" (ibid., p. 9) and to seek ways to opt for *life* in the omnipresent reality of death.

The brief treatment of "theology and the social sciences" emphasizes that while some materials for Christian reflection come from Marxist analysis, the social science resources are much broader than that, and that any theological appropriation from the social sciences must be made in a critical and tentative fashion.

The concluding portion of the lecture affirms the need to bear witness to the resurrection, and seeks to clarify the various levels on which liberation is affirmed: (a) a gift from God that provides liberation from sin; (b) liberation for love and communion; and (c) differentiation between historical embodiments of human liberation and the coming of the kingdom of God.

The final paragraph on the eucharist bears repeating, for detractors of liberation theology usually claim that such emphases are lacking:

> The eucharist [is] the primary work of the ecclesial community. When we share the bread we commemorate the love and fidelity that brought Jesus to his death, as well as the resurrection that put the seal of approval on his mission to the poor. The breaking of bread is at once the point of departure and the point of arrival of the Christian community. In the breaking of bread the community expresses its radical sharing of the human suffering that is caused in many instances by the lack of bread; it also joyfully acknowledges the presence of the risen Lord who gives life and sustains the hope of the people whom his actions and word have called together [ibid., pp. 17-18].

The afternoon colloquium, if not exactly a love feast, must have been a rewarding change for Gustavo after the grillings he had been enduring in Rome. The questions were probing but fair, and enabled him to clarify emphases in his writing that were at that time subject to misunderstanding.

After the interrogation, the academic jury retired, and shortly returned to announce that it had awarded Gustavo the degree doctor of theology *summa cum laude,* a decision dependent upon unanimous agreement of the jurors.[11]

An "up" day after some "down" months.

Another "up" event was the celebration at a sixtieth birthday festival for Gustavo at Maryknoll School of Theology in the summer of 1988. The event also celebrated the twentieth anniversary of the Medellín conference (in which Gustavo played such a central role), and the fifteenth anniversary of the English publication of *A Theology of Liberation,* which was unveiled in a new anniversary edition for the occasion. In addition to the Gustavo Gutiérrez Annual Ice Cream Festival (to be described later), there was the formal presentation of the manuscript of a huge festschrift, *The Future of Theology: Essays in Honor of Gustavo Gutiérrez* (Orbis Books, 1989)—a massive volume containing fifty essays from all over the world on Gustavo's theological contribution, along with shorter tributes from bishops, Nobel Prize winners, and church leaders. The mood of the week is epitomized in a limerick that surfaced on the final evening:

> Gustavo's an orthodox thinker,
> With heresy he does not tinker.
> His views are all sound—
> Which is what *we* propound
> To His Eminence Cardinal Rat*zing*er.

Gustavo—A Personal Portrait

At a recent meeting of the editorial board of *Concilium* a Catholic publishing venture, Gustavo and a North American priest-writer (who had described him as a fomenter of revolution) met for the first time. Whatever image the American had harbored of Gustavo was quickly dispelled by the reality. Commenting later on his surprise, the North American said to a friend, "He certainly doesn't *look* like a violent revolutionary!" To which the friend replied, "The image of Gustavo as a 'violent revolutionary' is held only by people who read writers like you."

Gustavo is often type-cast by those who are looking for a theological villain, and the rest of this chapter will try to let the true person emerge.

Many nouns can be used to describe Gustavo: theologian, professor, activist, scholar, priest, writer, teacher, lecturer. All of them "fit" one aspect or another of his personality. But the most all-embracing word is "pastor," one who lives for others and puts himself at the disposability of those for whom he works and with whom he lives. *Gustavo's teaching and writing are subordinate to his pastoral work,* not the other way around. Here is how he described their interrelationship in an interview with Fr. James Brockmann, S.J.:

> Theology is for my free time. I have never been a full-time teacher. ... I live in a parish and I work with Christian [base] communities and their pastoral agents. ... In Peru no one would think of calling

me Professor Gutiérrez. . . . The pastoral work is what I enjoy most. That is my primary function as a priest, I feel. I was ordained not to "do theology," but to proclaim the gospel. I consider theology only a help toward that, nothing more [*Christian Century,* October 19, 1983, p. 933].

He concedes that "abroad, sometimes, I do wear a theologian's hat," and it is a patent fact that he writes important books, despite his disclaimer:

My aim has never been to publish books. Not that there is anything wrong with publishing. It's just not my vocation, which is fundamentally pastoral. But when I do theology, I try to do it as seriously as possible. I regard that as an obligation. *A Theology of Liberation* was carefully thought out, and it confronted contemporary thought. That's why there are so many references, not to show how much I had read but to expose my thought to that of others [ibid., p. 935].

The priority of the pastoral calling is clear when people want to interview him. Elsa Tamez, a biblical scholar from Costa Rica who frequently works with Gustavo, describes the circumstances of an interview with him about the role of women in the church:

On a Sunday I went with my tape recorder to the Mass that Gustavo Gutiérrez was celebrating with a Christian [base] community. It was good to see him in his priestly vestments with bread and wine in his hands. He winked at me from the altar, and then at the kiss of peace we greeted each other with an *abrazo* and agreed on a time to meet. After Mass I went with him to the hospital to visit a parishioner who was sick [Tamez, *Against Machismo,* p. 39].

Only after Mass and the hospital visit was there time for Elsa Tamez to set up her tape recorder. The pastoral work came first. And the pastoral role is not limited to Lima. Gustavo is a priest and pastor wherever he goes. I know people in New York City who, when he taught there, would not have survived without the pastoral help of this short, unpretentious, eminently kind man. There must be thousands of such people in Latin America.

Often the role of "pastor" shades imperceptibly into the role of "teacher." Most of the teaching Gustavo does in Peru is with the "people," most notably in the annual two-week "summer course" given at the Catholic University in Lima. Over two thousand lay persons come to this course each year. Since the government considers "theology" a subversive topic, it is frequently touch-and-go as to whether the upcoming summer course will be permitted.

When Gustavo lectures, there are three requirements (in addition to some students): a blackboard, a lot of chalk, and an eraser. A point is written on the blackboard. As it is exposed, examples are given and subpoints gradually fill up the space under the main point. Then all but the major heading is removed in a series of swirling and esthetic but rather inefficient erasures. A second point is written on the board. After exposition, examples, and subheadings, there is another esthetic interlude with the eraser as the subheadings disappear to make room for a third major point, and refinements of the argument are noted in the diminishing space.

There are always three points. Dissertations will someday be written on whether this is a subtle appeal to trinitarian theology, an example of Hegelian methodology, or an acknowledgment that the human mind is capable of absorbing only three points in a given period of time. (I once teamtaught a summer course with Gustavo and prior to his arrival I had to devise a five-day course outline. I had him trapped, I thought: "How can you spread three points over five days?" "Is very easy," he replied, counting off on his fingers, "Introduction, three points, conclusion. Five days.")

To get any writing done, as I have already noted, Gustavo must occasionally get away from Lima, where he is otherwise on 24-hour call. Final documentation for the book on Job was done in the Graduate Theological Union Library in Berkeley; discovery of the surprising affinities between Walter Rauschenbusch and the concerns of liberation theology were explored in the stacks of Union Theological Seminary in New York City; extensive research on Bartolomé de Las Casas was done at the University of Michigan in Ann Arbor, and almost completed during a three-month residency at the University of Cambridge, England, in the winter of 1989.

Our *Who's Who* excursion at the beginning of this chapter noted a number of degrees from prestigious universities, and in later years these have given him some leverage in his ongoing battles with Rome. But such honors are worn lightly. There is a well-verified story (though Gustavo is not its source) that Yale University voted to give him an honorary degree several years ago. Yale requires that the recipient receive the degree in person, and stipulates that the offer will be made only once. Gustavo just could not make it to New Haven on the appointed weekend. He had already agreed to lead a retreat for lay persons.

I once moderated a panel in which Gustavo and a well-known pacifist debated the issue of violence in Christian ethics. The pacifist had ready responses for every question; to do him justice, he had been answering them all for years, but as a result there was no evident pain or anguish. Gustavo responded to each question with both pain and anguish. He wrestled with the moral dilemma that he and other Christians might find some day that all the alternatives to violence had been exhausted. It was an ongoing struggle he shared with his listeners. It was authentic.

"Authentic" is a good word for Gustavo. In keeping with the priority he gives to his pastoral ministry, he does not live in the pleasant university area in Lima, but in a third-floor apartment over the Bartolomé de Las

Casas Center in Rímac, the slum area of Lima, not far from where he was born, and where he spends the bulk of his time as pastor of the parish church. The quarters are spartan, though there is a roof where one could sit in the evening, if there were ever time for such diversion. The second floor is the center itself, with a study, conference room, kitchen, and library. The latter consists mainly of books in many languages that Gustavo transports home in backbreaking suitcase-fulls whenever he returns from another part of the globe. The first floor houses the shop of a local merchant.

As far as I have been able to discover, Gustavo's recreational pleasures are three: he confesses to being a chess addict from his youth, and laments that there is never sufficient time to indulge this whim; he is fond of swimming, good therapy for his shortened leg, and one bonus to his frequent lecturing at the New York State Maryknoll School of Theology is unlimited access to the pool; but more than anything else, he is inordinately, intemperately, immoderately, and ravenously fond of ice cream. Any flavor. In at least three places where he occasionally teaches in the United States, it has become the custom to end the term with the Gustavo Gutiérrez Annual Ice Cream Festival.

What comes next in Gustavo's story? In a volatile world, no one holding "controversial" positions is going to have a clearly charted future. The deteriorating political situation in Peru will make things more difficult for him. The increasing right-wing situation in the church in Peru will make things even more difficult. But whatever course Peruvian politics or Peruvian church politics takes, one can be sure that Gustavo will continue to be found among the poor, whoever and wherever they are. If it comes to a choice between being with them or writing another book, or even eating ice cream, the book and the ice cream will have to wait.

CHAPTER 3

Act One:
Commitment to the Poor (Praxis)

I want to inspire hope in you. To tell you you should love the land with its fruits—your seed, your animals, your tools. . . . I want to tell you you should love your culture, your songs, your language, your way of doing things, your family, your landscape. That along with the other poor you should make preparations and organize, because in unity alone is there strength. That sooner or later you or your children will possess the entire land because God has given it to all as a gift and a task. God is the sole owner of the fields.

— Archbishop Luis Vallejos, cited in
We Drink from Our Own Wells, p. 156

Theology in Latin America today will be a reflection in, and on, faith as liberation praxis. It will be an understanding of the faith from an option and a commitment. It will be an understanding of the faith from a point of departure in real, effective solidarity with the exploited classes, oppressed ethnic groups, and despised cultures of Latin America, and from within their world. It will be a reflection that starts out from a commitment to create a just society, a community of sisters and brothers, and that ought to see that this commitment grows more radical and complete. It will be a theological reflection that becomes true, veri-fied, in real and fruitful involvement in the liberation process.

— Gustavo in *The Power of the Poor in History,* p. 60

After describing his eight years of working among the desperately poor in the Peruvian altiplano—"people who have lived on the margins of sub-sistence for centuries"—Curt Cadorette, a Maryknoll priest, comments, "My interest in Gutiérrez's theology is not the result of mere intellectual curiosity. Rather *it flows from a privileged experience of having lived among the men and women who provide the raw material of his theology—the poor and oppressed of Peru*" (Cadorette, p. xi, italics added).

"The World Should Not Be the Way It Is"

Most of us have not had the "privileged experience" of living with the poor, in Peru or elsewhere. To the degree that we lack such experience, we will be unable fully to understand Gustavo's claim that the "first act" is not to develop a theology, or create a worldview, or do graduate work. Such activities can be components of the "second act," but they will be impoverished and even false to the extent that they have not been informed by the first act, which is not a "head trip," but a "foot trip," to engagement and identification with the poor, the victims, the marginated. Those who read (and write) books like this already have education, contacts, and resources that preclude full identification with the poor, but we must make as empathetic an attempt as we can to see and hear the people and voices and situation out of which the "second act" — the creation of a theology of liberation — later emerges.

There is a test by which we can determine whether or not the venture is really possible for us. Juan Luis Segundo, a Jesuit from Uruguay, has suggested that the starting point for all liberation theologies is a very simple claim: *the world should not be the way it is.* If we believe that the world is all right the way it is (with possible minor adjustments here or there), then, Segundo insists, we will never understand what liberation theology is all about. That the world should *not* be the way it is is the unassailable bottom-line for those who are victims, those who have been exploited, those who are . . . poor.

Involvement with that reality is the stuff of Act One.

Starting with the Situation of the Poor

Anglican Bishop Charles Gore once defined love as "the ability to read statistics with compassion." Measured by such a standard, few of us would qualify. Even if we did, we would have to remember that statistics are a dime a dozen (to employ a statistical measurement) and suffer from at least three shortcomings. (1) *Statistics depersonalize.* When we confront numbers rather than human beings, we can avoid personal involvement. (2) *Statistics immobilize.* No one can really internalize such statistics as "15,000 persons starve to death every day on plant Earth," or "in six years, 70,000 persons in El Salvador were murdered by death squads." (3) *Statistics are manipulable.* By clever and selective use of statistical data, almost anything can be "proven." (Statistic: the U.S.A. significantly reduced its megatonnage of nuclear weapons in Europe at a time when Russia was doing the reverse. Presumed conclusion: the U.S.A. was working for peace, the Russians for greater nuclear capability. Omitted statistic: the U.S.A. "reduced" its tonnage by replacing heavier weapons with newer and more sophisticated *and lighter* weapons. True conclusion: the U.S. capacity for nuclear attack was increased rather than decreased.)

So we will not rely too heavily on statistics to describe the world of the poor, but we will cite enough to open the minds of all but the most hardened. As to the "reliability" of such statistics, let us fashion a rule of thumb from Segundo's assertion that "the world should be the way it is." If statistics make us feel comfortable with "the world . . . as it is," we must be suspicious of them. Some noncomforting statistics:[1]

• In Brazil, the top 2% of the landowners control 60% of the arable land, while 70% of the rural householders are landless or nearly so. In Colombia the top 4% of landowners control 6% of the arable land, while 66% of the rural households are landless or nearly so. In El Salvador the top 1% of landowners control 41% of the arable land, while 60% of the rural householders are landless or nearly so. In Guatemala the top 1% of the landowners control 34% of the arable land, while 85% of the rural households are landless or nearly so. (One reason for the Guatemala statistic may be that Del Monte owns 57,000 acres but cultivates only 9,000 acres.)

• The cash income of farmers in the Chuchito area of Peru is $100 per year, and tenant farmers are allowed to retain only one-third of the crops they grow.

• Every week 2,000 to 5,000 persons move to Lima from the countryside, hoping to find work, at a time when only 37% of the adult population of Lima has steady work.

• Between 1980 and 1985, 70% of Peru's export earnings were used to pay *interest* on overseas loans.

• Whenever the interest rate on international loans is raised by 1%, the indebtedness of the Latin American nations rises by $2.5 billion.

• Workers in Peru who used to be breadwinners for six persons must now provide for eight persons on less than half the income they formerly had.

• Over half the children born in Peru die before reaching age five.

• The United States gives El Salvador over $1 million a day, most of which goes to sustain the army and the death squads.

• In El Salvador a family of six needs $333 per year to survive, but over half the population earns less than that.

• In 1800 the gap between the per capita incomes of the richer and poorer nations was about two to one. It is now about twenty to one.

• In 1960 a farmer could buy a tractor for the equivalent of three tons of bananas. In 1970 it took eleven tons.

What *human* realities lie behind such statistics? These things at least:

1. The distance between the few who are very rich and the many who are very poor is unimaginably great. While a few enjoy lavish circumstances, the overwhelming majority live in indescribable poverty. And despite good intentions — the Decade of Development, the Alliance for Progress, and

many philanthropic attempts to "help the poor"—the gap between rich and poor increases annually.

2. The poor are not only economically powerless, without adequate income to support their families, but are politically powerless as well, victims of rigged elections, military intimidation, and social structures that function as though the poor did not exist except for purposes of exploitation by the rich. Attempts by the poor to organize are routinely destroyed with whatever degree of brutality a given situation demands. Threats, "disappearances," assassinations, massacres and torture are run-of-the-mill responses.

3. Latin American countries are so indebted to international banking and business interests that they cannot pay off even the interest on their loans, let alone decrease the principal. The interest due annually is often greater than the total income of the country. (Monetary powers in the First World are beginning to come to terms with this reality, and various forms of debt forgiveness are being explored as a practical necessity, to forestall the collapse of the entire structure.)

4. It is common for the military to run the countries either through overt control or "puppet" civilian leaders who survive in public office at the pleasure of the military. The military, in turn, maintain control because the United States (and other First World powers) provide the necessary money, tanks, ammunition, and military training.

5. The reality to which all the statistics point is *poverty*—endless, grinding, destructive, dehumanizing—with no apparent hope of being overcome. As Gustavo describes it:

> I believe that to be poor is to be insignificant, to be just another number. It is to wait in line for days to have a toothache taken care of. It is to feel you have no way of responding to your family's needs, not to have the money even for an aspirin [*Latinamerica Press,* May 20, 1984, p. 5].

Statistics will never acquaint us with the real situation, for the poor *as people* can be ignored. In a rare moment of eloquenee, the bishops at Puebla, rather than pondering one more chart or sheaf of statistics, conjured up the faces of the poor as the only true way to "see" the world:

> This situation of pervasive extreme poverty takes place on very concrete faces in real life. In these faces we ought to recognize the suffering creatures of Christ the Lord, who questions and challenges us. They include:
> —the faces of *young children,* struck down by poverty before they are born, their chance for self-development blocked by irresponsible mental and physical deficiencies; and of the *vagrant children* in our

cities who are so often exploited, products of poverty and the moral disorganization of the family;

— the faces of *young people,* who are disoriented because they cannot find their place in society, and who are frustrated, particularly in marginal rural and urban areas, by the lack of opportunity to obtain training and work;

— the faces of the *indigenous peoples,* and frequently of the Afro-Americans as well; living marginalized lives in inhuman situations, they can be considered the poorest of the poor;

— the faces of the *peasants*; as a social group, they live in exile almost everywhere on our continent, deprived of land, caught in a situation of internal and external dependence, and subjected to systems of commercialization that exploit them;

— the faces of *laborers*, who frequently are ill-paid and who have difficulty in organizing themselves and defending their rights;

— the faces of *the underemployed and the unemployed*, who are dismissed because of the harsh exigencies of economic crises, and often because of development-models that subject workers and their families to cold economic calculations;

— the faces of *marginalized and overcrowded urban dwellers*, whose lack of material goods is matched by the ostentatious display of wealth by other segments of society;

— the faces of *old people*, who are growing more numerous every day, and who are frequently marginalized in a progress-oriented society that totally disregards people not engaged in production [*Puebla*, §31-39, italics added].

Another approach to the reality of the poor, which seeks to understand them through their faith as well as their faces, is through "popular religion," meaning not the latest fad, but the religion of the people, the *populus*. This folk religion is an amalgam of the Spanish Catholicism imposed by the conquerors and the Amerindian religions that were there long before the conquerors and were never fully extinguished, even by assiduous missionaries.

It has been the custom to dismiss folk religion as superstition and magic. But new appraisals have been developing, partly the result of studies undertaken at Gustavo's Bartolomé de Las Casas Center that accord new dignity and importance to folk religion. As Gustavo says:

I think that to consider it only a second-class Christianity is a mistake. Respect for it is at bottom a respect for the Lord's presence. Just as we say the church has a lot to learn from the world, so we have a lot to learn from folk religion. . . . Folk religion is an expression of a poor people, and [the bishops at] Puebla recognized that the poor are the bearers of the gospel. To be a bearer of the gospel is to evangelize.

... Folk religion reminds us of many aspects of the life, of the sufferings and joys, of poor people, and other sections of the church need to be reminded of that for a better understanding of the gospel [Brockmann interview, *Christian Century,* pp. 33-34].

As early as 1971, when *A Theology of Liberation* was first published, Gustavo included in his notes a significant bibliography on folk religion (cf. p. 93, n. 20 [pp. 74-75, n. 20]).

As John McCoy has pointed out, there have been three important expressions of folk religion: miracles, fiestas, and patron saints of an area. Belief in miracles helps those in hopeless situations continue to hope; fiestas create a sense of community where social bonds can be renewed and reinforced; and patron saints provide a sense of history and perspective for the present.

Traditionally, folk religion has been seen as a means of "escape" from the injustices of life, and consequently as politically innocuous, but as Diego Irarrázaval, of the research team at the Las Casas center, notes:

To the extent to which they feel protected by God and His Saints and spirits, the poor feel capable of rising up and challenging a social order that they know is almost invincible. For they know that God is on their side [McCoy, *America,* December 31, 1988, p. 534].

Devotion to the Virgin of Guadalupe is a good example of interweaving Christianity and earlier folk religion to create social consequences. When a Mexican peasant claimed to have been visited by an apparition of the mother of Jesus, Mary was perceived not as an Aztec goddess or as a Spanish lady of high society, but as "a humble Amerindian woman," pointing beyond a destroyed culture (Aztec) and an imposed culture (Catholic Christianity), so that she became a rallying point for piety and action by poor persons who could not have responded to the "destroyed" or "imposed" alternatives. Leonardo Boff insists that this is the way the gospel must be preached, "not in European, white, dominating, or colonizing ways, but in ways that express incarnation in a struggling people" (ibid., p. 536).

Three Meanings of Poverty

We are always tempted to depersonalize matters that threaten us. We would feel relieved if we could shift the discussion from "poor persons," flesh and blood human beings whose plight makes us feel uneasy, to "poverty," an impersonal concept about which we can reflect, write paragraphs, and keep at a distance.

Gustavo analyzes three meanings of poverty that will not allow us such an escape, but will involve us at a deeper and more personal level than before.[2]

Our first task is terminological, because, as Gustavo points out, "poverty is an equivocal term" (*TheoLib,* pp. 162 [287]). In Catholic circles, poverty is one of the "evangelical counsels," along with chastity and obedience, for those who make profession in a religious order. In this context it is a high-order virtue, beyond the reach of garden-variety sanctity. Certain strains of Christian spirituality have also exalted poverty in ways that neutralize the need to challenge or remove it; since it holds such an important place in Christian thought, poverty must be "good." It is to overcome such confusion that Gustavo differentiates three meanings of poverty.

1. *Material poverty* is "the lack of economic goods necessary for a life worthy of the name" (ibid., pp. 163 [288]), a subhuman condition that must always be opposed. Even so, many conventional Christians want to make a virtue out of it . . . for others. Those who are themselves victims of material poverty, however, are less and less willing to look on their situation as a disguised blessing, and more and more determined to repudiate it as appropriate for anyone.

2. *Spiritual poverty,* often understood as "an interior attitude of unattachment to the goods of this world," can nevertheless lead, as Gustavo points out, "to comforting and tranquilizing conclusions." According to this reading, one can possess many material goods as long as one is not "overattached" to them. The flip side of the coin is that one need not be overconcerned about those who lack material goods, for material goods always threaten to dominate their lives. It has even been argued that it is better for most people (i.e., people other than those arguing the point) *not* to have too many material goods, for fear they will become enamored of them and place their salvation in jeopardy.

3. Gustavo argues that there is a *biblical understanding of poverty* as well, and that there are two major ways of understanding it. On the one hand, the bible views material poverty as "*a scandalous condition* inimical to human dignity and therefore to the will of God" (ibid., pp. 165 [291]). Jesus and the prophets inveigh against the oppressiveness that results when the rich exploit the poor, and Gustavo offers copious examples of this conviction throughout Scripture (cf. Job 24:2-12; Amos 2:6-7; 10:1-2; Exodus 16:6-8; etc.). Poverty contradicts the meaning of the Mosaic religion, which was to give people dignity; the mandate of Genesis, which was to provide fulfilling work; and the sacramentality of the human person, who is to know God by acting justly toward other human persons.

On the other hand, however, the Bible also understands poverty as *spiritual childhood,* an attitude opposed to pride or self-sufficiency, synonymous with faith and trust in the Lord. So when the gospel says that the poor are "blessed," it is not condoning poverty on the grounds that injustice will someday be overcome in the kingdom of God. Rather:

> The elimination of the exploitation and poverty that prevent the poor from being fully human has begun; a Kingdom of justice which goes

even beyond what they could have hoped for has begun. They are blessed because the coming of the Kingdom will put an end to their poverty by creating a world of fellowship [ibid., pp. 171 (298)].

Gustavo feels that these two biblical notions, of material poverty as a scandalous condition, and spiritual poverty as "an attitude of openness to God," converge in a third understanding of *poverty as a commitment of solidarity and protest.* This is the true biblical understanding.

Christians are not to idealize poverty but to oppose it: "Christian poverty, as an expression of love, is *solidarity with the poor* and is a *protest against poverty*" (ibid., pp. 172 [300-301]). There are important, even conflictive, results when this is taken seriously, for identification with the poor means that "to be with the oppressed is to be against the oppressor." It means taking sides, it means political engagement in a struggle against the structures of society designed to keep the poor poor so that the rich can become richer. This also defines the task of the church, and provides it with a vocation that is uniquely its own, "by rejecting poverty and making itself poor in order to protest against it" (ibid., pp. 173 [301-2]).

So the outcome of a biblical excursion into the meaning of "poverty" means a deeper engagement with the poor than before:

> Only authentic solidarity with the poor and a real protest against the poverty of our time can provide the concrete vital context necessary for a theological discussion of poverty. The absence of a sufficient commitment to the poor, the marginated, and the exploited is perhaps the fundamental reason why we have no solid contemporary reflection on the witness of poverty.
>
> For the Latin American Church especially, this witness is an inescapable and much-needed sign of the authenticity of its mission [ibid., pp. 173 (302)].

"A Preferential Option for the Poor"

When the United States Roman Catholic bishops issued the first draft of their pastoral letter, "Economic Justice for All" in 1984, there was widespread dismay among conservative Catholics. (So great was the apprehension that one group issued a "response" to the bishops' letter even before it had been released.) The apprehensions frequently focused on the bishops' conviction that the church should make "a preferential option for the poor."

The phrase was new to North American Catholics, but it was not new to North American bishops, who were simply claiming as their own a perspective increasingly axiomatic in the southern hemisphere.

Although Vatican II exhibited a new degree of openness to "the modern

world," that world was still the world of "bourgeois society," as Gustavo
pointed out in an analysis of the documents: "The theme of poverty . . .
knocked on the Council's door but only got a glimpse inside" (in Greinacher
and Muller, *The Poor and the Church,* 1977, pp. 12-13). When the Latin
American bishops met at Medellín three years later, however, those knock-
ing on the door were by that time so close to home that they could neither
be ignored nor resisted. One of the Medellín documents was "Poverty in
the Church" (cf. Medellín proceedings, vol. 2, pp. 213-20, and Hennelly,
document #10). A summary of its highlights will indicate the beginning of
a new direction:

The church (the bishops acknowledged) can no longer remain indifferent
to the social injustices that condemn most Latin Americans to abysmal
poverty. The church is frequently charged with being allied with the rich,
and even though many bishops, priests, and religious are actually poor, the
prevailing image is of an affluent church in lockstep with the affluent portion of society.

To remedy this situation, the church must distinguish between (a) poverty as a lack of material goods, which is always evil, (b) spiritual poverty
as an attitude of openness to the Lord, and (c) poverty as an identification
with the poor in order to bear witness against the evils under which the
poor are ground down and destroyed. (One cannot fail to notice the sym-
metry between this analysis and the "three meanings of poverty" discussed
in the preceding section of this chapter, nor fail to conclude that the two
analyses flowed from the same pen.)

All this means that "a poor church must denounce the injustice manifest
in the inequities between rich and poor, and bind itself to a life of poverty
among the poor, following the example of Christ who, though rich, 'became
poor for our sakes.' " The church must also employ its resources and per-
sonnel to "give *preference* to the poorest and most needy sectors" (§9, italics
added). This new solidarity "has to be concretized in criticism of injustice
and oppression."

In addition, church buildings should be modest, clothing simple, institutions functional and without ostentation, titles of honor foresworn, and
"fees" for the administration of sacraments refused. Servants of the church
should give testimony to poverty by their own detachment from material
goods.

It would be idle to pretend that all the provisions for change envisioned
in this document had been achieved before the bishops met again at Puebla,
but they presaged a new awareness in the life of the church, and, without
quite employing the actual phrase, gave credence to the notion that the
church must make a preferential option for the poor. The emergence of
the "base communities" in the interval between Medellín and Puebla
helped to spread such notions in the life of everyday people, and speed
their implementation. Whatever else they were, the base communities rep-

resented the poor organizing among themselves and rooting their concerns in the church's witness to social justice.

As a result, when Puebla convened, the time was ripe for further clarification and with Gustavo's help an advance was registered.

The most concentrated treatment of the theme is in the concluding section of the overall document, "A Missionary Church Serving Evangelization in Latin America" (*Puebla*, §§1134-65). The bishops affirmed their intention to continue in the spirit of Medellín, and the consequent "need for conversion on the part of the whole Church to a preferential option for the poor" (§1134). In the last decade, they note, the poor have begun to organize, the church has been more forthright in its denunciation of social injustice, and the result has been tension and conflict.

There are three reasons for the need of a preferential option. The *first* is the example set by Jesus, who identified with the poor by becoming one of them, and the need for a church serving in his name to make a similar commitment. Whenever the image of God in the poor is dimmed and defiled, "God takes on their defense and loves them" (§1142).

A *second* reason for the preferential option is that service to the poor is what Christ taught his children to do. An important insight from Vatican II is cited to give this concern specificity:

> The demands of justice should first be satisfied, lest the giving of what is due in justice be represented as the offering of a charitable gift. Not only the effects but also the causes of various ills must be removed. Help should be given in such a way that the recipients may gradually be freed from dependence on others and become self-sufficient [AA, 8, cited §1146].

When this happens, a reversal takes place: not only does the church evangelize the poor, but *the poor evangelize the church,* challenging it, summoning it to conversion, and incarnating "evangelical values" (§1147).

A *third* reason for the preferential option is that the connection between the gospel and poverty demands a connection between the church and the poor. "Evangelical poverty" is a call to all to combine trust in God with an austere lifestyle, and to carry out in practice "the giving and sharing of material and spiritual gifts" (§1150).

Certain pastoral guidelines follow these considerations: recognizing "the scandalous reality of economic imbalances," Christians must find new ways "to construct a just and free society" (§1154). This means both inner and outer transformation: "the required change in unjust social, political, and economic structures" must be accompanied "by a change in our personal and collective outlook" (§1155).

The church as church must therefore reexamine its own structures and collectively embrace "an austere lifestyle," so that, being "authentically poor," it can become a place "where the poor have a real chance for participation and where their worth is recognized" (§1158).

Concretely, the bishops condemn extreme poverty, pledge to denounce mechanisms that generate it, offer to work in solidarity with all "people of good will" in order to uproot poverty, support the overall right of the poor "to share in the decisions that affect their lives," and specifically the right to organize "to defend and promote their interests" (§§1159-63). These themes are not located exclusively in part 4, but permeate the document as a whole (cf. §§382, 707, 711, 769, 1217 for examples).

It is one of the best kept secrets of the Puebla Conference that the chapter immediately following "A Preferential Option for the Poor" is entitled "A Preferential Option for Young People," and is actually longer than its predecessor. This should dispose of the false charge that "the preferential option for the poor" is meant to be exclusive. To speak of "a preferential option for the poor" is *not* to speak of an "exclusive option for the poor," as though God loved only the poor and hated everybody else, especially the rich. This point is insisted upon so frequently in the document that any charge of "exclusiveness" simply betrays the assailant's lack of knowledge of the text. What *is* being claimed is that in responding to the long-range concern God has for all people, one starts with an immediate concern for, and involvement with, the poor. To the degree that the cries of the poor are heard, and are given priority over the complaints of the rich, there can be movement toward a more just society. As the poor are liberated from their scandalous poverty, new conditions will be created in which the rich will no longer be able to act as oppressors, and new relationships will be possible in a community in which all can share. To start with a preferential option for the poor is finally to include the rich as well. To start at the opposite end with a preferential option for the rich, as the church did for centuries, cuts the church off from the poor, for the concern of the rich will always be to keep the poor from threatening them, and creative relationship will be impossible.

Using the "preferential option for the poor" as a basis for judgment, we can now examine some attempts to transform the situation of the poor.

"Development": A False Remedy for a Real Problem

In 1955 an international conference was held in Bandung to face the unacceptable inequities between rich and poor nations, or, as they soon began to be called, the "developed" and "underdeveloped" nations. The conference had many delegates from Asia and Africa who found themselves confronting a "First World" (the United States), a "Second World" (Russia), and not wanting to align with either. So the "unaligned" nations became, almost by terminological accident, a "Third World" — nations that (with whatever dissimilarities) shared at least that they were poor, dark-skinned, and generally from the southern rather than northern hemisphere.

How were the inequities to be overcome? The proposal that emerged, not solely out of Bandung but out of many other conferences, agencies, and sponsorship by the United Nations was commitment to a "Decade of Development," during which the rich would provide to the poor, either by outright gifts or long-term loans, sufficient capital for them to replicate the processes that had brought prosperity to First World nations.

The misfortunes of this experiment are described by Gustavo in the early pages of *A Theology of Liberation* (chapters 2 and 6, pp. 13-25 [21-42], 49-57 [81-99]). "Developmentalism," as it came to be called, was to provide a means for economic growth, a total social process, and a humanistic perspective. It was a "given" that the way in which the wealthy had accumulated wealth was to be a model for the rest, and that the way was the way of market capitalism. An outside model was thus imposed on the "backward" nations, instead of exploring whether other models might work better in non-European, non-North American situations.

As Gustavo points out, "reformism" was the device that, as he also pointed out, represented nothing more than "timid measures, really ineffective in the long run, and counterproductive to achieving a real transformation" (ibid., pp. 17 [26]). There was no attack on the root problems, nor was there willingness on the part of the donors to allow challenges to the status quo. Result: after the "Decade of Development," the gap between rich and poor nations had actually increased rather than diminished. Whatever benefits those at the bottom accrued were disproportionately small compared to the large benefits of those at the top.

There are at least two historical reasons why attempts to make the poor replicate the patterns of the rich were doomed:

1. Earlier societies, at the time of capitalist expansion, had had wideopen geographical frontiers — that is, unsettled areas with unbelievably rich natural resources — that could be plundered on the cheap by those who got there first and had sufficient military strength to quell others who sought similar rewards. There were no comparable uncharted frontiers left in the 1950s and 60s.

2. The so-called unsettled areas of the world had not actually been unsettled; indigenous peoples had lived within them for centuries. This meant confronting the "natives" as less than fully human, so that they could either be exploited if cooperative, "relocated" if uncooperative, or destroyed genocidally if aggressively uncooperative.

Consequently, to offer past experience as a model for contemporary success was historically and morally flawed from the beginning.

Several flaws of a different order emerge when one tries to assess the developmentalist approach today:

1. Development is *tokenism*. It does not fundamentally challenge a system concerned more about profits than about persons, and is content with "cosmetic" changes that may initially look impressive but really transform nothing. Swinging hard, Gustavo points out that such gentle measures are doomed from the start:

Only a radical break from the status quo, that is, a profound transformation of the private property system, access to power of the
exploited class, and a social revolution that would break this dependence would allow for the change to a new society, a socialist society—
or at least allow that such a society might be possible [ibid., pp. 17
(26-27)].

2. Development is *exploitive.* It erodes the inner life of the "dependent"
nation. Aid that goes to needy countries frequently shores up oligarchies
already in power, usually repressive regimes bent on remaining in power.
Brazil, for example, was heralded with having achieved an "economic miracle" because of the rapid rise of its Gross National Product, but the new
revenues went into the pockets of those already at the top of the heap,
while the actual purchasing power of the rest *declined* by almost 25 percent
during the same period. The "miracle" benefited the few but not the many.

Overseas investors favor countries with "stability"—that is, the promise
of no social upheavals that might threaten profits, no worker "agitation"
for higher wages that might threaten profits, no pressing for safe working
conditions that might threaten profits. But "stability" and dictatorship work
hand in hand. So the Philippines under Marcos was handsomely rewarded;
Nicaragua under Somoza was handsomely rewarded; a succession of puppet
civilian rulers in El Salvador was handsomely rewarded. In all these cases,
loans lined the pockets of the military and enabled them to purchase even
more sophisticated military hardware that would keep them in power,
whether overtly or covertly.

The exploitation had another consequence. As we have seen, interest
on loans began to pile up, and when the "economic miracles" did not occur
(save for the few), the small countries had to negotiate new loans to pay
interest on the old loans. Over a decade and a half, the indebtedness of
the poor countries to the rich nations reached unbelievable proportions.
As already noted, it is now the case that the annual income in many Third
World countries is less than the *interest* due annually on their accumulated
loans.

3. Development is *paternalistic.* Those who pay the piper call the tune.
Decisions about what a small Latin American country should manufacture,
export, import, what political party should hold power, what its foreign
policy should be—such matters are decided less in San Salvador or Lima
or Managua than in New York or Bonn or London. Small nations discover
that they are mere pawns on a chess board of international finance, without
power to move themselves, or even recommend the moves that others make
on their behalf.[3]

The Choice between "Superversion" and "Subversion"

The difficulty with development as a remedy for human inequities is that
it imposes new patterns from above, created by those in power, who may

be willing to do a few things *for* the poor, but seldom want to work *with* the poor, and almost never acknowledge that the poor have a right to make their own decisions and be the architects of their own destiny.

The word for this posture is *superversion,* the root of which is the Latin *vertir*, meaning "to change direction, turn about, overthrow, redirect." The prefix *super* means "above, on top of." Thus super-version means "to change things from above," to allow those on top to direct the course of events. It is an attitude that says, "We see the plight of those on the bottom, and we are willing to make a few minor changes so that their plight will be less catastrophic." Many "good works" are done in the name of superversion, and church people are often at the heart of such efforts. The modern "trickle down" theory of economics is a contemporary instance of super-version: if the rich are allowed to make lots more money, some of it is bound to "trickle down" to the poor.

The problem with superversion is that *nothing significant changes.* There is no historical evidence to suggest that those with power or money will share them voluntarily. Whatever changes ensue, therefore, will be token changes, cosmetic adjustments that are minor palliatives at best and further reintrenchment of unjust social structures at worst. Superversion changes superficially from above, rather than radically from below, and it does so in the interests of the few on top rather than the many on the bottom.

If superversion will not meet the need, the alternative is *sub*-version, or "change from below," by those dwelling in what Gustavo calls "the underside of history." To hear him correctly, we must rid ourselves of the notion that to be "subversive" means to engage in cloak-and-dagger operations or clandestine maneuvers, though in extreme cases of injustice such activity might be necessary. Instead of remaining content that history be "written by those with white hands," in Leonardo Boff's phrase, Gustavo believes that history must be rewritten "from below"—which means remade—by those who have been its victims. He is insistent on reclaiming the word as a description of the history of the poor:

> It will be a subversive history. History must be changed around, not from above but from below. There is no evil in being a subversive, struggling against the capitalist system, rather what is evil today is to be a "superversive," a support to the existing domination [*LibChange,* pp. 92-93].

If superversion means that the rich see to it that their privileged position is not challenged, subversion means that the poor take charge of their own lives. There is no doubt in Gustavo's mind which form of action the gospel demands. Mary clarified the choice long ago in her song when visiting Elizabeth:

> God has put down the mighty from their thrones,
> and exalted those of low degree.

> God has filled the hungry with good things
> and the rich God has sent empty away
> [Luke 1:52-53].

During the Somoza regime in Nicaragua, to carry these words on one's person in a little amulet was to risk the death penalty. With all their demonic power, the Somozas knew when a real challenge confronted them.

Gustavo's personal discovery, as traced in chapter 2—that poverty is the result of unjust social structures rather than simply lack of initiative by the poor—has the consequence that commitment to subversive action with the poor will mean commitment to changing the social structures that keep them poor.

This recognition brings another initially threatening word into the discussion, the word "radical," which comes from the Latin *radix,* meaning "root." To look at a problem "radically" is to try to get to its "root." And the "root" of the problem for Gustavo is that present social structures exploit the many poor for the sake of the few rich. To one who accepts this analysis, the only effective way to deal with such structures is to "up-root" them, so that other, more just, structures can replace them. Deep-rooted problems call for deep-rooted remedies:

> Solidarity cannot limit itself to just saying no to the way things are arranged. It must be more than that. It must be an effort to forge a society in which the worker is not subordinated to the power of the means of production, a society in which the assumption of social responsibility for political affairs will include social responsibility for real liberty and will lead to the emergence of a new social consciousness.
>
> Solidarity with the poor implies the transformation of the existing social order [Geffré, p. 60].

By recasting one of Gustavo's prose statements into blank verse, we can see more clearly the kinds of choices to which he feels Christians are called:

> The Latin American poor
>   seek to eradicate their misery,
>   not ameliorate it;
> hence they choose
>   social revolution rather than reform,
>   liberation rather than development,
>   and
>   socialism rather than liberalization
>   [*Emergent,* p. 240].

This means a new praxis of the poor.

The Praxis of the Poor[4]

The word "praxis" has appeared frequently in our discussion. It is an important — and difficult — word we must now try to clarify. The end result will be a fresh way of looking at the world.

Like many theological concepts, the word itself is simply a transliteration of the Greek word *praxis*. Dictionaries often define it by its English cognate "practice," frequently setting up a contrast between "theory" and "practice." But in liberation theology the word is more richly nuanced.

While praxis does resemble "practice," we must not use the apparent similarity to fortify a contrast with "theory," but insist on a special affinity between them. Thus a "praxis situation" is one in which theory and practice are *not* separable. Each continually influences, and is influenced by, the other; as the mutual interchange goes on, they are not only constantly transforming one another, but are transforming the overall situation as well.

A rudimentary example of a "praxis situation" is the familiar cartoon of two donkeys, tethered to each other between two feeding troughs, but on a rope so short that if Donkey A is to eat from his trough he must pull Donkey B away from *his* trough and vice versa:

Donkey A reflects: "I'm hungry, and there's food in my trough."

Donkey A acts by trotting toward his trough. He gets part way when the rope tightens around his neck and starts to choke him.

Donkey B reflects: "What is he trying to do, pulling me that way? Whatever it is, I'm not buying it."

Donkey B acts by digging in his heels.

Donkey A reflects: "This is more complicated than I thought. I'll have to pull even harder."

Donkey A acts by trying to drag Donkey B in his direction.

Donkey B reflects: "Ouch! Now he's pulling the rope harder than ever. I don't like that."

Donkey B acts by digging in his heels even harder than before and refusing to budge.

Donkey A reflects: "This is getting nowhere. I'll have to try something else."

Donkey A acts by moving slowly toward Donkey B, turning around suddenly, and running hard toward his trough, hoping to throw Donkey B off balance.

Donkey B reflects: "He wants to get to his food. But I want to get to *my* food just as much as he does."

Donkey B acts by dashing toward *his* trough, but Donkey A is already braced and the two of them tumble in the dirt.

Donkey A reflects: "Now I *am* in a fix. I need strength, which I can't get without food, and I need food, which I can't get without strength. ... On the other hand, what I *really* need is a new game plan. What if I were to let him go to his trough and eat? Would he let me go to mine?"

Donkey A acts by letting the rope go slack and following Donkey B to his trough.

Donkey B reflects: "Hmm. These are good oats. Maybe if I share mine, he'll share his."

Donkey B acts by moving over to make room at the trough for Donkey A.

Donkey A reflects: "A nice gesture. ... When we finish eating at his trough we can go over and eat at mine."

Donkey A acts by walking to his trough with Donkey B and sharing with him.

Of course, that is only one scenario, and human beings are not usually as reasonable as donkeys. But the point of this oversimplified episode is that *action and reflection are interrelated.* Nothing happens that is not thought about, nothing is thought about apart from what has happened or might happen. How the donkeys act is the result of reflecting on the situation; how they reflect on the situation is the result of how they have acted. The situation is always changing because of what they have done ... and thought.

The process is never-ending. Perhaps someday Donkey A's pile will be bigger than Donkey B's and a crisis will ensue: How to cope with this new situation? Or there will be no oats at all, and they will have to find a way to get out of the corral to forage elsewhere. Someone once quipped that "praxis makes perfect," but that is unfortunately not the case, for a new situation produces not a perfect resolution but only ... a new situation.

Let us see why praxis is so important in liberation theology. For Christians, the notion of praxis is not entirely new. Christians have always struggled with the tension between reflection and action, prayer and picketing, devotions and deeds. Even the classic twelfth-century statement by St. Anselm, "I believe in order that I may understand," is, as Gustavo has pointed out, a praxis utterance, affirming that reflection (understanding) can take place only in the midst of commitment (believing). (See *Wells,* pp. 35-36, and *TheoLib,* xxxiii.)

But there is something new in liberation theology's appeal to praxis. For Gustavo, praxis is not just any old praxis but *the praxis of the poor.* There is a difference between an overall methodology, and the location in which the methodology is practiced. As far as *the methodology* itself is concerned:

Liberation theology has maintained that active commitment to liberation comes first and theology develops from it. ... Liberation theology reflects on and from within the complex and fruitful relationship between theory and practice [the praxis situation] [*Emergent,* p. 247].

There would be considerable agreement with Gustavo that commitment precedes theological reflection and that it is developed in what he calls "the complex and fruitful relationship between theory and practice." Anselm committed himself to love God, and found God in the midst of ontological reflection.

But *the location* in which the methodology is practiced points to a striking difference:

> Liberation theology's second central intuition is that God is a liberating God, revealed only in the concrete historical context of liberation of the poor and oppressed. This second point is inseparable from the first. . . . It is not enough to know that praxis must precede reflection; we must also realize that *the historical subject of that praxis is the poor* — the people who have been excluded from the pages of history. Without the poor as subject, theology degenerates into academic exercise [ibid., p. 247, italics added].

At this point, the distinction is very simple: Gustavo, like Anselm, commits himself to love God, but his place of meeting God is not in the midst of ontological reflection but in the midst of the poor. Unless we understand praxis as the praxis of the poor, we will co-opt Gustavo's theology into a nonthreatening middle-class intellectual exercise.

The praxis of the poor is also *a praxis committed to change.* We can trace this theme back to the early Marx. The main point of his "Eleven Theses Against Feuerbach" was to rescue thought from the realm of abstraction and theory, and return it to the "world of human activity" (which is how Marx defined praxis). The human "essence," Marx believed, is not abstract, but is found in "the totality of social relations." And since human work has become alienated, only revolutionary praxis will restore meaning to life. The culminating eleventh thesis "against Feuerbach" is the one for which Marx is best remembered: "The philosophers have only *interpreted* the world in different ways; the point is to *change* it" (cited in Bloch, *On Karl Marx,* Herder and Herder, New York, 1971, p. 57). Ernst Bloch provides important correctives against understanding the assertion simplistically, particularly in his reminder that both italicized words in the quotation are important. The type of action needed to *change* the world will be partly dictated by the *interpretation* one has made of the world. As a later Marxist said, "The practical man takes the given order as permanent, while the man of praxis is revolutionary" (Megill, cited in Hoffman, *Marxism and the Theory of Praxis,* p. 17).

Urgency of action — action always understood in the light of reflection — is a central emphasis for Paulo Freire, a Brazilian Catholic lay educator, and a brief examination of his concerns can focus the discussion once more on Latin America. Freire's practical contribution has been a widely used literacy program that not only teaches the poor how to read and write, but makes them aware of socio-economic structures that have immobilized them, and provides tools for breaking out of such immobility. Freire's word for this process—conscientization—has become a symbol of the possibility of dignity and power among the poor, as they are "conscientized" to their actual situation and opt to change it. "Today I learned to write my name," a campesino proudly states, "tomorrow I can transform the world."

Freire's simplest definition of praxis is "reflection and action upon the world in order to transform it" (*Pedagogy of the Oppressed,* p. 36). He later amplifies this bare-bones statement:

> [Human] activity consists of action *and* reflection; it is praxis; it is transformation of the world. And as praxis, it requires theory to illuminate it. [Human] activity is theory *and* practice; it is reflection *and* action. It cannot . . . be reduced to either verbalism or activism [ibid., p. 119, italics added].

This denial of reductionism is of capital importance. For Freire, both "verbalism" (spinning out abstract theory—an exercise Freire calls a "blah") and "activism" (moving into a situation to "do" something without reflecting on its appropriateness) are destructive. Each needs the other:

> True reflection leads to action. On the other hand, when the situation calls for action that action will constitute an authentic praxis only if its consequences become the object of critical reflection [ibid., pp. 52-53].

"Action is human," in other words, "only when it is not . . . dichotomized from reflection" (ibid., p. 38). If either reflection or action is sacrificed or neglected, "the other immediately suffers. There is no true word that is not at the same time a praxis. Thus to speak a new word is to transform the world" (ibid., p. 75).

In summary, we can see some of the implications of a "praxis of the poor" for liberation theology:

1. Praxis avoids abstraction; it is grounded in *experience* of the world.

2. Thought is for the purpose of *change,* of transformation. Truth is something that is "done."

3. People are empowered to change *their own situations* rather than having solutions imposed on them.

4. The best praxis situation is *communal* reflection and action (a concern to which we will return in dealing with the "base communities").

5. Praxis is *never completed*; it contains the tools for ongoing correction and avoids settling into a rigid orthodoxy.

What praxis makes possible (to paraphrase Antonio Gramsci, a strong influence on Gustavo) is fewer abstract reflections on "the nature of truth," and more practical sorties into the real world, intent on social and political change (cited in Hoffman, *Marxism*, p. 18).

It is out of praxis that empowerment comes.

The Empowerment of the Poor

The quotation from Archbishop Vallejos at the beginning of this chapter unites two important impulses. The *first* is an exhortation to the peasants to love the earth with all its gifts and promises, a passage that is lyrical in its acknowledgment of the beauty of the earth. The *second* impulse is down-to-earth practical advice to the poor: Organize! These gifts that you love will be taken from you if you do not band together and realize that "in unity alone there is strength." The seemingly different impulses are united by a theological conclusion: God has given the land as a gift to be nurtured; "God is the sole owner of the fields."

The good news is that what Archbishop Vallejos was urging is already beginning to happen. The poor are discovering that they *can* organize, that they have the right to think and speak up, and that the more united they are, the more they will be heard. No longer are they waiting for someone to speak out for them, or to empower them; they are speaking themselves and creating their own empowerment. Gustavo frequently makes the descriptive comment that "the poor are speaking less and less through intermediaries and are beginning to have their direct way" (see, e.g., *PP*, p. 37).

This is more than simply a fact to be noted; it is a reality to be embraced:

> All our works must try to contribute to helping the poor take their history and their destiny into their own hands. . . . The goal is to work with the poor and help them to be more conscious of the reasons for their poverty and to look for some solution [interview in *The Other Side*, November 1987, p. 10].

Invoking another frequently employed image, Gustavo reminds us that "in spite of all vicissitudes, and however dramatic their setbacks, the hitherto 'absent from history' are beginning to be present in it" (*PP*, p. 76).

Good news to the poor, bad news to those who want to keep control:

> The most significant fact in the political and church life in Latin America in recent years is the active presence that the poor are coming to assume in it. As can be imagined, this does not fail to provoke fear and hostility [ibid., p. 131].

The "fear and hostility" will have to be endured, for an irreversible fact is emerging: the poor are beginning to speak and act *on their own behalf.*

Gustavo does not mince words about what it will mean for the church when the poor have fully claimed their rights:

> Evangelization, the preaching of the gospel, will be truly liberation only when the poor themselves become the preachers.
>
> Then, of course, the preaching of the gospel will become a stumbling block and a scandal. For then we will have a gospel that is no longer "presentable" in society. It will be expressed in the vernacular; it will not sound nice; it will not smell good; and the "educated" of this world will find it "unrefined." But it will be the Lord, the Servant of Jahweh, who scarcely looks like a human being at all (cf. Is. 52:14), who will be speaking to us from among the poor. Only by listening to their voice will we hear his voice, and recognize him as our liberator [conflated from *PP*, pp. 22 and 208-9, and Greinacher, *The Poor in the Church,* p. 15—three passages clearly deriving from the same source].

This new reality will not only affect the way the gospel is proclaimed. It will also affect the very doing of theology, something that may initially be difficult for professional theologians to accept:

> We will not have an authentic theology of liberation until the oppressed themselves are able freely and creatively to express themselves in society and among the people of God. . . . We shall not have our great leap forward, into a whole new theological perspective, until the marginalized and exploited have begun to become the artisans of their own liberation—until their voice makes itself heard directly, without mediations, without interpreters—until they themselves take account, in the light of their own values, of their own experience of the Lord in their efforts to liberate themselves. We shall not have our quantum theological leap until the oppressed themselves theologize [ibid., p. 65; see also *LibChange,* p. 87].

In addition to these immediate changes and challenges, threatening in the utmost to many, the long-range implications of the empowerment of the poor will be to create a new church very different from the present one:

> Instead of talking about the church of the poor, we must be *a poor church*. And we flaunt this commitment with our real estate, our rectories, and other buildings, with our whole life style [*Between Honesty and Hope,* p. 142, italics added].

Still more is involved, and Gustavo offers an image even wider and more inclusive:

It is not a question of the church being poor, but of the poor of this world being the People of God, the disturbing witness to the God who sets free [in Geffré, p. 13].

Disturbing indeed. Life in the church in the years ahead may not be simple. But it will certainly not be dull.

Another thing that militates against dullness is the slow but sure empowerment of women, beginning to escape from what the Puebla document described as being "doubly oppressed," both as *poor* (victims of economic exploitation in a capitalist society), and as *women* (victims of sexual exploitation in a macho society) (§ 1135). Many women would expand the analysis to include a third oppression: they are also *Catholics* (victims of ecclesiastical structures that appear firmly committed to keeping women second-class citizens in the Body of Christ).[5]

Gustavo's estimate of Puebla's treatment of women is generous: "The condition of women is treated in several places in the Puebla documents, and the treatment constitutes without a doubt one of the conference's remarkable contributions" (*PP*, p. 161, n. 11). There are some grounds for this. At Puebla women got the same treatment as liberation theologians—almost all were barred from the official meetings—but they responded much as the liberation theologians did, by working "outside the walls," and counting on friendly bishops to introduce their proposals. Rosemary Ruether, a North American Catholic theologian, who was part of this group, and has a track record of dealing trenchantly with male hierarchies, gives a positive assessment as well. Summarizing material in the report of the Commission on the Laity (§ 834-49), she says:

The section speaks of the oppression and exploitation of women in many areas. It begins by mentioning the traditional marginalization of women by economic and cultural structures (machismo, unequal salaries), which results from their almost total exclusion from political, economic, and cultural life. It goes on to note that new forms of marginalization arise in a consumer society that uses women as objects of commercialization, masking their exploitation under the cover of progress. It talks of the connection between increased female prostitution and oppressive economic conditions; of the ineffectiveness of laws intended to protect women; of the near absence of organizations to protect womens' rights; of the double burden of jobs and domestic labor that women bear, who often have to assume full economic support of the family alone. The section also mentions the exploitation of women as domestic servants.

The Puebla document then goes on to affirm the equality and dignity of women in the gospel perspective. Woman is man's co-equal in the image of God and co-creator with him in continuing the work of creation. Woman is in no way second in the order of creation, but an equal partner. In the New Testament women share equally in the prophetic gifts. They are represented by the women who understood Christ's message, such as the Samaritan woman, the women who followed Christ, who remained faithful at the cross, and who were sent to the apostles by Jesus to announce his resurrection. They were also present in the women of the early Christian communities and especially in Mary, who announced the liberation of the children of God in the Magnificat.

The bishops affirm the need to use women's abilities more fully in the ministry and mission of the church, without, however, including ordination. Women are called to participate in new nonordained ministries [*Christianity and Crisis,* April 2, 1979, pp. 78-79; also cited in *Puebla*, pp. 334-35].

In a culture characterized by machismo, and in a church dominated by a male hierarchy safeguarding its leadership prerogatives, these gains are indeed steps forward. But with Latin American women becoming increasingly conscientized about their deserved social roles, we can assume that "the revolution of rising expectations" will not lag in the future.

At the first "Theology in the Americas" conference in Detroit in 1975 only one of the Latin American theologians was a woman; at the first Ecumenical Conference of Third World Theologians (EATWOT) in Dar es Salaam in 1976 only one woman from the entire Third World was present. (In both cases the woman was Beatriz Melano Couch of Argentina.) Fortunately, such situations are more and more the exception, and when they are offered as the rule there is instant recognition that something is amiss.

A fascinating account of changing attitudes toward women on the part of male theologians in Latin America is contained in Elsa Tamez's interviews with Third World theologians, entitled *Against Machismo.* Two of Gustavo's comments are pertinent:

First, like any profound oppression, the oppression of women damages all of society in an intolerable way. Not only are women marginalized and oppressed, but also a sick human society results. . . .

Second, not only must we be sensitive to the intolerable situation of women in society today, but we must also be sensitive to all that human society is losing because of this oppression. I'm very much afraid that by speaking of their oppression we will approach women in a condescending way: "The poor little thing is so marginalized and oppressed, we need to help her out." I think we need to join in solidarity with women's demands because otherwise we miss out on too much ourselves [in *Against Machismo,* p. 41].

The most important gift for women, of course, is not that men are now acknowledging their worth, but that women are beginning to take charge of their lives. This has been particularly characteristic of the base communities, where the preponderance of local leadership has been female, to such a degree that Gustavo acknowledges, "I cannot conceive of the popular Christian communities without women" (ibid., p. 42). Inasmuch as these communities are the most important reality in the Latin American church today, the increasing empowerment of women through them is an important key to the church's future.

The Joy of the Poor

When Gustavo addressed the second conference of "Theology of the Americas" in Detroit in 1980, his topic was "The Historical Project of the Poor in the Context of the North American Church."[6] Such a title might have augured a straightforward performance, and Gustavo spoke first and predictably about the need "to understand the meaning and reality of the historical project of the poor."

But he then moved in a direction unanticipated by his largely North American audience. He spoke about the need "to recognize the joy of the poor" (p. 82). On the lips of a North American, speaking out of a life of relative affluence, the theme would have sounded romantic or callous. But coming from within Gustavo's lifelong immersion in the midst of the poor, it opened some new doors to his hearers.

It is not enough, he reminded them, to recognize only the sufferings of oppressed persons, real as they are. It is also necessary to recognize that "the poor know joy." It is a joy expressed in songs, festivals, poetry, the reenactment of old customs, and religious ceremonies. It is a joy that does not ignore or forget past indignities; indeed it grows out of them by affirming that they are not the last word. The last word belongs not to indignities, but to God. And the poor know that God's word, however long deferred, is a *good* word, and that history finally belongs to God, not to the oppressor. This is "a paschal joy which God has bought through pain and death, but which expresses a prophetic hope . . . a confidence found in the songs of Hannah and Mary, a confidence in which the poor live" (p. 82). So there is laughter — "an expression of present confidence in the Lord."

Oppressors cannot understand this laughter and are unnerved by it. The suffering of others can sometimes elicit compassion and sensitivity even among those with hardened hearts. But joy? Such a response is incomprehensible and even frightening to those whose ears are closed to a message that the future belongs to the poor rather than to them.

So, this joy is *subversive*. It rejects the notion that the present situation will remain normative; it is a vote for change. It affirms an open future to which it looks forward in confidence because in the eucharistic celebration that future has already broken into the present: "In the breaking of the bread, the bread which is lacking to the poor, the life of the resurrection becomes present. This life is the assurance that death will not triumph, that sin and injustice will be abolished" (p. 83).

The poor have a secret that enables them to be joyful. And that changes the whole tilt of the world:

> The joy of the poor is always a challenge to the powerful, and raises questions they are incapable of understanding because all they see is deep suffering. But the poor know how to be joyful. They know how to have parties, and in the religious sphere they know how to celebrate the presence of God.
>
> I would wager that the powerful of this world feel more serene when the people are silent, when they are resigned, even when they weep. What is disturbing to them is that the poor laugh in the midst of their situation.
>
> But as the Gospel of Luke says, "Those who suffer today shall laugh tomorrow." And tomorrow has begun today! [in *Latinamerica Press*, May 10, 1984, p. 8].

Subversive news: tomorrow has begun today. . . .

CHAPTER 4

Act Two, Scene One: Theology as Critical Reflection on Praxis (Method)

Liberation theologians do not think themselves into a new way of living, but live themselves into a new way of thinking.
— Henri Nouwen, *¡Gracias!*, p. 159

Faith in God does not consist in asserting God's existence, but rather in acting on [God's] behalf.
— Gustavo in *Liberation and Change*, p. 89

In *The Liberation of Theology*, Juan Luis Segundo notes that the enduring contribution of liberation theology is not a new *content* to Christian faith, but a new *method* for understanding it. The reader can test that claim after reading this chapter and the next in tandem. We can take for granted that the question of methodology is central. Gustavo argues, in fact, that his book *On Job* centers on the relationship of methodology and spirituality, and that the book as a whole "raises the question of theological method" (in Tamez, *Against Machismo*, p. 48).

We established in chapter 3 that the "first act" is commitment to the poor, and that no amount of subsequent theologizing can displace that fact. As we move into a consideration of the "second act," the realm of speculation, we must anchor ourselves firmly in Gustavo's reminder at the conclusion of his own major speculative venture:

All the political theologies, the theologies of hope, of revolution, and of liberation, are not worth one act of genuine solidarity with exploited social classes. They are not worth one act of faith, love, and hope, committed — in one way or another — in active participation to liberate humankind from everything that dehumanizes it and prevents it from living according to the will of God [*TheoLib*, p. 174 (308)].

75

Our procedure will be to take as our yardstick Gustavo's definition of the "second act": theology as *"critical reflection on praxis* in the light of the Word of God." In this chapter we will examine the italicized portion of the definition, which we can call "act two, scene one." In the next chapter we will italicize the remaining portion of the definition and repeat the process, which we can call "act two, scene two." There is, of course, an artificiality about this distinction — how can one talk about method without also talking about content? — and our escape from this dilemma will be a reminder that chapters 4 and 5 (act two, scenes one *and* two) can be understood only together.

The phrase "critical reflection on praxis" initially sounds redundant: inasmuch as praxis is a uniting of "reflection and action," Gustavo seems to be suggesting that theology is "critical reflection on 'reflection and action.' " This is, in fact, descriptively the case: theology is a *second* reflection, so to speak, about what has already been going on — that is, the commitments we have made and the reflections we have engaged in about them. But this is now going on from within a *theological perspective* — that is, "in the light of the Word of God" — that portion of the overall definition we are temporarily bracketing; a further reminder that the division between chapters 4 and 5 is only temporary.

God-Talk—And the Suffering of the Innocent[1]

The book of Job is not the first place one would look for a liberation tract for the 1990s. It seems far removed from problems of social justice — a book of literary fiction and poetry rather than a message of exhortation to the oppressed. Gustavo is aware of such misgivings (*Job*, p. xvii), but feels they are based on a misreading. Recognizing that we are entitled to bring our own concerns to scripture, and read scripture in their light, he insists that the Book of Job relates not only to an age-old problem, "How are we to talk about God?," but even more to a contemporary problem, "How are we to talk about God from within a specific situation — namely, the suffering of the innocent?" (p. xviii). Job's cries are the cries of suffering and oppressed persons everywhere; his protestations of innocence illumine "the innocence of an oppressed and believing people amid the situation of suffering and death that has been forced upon it" (p. xviii). Out of such concerns, Gustavo paints an important tapestry illustrating theological method.

Theology, "God-talk," is talk about a mystery, but a mystery that must be communicated — a mystery, indeed, that *has* been communicated, that "was secret for long ages but is now disclosed" (p. xi). The starting point is God's self-communication, God's revelation or self-disclosure, and there are two important things to say about its relation to theological method:

1. There is a relationship between *revelation* and *gratuitousness*, the "graciousness" of God's reaching out to the least likely, God's assigning of "a

privileged place to the simple and despised" (p. xi). Jesus thanked God for hiding the truth from the learned and sharing it with "little children" (Matt. 11:25–26). The Greek word in this passage, *nēpioi*, refers to the weak, the unlearned, the ignorant, as well as (drawing on its biblical usage elsewhere) the afflicted, the hungry, those "not invited to the banquet," "the poor of the land," those least likely to be acknowledged as having worth. "The scorned of the world," Gustavo concludes, "are those whom the love of God prefers" (p. xii). God loves every human person, but God especially loves the poor and forgotten. By declaring such a preference, God indicates that "an entire social and religious order is hereby turned upside down" (p. xiii).

2. This naturally has implications for *the way we speak about God*. We are called first of all to be silent, to engage in contemplation in the face of such a mystery. (Bonhoeffer starts at this same point in his treatment of Jesus in *Christ the Center*.) Then we are to seek to do God's will—all before we reflect or speak ourselves:

> Contemplation and practice together make up a *first act*; theologizing is a *second act*. We must first establish ourselves on the terrain of spirituality and practice; only subsequently is it possible to formulate discourse on God in an authentic and respectful way [p. xiii].

Although the above summary draws chiefly from the book *On Job*, we have seen that the same themes are present in Gustavo's earlier volume, *El Dios de la vida*, not yet translated into English, where he diagrams the relationship just described:

Diagram 1
First Act/Second Act

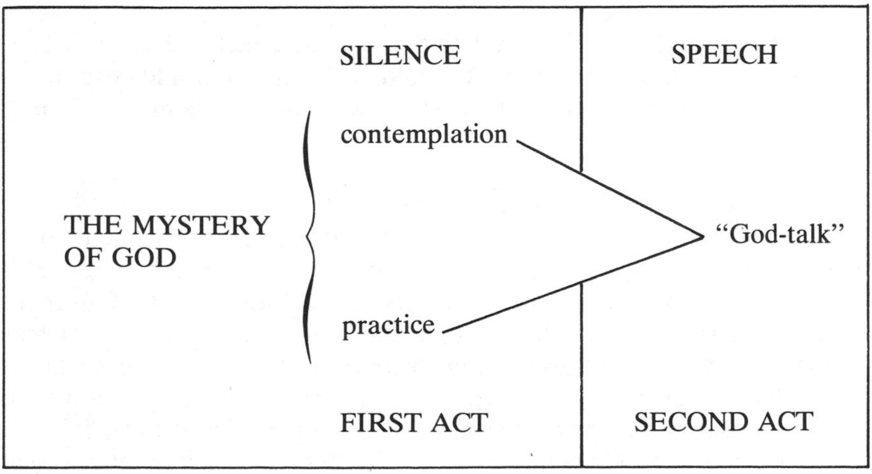

Gustavo distinguishes four "key questions" that must be faced by any theology trying to engage in "critical reflection on praxis" among the suffering innocent:

1. How are we to talk about a God who is revealed as love in a situation characterized by poverty and oppression?

2. How are we to proclaim the God of life to men and women who die prematurely and unjustly?

3. How are we to acknowledge that God makes us a free gift of love and justice when we have before us the suffering of the innocent?

4. What words are we to use in telling those who are not even regarded as persons that they are daughters and sons of God? (p. xiv).

Following Adolphe Gesché, Gustavo differentiates the "evil of *guilt*" (for which one can be held accountable and in response to which judgment can be expected) and the "evil of *misfortune*" (evil suffered by the innocent, or, as Gesché puts it, "widespread, objective evil that entails no fault in the sufferer"). While we must not forget the responsibility of those who cause suffering to the innocent, we must not blind ourselves to the terrible fact that massive suffering is endured by those *who are innocent*. There is no way to assign guilt to them so that their misfortune would be "deserved," a problem compounded by the fact that the innocent are often believers: "The silence of God is hardest to bear for those who believe that the God of our faith is a living God" (p. xv, see also pp. 105-10).

Gustavo next examines the opening episodes in Arguedas's novel *Deep Rivers* (which we have already looked at in chapter 2) to personalize the abysmal suffering of so many poor persons, who have not only done nothing to deserve misfortune, but have lived lives of such gentleness in the face of raw brutality that they would seem on any scale of divine accountability to merit at least a cessation of hardship, if not reward. It is in the midst of such realities that we must search for ways to affirm, when the evidence gives us so many reasons to deny:

> The center of the world—so called because the crucified Jesus dwells there, and with him, all who suffer unjustly, all the poor and despised of the earth—is the place from which we must proclaim the risen Lord [p. xvii].

Let us move to the text of Job itself.

There is a wager between God and "the accuser": "Are human beings capable, in the midst of unjust suffering, of continuing to assert their faith in God and speak of God without expecting a return?" (p. 1). Can there be a "disinterested" faith in God that does not look for rewards or fear punishment? Gustavo lets us know in advance that "God wins the wager"—not to destroy our interest in the plot, but to offer the journey of Job from the very outset as a route along which others might be able to walk.

Job is an enticing character to put to the test. He is a man of personal integrity, a "just" man, comfortably situated. But would he retain his integrity if he were stripped of all that is dear to him? Surely, the accuser argues, Job's faith is predicated on the blessings God has given him, and is not really "disinterested" at all. Take away the blessings, make Job the victim of unjust suffering, and will he still speak well of God?

The accuser is permitted to test the proposition. Job's family, friends, and possessions are all taken from him. He remains faithful. With divine permission, the ante is upped and Job is further afflicted with terrible illness—a sick man, now, as well as a poor one, an outcast from society, alone in a garbage dump. Even so, Job refuses to "curse God," a course of action that, given the circumstances, seems eminently appropriate to his wife. Job's faith is still "disinterested," despite all that has happened to him. He does not make faith in God dependent on his material well-being. "His response is sincere," Gustavo comments, "but it will have to reach a deeper level" (p. 7).

Enter three "friends"—a noun richly deserving inverted commas, for they rebuke Job at every turn. But before they can take him on, Job indulges in a long monologue. He still does not curse God, but he does curse the day of his birth, and engages in an extended complaint to God: God's universe, if not fully malevolent, is at least chaotic, and it would be better never to have been born into it. This is not just sophisticated existential pique; it springs from deep misery, and an anguish that cannot fail to touch the hearer. His suffering, Job believes, is undeserved and has no intelligible cause, and in so concluding, the once-rich man is speaking a language the poorest of the indigenes in Latin America can understand, for they too, though they would use different words, have seen "the vital framework of their world collapsing" (p. 10).

The impulse to deny is almost overwhelming, but Job remains a "rebellious believer," his rebellion focusing on "the suffering of the innocent," of whom he considers himself one (an estimate with which God seems to concur). Only if "speaking of God" can survive in the crucible of the deepest human suffering, will it be worth taking seriously.

So there is a "wager." But it is on a deeper level than Pascal's famous intellectual wager. Pascal addressed the "nonbelievers" (the "winners" in history who have time for abstract speculation), whereas Job addresses the "nonpersons" (the "losers" in history for whom nothing remains)—a distinction we will explore below. But even before such exploration, we can make the blunt point blunter: the difference is that Job's locale is not a library, but a garbage dump.

Perhaps the Book of Job is a liberation tract after all.

Prophecy and Contemplation: Two Languages That Must Be Merged

Two important shifts take place as the book of Job unfolds:
1. Job discovers that what is at stake is not simply his own suffering, but

the suffering of *all* poor people. Consequence: "Those who believe in God must therefore try to lighten the burden of the poor by helping them and practicing solidarity with them" (p. 16).

2. God's speeches make clear to Job that justice and grace cannot be separated: "The world of justice must be located within the broad but demanding horizon of freedom that is formed by the gratuitousness of God's love" (p. 16).

These insights correspond to two ways of speaking about God that must be joined: the language of prophecy and the language of contemplation.

The Language of Prophecy

The language of prophecy emerges from Job's struggle with his "friends," who relentlessly try to beat him into submission with a verbal club called the traditional doctrine of retribution:

> God punishes the wicked and rewards the upright.
> Job is being punished rather than rewarded.
> Therefore Job is wicked.
> Q.E.D.

The remedy? Repent.

The doctrine assures the rich that God is rewarding them, and induces guilt on the part of the poor, who interpret their misfortunes as God's punishment for their wrongdoing.

But the doctrine does not work with Job, who continues to assert his innocence in the face of his misfortune. He does not claim to be sinless, but "he finds no sin that merits so great a punishment" (p. 24).

A crucial shift begins. Job discovers not only that his own suffering is unjust but so also is *the suffering of others*. He does not use this insight to deny God, but rather to challenge a human understanding of God based solely on the doctrine of retribution. The "friends" deal only with a doctrine of suffering, never with suffering people. They "believe in their theology rather than in the God of their theology" (p. 29).

Job's viewpoint broadens beyond his own personal misfortune; he discovers that there are other sufferers as well, and that their lot and his are intertwined. "Job realizes that he is not the only one to experience the pain of unjust suffering. The poor of the world are in the same bind as he is" (p. 31). So Job begins "to free himself from an ethic centered on personal reward and to pass to another focused on the needs of one's neighbor" (p. 31). This, Gustavo says with wry understatement, "is a considerable shift" (p. 31).

Job has to find another way to account for the misery of the poor:

> He sees now that this poverty and abandonment are not something fated but are caused by the wicked, who nonetheless live serene and

satisfied lives. . . . The wicked are both rejecters of God and enemies of the poor—two sides of the same coin [p. 32].

So Job utters what Gustavo considers the most radical description of the wretchedless of the poor in the entire Bible, along with "a harsh indictment of the powerful who rob and oppress the poor" (p. 32). The passage—Job 24:2–14—is stinging in its recognition that poverty is not deserved, but is "a state of affairs caused by the wickedness of those who exploit and rob the poor" (p. 33).

Job realizes that to be related to God also means to be related to the poor and to struggle on their behalf: God wants "uprightness" or justice (*sedekah*) and judgment (*mishpat*), and Job has always practiced these in relation to the unjust situation of the poor of the land. He sees the poor as God's friends; "to give to the needy is therefore to give to God" (p. 40). A defense of the poor necessitates their being freed, and Job has tried to cultivate solidarity with them. "He wanted his life," Gustavo interprets, "to be one of surrender to the God who has a preferential love of the poor. Therefore he tried to be attentive to the needs of the poor" (p. 48).

Job had first turned inward, concerned only with his own suffering and the injustice he felt had been done to him. The ancient doctrine of retribution did not "work" in his case; it was not because he was evil that suffering had come to him. He then realizes that there are many others like himself, and that the doctrine of retribution does not "work" for them either; their suffering is not due to their faults. They, too, are innocent, and Job realizes that he must enter into solidarity with them. As he experiences their lot, he finds firmer ground for prophetic speech:

> To get out of himself and help other sufferers (without waiting until his own problems are first resolved) is a way to find God. . . . He now begins to see that he may not let his own unjust situation be an obstacle to immediate commitment to the poor. The needs of others cannot be left in abeyance until everything has become clear [p. 48].

The shift is an important advance in Job's understanding of his situation. But it is not yet enough.

The Language of Contemplation

Job's religion has remained "disinterested"; his trust in God has been shown not to be dependent on material prosperity. Such a conviction, Gustavo notes, is frequently found on the lips of believers who are poor—a conviction that somehow everything belongs to God and comes from God. The conviction can be manipulated into a resigned acceptance of evil, but that need not be the case. Job discovers that his real quarrel is not with his friends but with God. While the friends continue to talk *about* God, Job begins to address himself *to* God. This is what characterizes the language of contemplation, which is needed to supplement the language of prophesy.

Job enters into a spiritual struggle with God. He finds that he needs God in three ways. Because he is, in effect, instituting a "lawsuit" with God, he needs an *arbiter* who can mediate between himself and God. But the only such arbiter can be God. Because there will also be direct debate between himself and God, Job needs a *witness*. And because the witness also is in heaven rather than on earth, the crucial need is for a *liberator* or *defender*, a *gō'ēl*, through whom Job can hope to receive vindication. The Hebrew word *gō'ēl* comes "out of the Jewish experience of solidarity and had the family for its initial setting" (p. 64). The verb to which it is related means "to liberate, to ransom, to redeem." It is the obligation of the nearest relative of the unjustly treated to be that person's *gō'ēl*. And within the covenant, "God is the nearest relative," the one who must rescue (p. 64). The ultimate appeal is not to some third party but to God; the God who judges must also defend. The one who seems an enemy must be claimed as a friend. "God is the defender of all those who suffer injustice" (p. 65).

This is a conviction mirrored in the lives of the poor. Caesar Vallejo captures it when he writes on behalf of the poor, "Whatever be the cause I must defend before God after death, I myself have a defender: God" (cited pp. 65, 121). To speak in such fashion is to have a *gō'ēl*, a liberator, to acknowledge that God's judgment and God's mercy do not work at cross-purposes.

Gustavo pursues the theme at greater depth in a discussion of "The Mysterious Meeting of Two Freedoms" (pp. 67–81), the most difficult and perhaps the most important chapter in the book. The "friends" are gone; Elihu, the late arrival, is gone; it is down to Job and God. Job is naturally a little fearful as the denouement approaches, but his fears are groundless. For God does not come to crush, but to announce the divine greatness, which is "the gratuitousness of creative love" (p. 69). Gratuitousness is the opposite of retribution; it is "the hinge on which the world turns" (p. 72).

This is a way of talking about God's freedom. God will not be bound by the theories of Job's "friends," who insist that God conform to their rigid doctrines. No! God is free of all the constraints with which humans try to bind and control God's power. Some odd analogies are proposed: just as the donkey has freedom to roam in the wastelands, just as the ostrich can "make fools of horse and rider," just as the horse can outmaneuver the wiles of humans—so, too, is God free of the petty limitations with which theologians seek to circumscribe divine activity.

God forces Job to look more openly at the exercise of justice in the world. God's free and gratuitous love can neither be imprisoned in theological concepts nor destroyed by human excess and defiance—though it can be sorely tested. The point is that justice and judgment exist not in contradiction to gratuitous love but within it. God respects human freedom, and to that degree the all-powerful God is "weak," but God also invites human collaboration in creating justice in the world.

Two kinds of freedom are operating here. The first is *God's freedom*, God's gratuitousness, God's freedom from human constraints, and God's freedom to love indiscriminately in working for justice. The second is *human freedom*, which establishes Job's freedom to complain and rebel. Job is free to encounter God directly, without the need of intermediaries; God is free to exercise the gratuitous love that is "the foundation of the world, within which justice must be exercised."

The relationship of gratuitousness and justice is "the key to the interpretation of the Book of Job" (p. 82), and it takes Job's final speech, in 42:1–6, to clarify it. At the conclusion of his encounter with God, Job can affirm four things (not three, as stated on p. 83):

1. Job sees that *God has plans and is carrying them out*. This is not a reassertion of divine retribution but a further repudiation of it, for God's plans are gracious rather than vindictive. God is greater than the theology of Job's "friends."

2. Job is now aware of *previously unrecognized aspects of reality*; God has given him "a glimpse of another world" (p. 84) containing marvels beyond his grasp. There is not just a "plan," but a plan of gratuitous love, and although Job is only beginning to discern it, he discerns enough to affirm.

3. Job has had "a joyous *encounter with the Lord*." Before, he knew of God only by hearsay, but now he has encountered God face to face. Before, Job had addressed God in complaint and protest: "now he does so in acceptance and submission that is inspired not by resignation but by contemplative love" (p. 85).

4. As a result, Job can *abandon his attitude of complaint*. Grasping the nettle of one of the most diversely interpreted phrases in scripture (Job 42:6), Gustavo concludes that Job, rather than deciding "to retract and repent in dust and ashes," is really saying, "I repudiate and abandon [change my mind about] dust and ashes." He rejects his former attitude of lamentation and complaint. Gustavo's conclusion: "In his final reply what Job is expressing is not contrition but *a renunciation of his lamentation and dejected outlook*" (p. 87). Job's concluding speech represents "a high point in contemplative speech about God" (ibid.).

Job has moved beyond justice, for "justice alone does not have the final say about how we are to speak of God" (ibid.). Grace does. Job learns "to situate justice within the framework of God's gratuitous love" (p. 88) rather than the other way around. Only gratuitous love makes it possible to understand God's preferential option for the poor, which is "the key to authentic divine justice" (p. 88): *God does not love the poor because they are good, but because they are poor*. That is a statement about the boundless love of God, not about the virtue or lack of virtue of the poor. So out of God's gracious love grows the reality that we must act for justice. What Job finally has is not a new "doctrine of God," but a new sense of "the presence of God."

One Language, not Two

Thus far Job.

But for Gustavo the journey is not quite over. The Book of Job has acquainted us with two languages, two ways of speaking of God. But we must not make this provisional distinction final. The two languages must become one:

> Two languages—the prophetic and contemplative—are required, but they must also be combined and become increasingly integrated into a single language [p. 94].

In a strong section (pp. 94–97), Gustavo demonstrates that the two languages are not complete in themselves. They need each other, they feed and correct each other. Negatively:

> Without the prophetic dimension, the language of contemplation is in danger of having no grip on the history in which God acts and in which we meet God. Without the [contemplative] dimension the language of prophecy can narrow its vision and weaken its perception of the God who makes all things new (Rev. 2:15). Each undergoes a distortion that violates it and renders it unauthentic [p. 96].

Positively:

> The language of contemplation acknowledges that everything comes from [God's] unmerited love and opens up "new horizons of hope" (Puebla §1165). The language of prophecy attacks the situation—and its structural causes—of injustice and deprivation in which the poor love, because it looks for "the suffering features of Christ the Lord" in the pain-ravaged faces of an oppressed people (Puebla §§31–39). Both languages arise, among the poor in Latin America as in Job, out of the suffering and hopes of the innocent [p. 97].

Conclusion: "[Contemplative] language expresses the gratuitousness of God's love; prophetic language expresses the demands love makes" (p. 95).

The theme is not limited to Job; the connection is vividly illustrated in Jeremiah as well:

> Sing to the Lord;
> praise the Lord!
> For he hath delivered the life of the needy
> from the hands of evil doers
>   [Jer. 20:13, cf. also Isa. 42:1–5].

The first two lines are contemplative, the last two prophetic. Song and deliverance are joined; contemplation and practice are intermingled; gratuitousness and justice are inseparable.

Nor is the theme a new one for Gustavo. As far back as 1981 he had anticipated this development:

We need a language that is both contemplative and prophetic; contemplative because it ponders a God who is love, prophetic because it talks about a liberator God who rejects the situation of injustice in which the poor live, and also the structural causes of that situation. As was the case in the book of Job, both idioms arise in Third World countries out of the suffering and hope of innocent victims [in Fabella and Torres, eds., *The Irruption of the Third World*, p. 232].

An Interlude for Stocktaking

We have just concluded a complicated and rather sophisticated theological journey. It has been, one hopes, useful and even illuminating. But a haunting question is at least half-formed: What has happened to the poor and unlettered in the course of these pages? Have they not been swept aside and drowned in this torrent of words? Have not we, in our turn, overintellectualized, after the fashion of Job's "friends"?

Let us acknowledge that the text of the book *On Job: God-Talk and the Suffering of the Innocent* is not likely to be a staple in the reading diet of the Quechua Amerindians of Peru's altiplano. But the text of the biblical book of Job itself will be such a staple, even in groups where illiteracy runs high and the story must be told and retold rather than read and reread. And the story itself is one to which the destitute can relate. They, too, are visited by one catastrophe after another. They, too, sit in the garbage heap; or, more likely, forage within it for scraps of still edible food for their children. They, too, have "friends," sometimes priests, who tell them to accept their lot with resignation as the pure outworking of God's will.

But they, too, as Gustavo frequently reminds us in the course of his exposition, have come to mature positions of faith, developed not by reading books but by reflecting in their own fashion on their own bitter experiences — reflections that parallel the increasing depth of Job's wisdom. They might not grace these convictions with the label "theology" or even "liberation theology," but with their hard-won wisdom they are closer to the God to whom "theology" only points, than the rest of us, with all our dialectical skills, will ever be.

The Nonbeliever and the Nonperson: Two Interlocutors Who Must Not Be Merged[2]

Reinhold Niebuhr claimed that there is nothing more irrelevant than the answer to an unasked question. We can extend his point by arguing that confusing the question one has been asked with the question one is prepared to answer is equally irrelevant. It is particularly important for theologians to recognize this temptation, for their readiness to provide answers often outweighs their willingness to listen before doing so.

Having just merged two apparently contrasting ways of talking about God — the prophetic and the contemplative — we must now examine a contrast that calls for a different resolution. Here the task is not to merge two concepts, but to insist upon their differentiation. This is the contrast, found throughout Gustavo's writings, between two kinds of interlocutors or questioners: the nonbeliever and the nonperson.

Most readers of this book are acquainted with *nonbelievers*, and may often be close to the position themselves. This does not mean they have totally rejected belief and become atheists, but that belief has become difficult, if not yet impossible, in the modern world they inhabit. The last four centuries have offered a continuous assault on what were once taken to be "eternal verities" that would survive though the heavens fell. But word has come that the heavens seem to have fallen and not much of what they symbolized has survived. Consider the catalogue: the industrial revolution; the Enlightenment, with its insistence that "the world has come of age" and no longer needs the "God-hypothesis"; the rise of modern freedoms, including freedom from the shackles of authoritarian religion; the rise of the bourgeoisie, with innate confidence in their ability to make a go of things; the spectacular success of modern science, which is "methodologically atheist"; the stress on individualism and the free play of private interests; satisfaction with reason at the expense of faith; the relentless critique of religion from every possible perspective — these and a host of other impulses seem to the once-faithful to be tolling a death knell for the life of faith.

The questions of the nonbeliever are many: How can I believe in God in an age of science that renders God unnecessary? How can I believe in God when once demonstrable proofs of God's existence have been disproved? How can I believe in God in a universe that gives no indication of being under providential care? How can I believe in God after reading Feuerbach? How can I believe in God when belief demands shutting out the forces of modernity? How can I believe in God when so many people live happy, well-adjusted lives without such belief?

These nonbelievers are often cultured, well-educated people, technologically proficient, who frequently (as Gustavo adds) have relatives who are theologians. They question not the modern secular world but the *religious* world they once inhabited, and their questions are a series of variants on the question with which Dietrich Bonhoeffer struggled, "How can we proclaim God in a world 'come of age' "?

But these are not the concerns and questions of those whom Gustavo calls the *nonpersons*, those who do not count, do not really exist, are not accorded the status of full personhood. They are the poor, the marginated, the victims. When they lie injured by the side of the road, no one stops, because no one notices them, or, noticing, decides they are not important enough to merit help. And so they begin to believe what is said about them as a result of how society treats them: they do not count.

Unlike nonbelievers, the nonpersons are not cultured. They may not even be literate. They probably smell. It is unlikely that they have relatives who are theologians. Their questions, in contrast to the nonbelievers, are not about the gradual erosion of a religious world they probably still inhabit, but about the actively destructive power of the political, economic, and social worlds that have ground them down for centuries.

So they have different questions: How can we see ourselves as persons in a world that denies our personhood and that of our children? How can we worship God as Lord of us all, when we are victims of other "lords" that dictate who among us will live, who will die, who will starve, who will be tortured? How can we see ourselves as brothers and sisters when everything in society denies us such status?

Gustavo, as one who is deeply involved in the plight of nonpersons, puts the problem thus:

> The question is not how we are to talk about God in a world come of age, but how we are to tell people who are scarcely human that God is love and that God's love makes us one family? [in *Emergent*, p. 241].

The issue, then, is not how to find room for God in a metaphysical framework where God no longer seems to be needed, but how to announce God as personal in an impersonal world that destroys the possibility of personhood. *It is crucial not to conflate these two kinds of interlocutors.* They are not variants within one world. They are inhabitants of two different worlds. And they exemplify different theologies.

The Break with "Dominant Theology"

The distinction between the nonbeliever and the nonperson provides access to another crucial theme of Gustavo's—the break with "dominant theology." We have already examined his personal discovery that European theology—what he called "dominant" or "progressive" theology—was not adequate for understanding the world of the poor or providing impetus to change that world, and had to be replaced by what eventually became "liberation theology."

Gustavo's treatments of dominant theology are detailed, subtle, and well-informed.[3] He has acquainted himself with theological trends from the sixteenth century to the present in a fashion that is fair (although this Protestant commentator is a little unhappy with his characterization of the Reformation as another triumph for individualism), comprehensive, and so nuanced as to defy easy summary.

The spirit epitomized by the Enlightenment is at the center of this recital, and Kant's claim that the world has "come of age" provides the touchstone from which innumerable attempts were spawned by "dominant theology" to salvage something of "the faith once delivered to the saints." Although ultimately critical, Gustavo is not scornful of these efforts, and he is particularly cordial to such Protestant theologians as Karl Barth and Dietrich Bonhoeffer. The latter was making an honest effort to explore how to speak of God in "a world come of age." Through his own experiences in the underground and in prison, Bonhoeffer recognized that God cannot save us through domination but only through suffering with us, and this acknowledgment of the "weakness" of God made it possible for Bonhoeffer, who was "a bourgeois of the bourgeois," to grasp the fact that for himself as well, identification with such a God could only be achieved by identification with the lowly of this world with whom God had already identified. Gustavo frequently quotes what he calls "a beautiful text of Bonhoeffer" to show how radical was the repositioning:

> We have for once learnt to see the great events of world history from below, from the perspective of the outcast, the suspects, the mal-treated, the powerless, the oppressed, the reviled — in short from the perspective of those who suffer [*Letters and Papers from Prison*, p. 17; cited in *The Power of the Poor in History*, in a different translation].

Bonhoeffer was martyred during the war and had no chance to test this discovery. But although ongoing dialogue with him is therefore not possible, there is another German theologian, the Roman Catholic Johann Baptist Metz, who has tried as have few others in Europe to be open to new theological currents from Latin America, and Gustavo's responses to him indicate both the strengths and weaknesses of the endeavor.[4]

In good European fashion, Metz deals with problems raised by the Enlightenment, which, by stressing that the modern world had gained autonomy, forced Christianity to retreat from the public and social realm, retaining only the "privatized realm" of interior faith. The *theology of secularization* played along with this, and settled for two realms, one public and the other private (what Gustavo elsewhere calls "the distinction of planes"), with religion relegated to the private realm. New versions of *progressive theology* settled for an uncritical conformism to the world. In opposition to both of these positions, Metz has called for a *political theology* that "deprivatizes" the faith and reinserts it once more in the public realm, but in critical rather than uncritical fashion. (Jesus' death, for example, is interpreted by Metz as due to his conflict with the political powers of his time.) Theology, as the "dangerous memory" of such biblical realities, must reaffirm a faith back in touch with the real world; Metz feels that theologians have been too remote from that world and should "allow themselves to be interrupted by the mute suffering of a people."

Gustavo affirms that this is admirable, particularly coming from one in

Metz's own situation, and believes that he "has explored a very rich vein for theology." But his admiration is tempered in two ways:

1. He feels that since Metz is "far from the revolutionary ferment of the Third World countries, he cannot penetrate the situation of dependency, injustice, and exploitation in which most of humankind finds itself" (*TheoLib*, p. 129 [224]). Since Metz and others like him have not directly experienced these confrontations and conflicts—or the consequent commitment to liberation that emerges from them—the analysis remains "rather abstract"; it would be helped by more attention to the social sciences, and especially to certain aspects of Marxism, perhaps as mediated by Ernst Bloch.

2. Despite Metz's important rejection of the political conformism of the "theology of secularization," Gustavo feels that he has not completely shaken it off, and as a result extrapolates too easily from the European situation, assuming "the universal existence of a secularized world and the privatization of faith" (ibid.). What Metz describes as true for Europe is simply not descriptively true for Latin America, where religion, rather than being "privatized," plays a central and public role, albeit very pro-establishment.

So one must be careful not to take Metz's analysis and simplistically transplant it elsewhere. It does not work on the Latin American scene. (This is an important rejoinder to critics who charge that liberation theology is nothing but "transplanted European political theology.") Those who follow Metz with his new political theology must be ready to engage in more robust critique of advanced capitalist society, and not let themselves be seduced into too narrow an ecclesiastical framework.

Metz hears such concerns and in a number of more recent works, such as *Faith in History and Society* (where he writes about "the primacy of praxis") and *The Emergent Church*, he offers the next round in the exchange. Furthermore, Metz has broken sufficiently out of the "Germanic" mold to have gotten into trouble with his bishops, which can only be taken as a sign that he is doing something right.

The inadequacy of dominant theology to deal with the realities of the Third World led to the need for an alternative. In chapters 1 and 2 we traced some of Gustavo's steps in formulating such an alternative. And since chapter 5 will deal with the content of a developed liberation theology, it will be sufficient here to note what Gustavo sees as "two fundamental insights" of liberation theology that have been present from the beginning, no matter what other things have been embroidered around it, and that speak to needs the dominant theology was not able to meet. These are (1) its theological method and (2) its perspective of the poor. The distinctions are important enough to justify an extended quotation, which can also serve as a summary of where we have come thus far in our study:

From the beginning the theology of liberation posited that the first act is involvement in the liberation process, and that theology comes afterward, as a second act. The theological moment is one of critical reflection from within, and upon, concrete historical praxis, in confrontation with the word of the Lord as lived and accepted in faith. . . .

It is not a matter of setting an inductive method over against the deductive method of such and such a theology. That would be an oversimplification. It is rather an attempt to situate the work of theology within the complex and proliferous context of the relationship between practice and theory.

The second insight of the theology of liberation is its decision to work from the viewpoint of the poor—the exploited classes, marginalized ethnic groups, and scorned cultures. This led it to take up the great theme of poverty and the poor in the Bible. As a result the poor appear within this theology as the key to an understanding of the meaning of liberation and of the meaning of the revelation of a liberating God.

This second point, of course, is inseparable from the first. If theology is to be a reflection from within, and upon, praxis, it will be important to bear in mind that what is being reflected upon is the praxis of liberation of the oppressed in this world. To divorce theological method from this perspective would be to lose the nub of the question and fall back into the academic.

It is not enough to say that praxis is the first act. One must take into consideration the historical subject of this praxis—those who until now have been the absent ones of history. A theology thus understood starts off from the masses and moves from within their world. It is a theological reasoning that is veri-fied—made to be true—in a real, fertile involvement with the liberation process.

The inseparability of these two prime intuitions, furthermore, is what enabled liberation theologians to see from the very beginning that they were not going to be able to build a theology of any substance if the poor had no grasp of the hope that was theirs. . . . This is important. The only way to come to a new theological focus and language was to sink our roots in the social life of the Latin American people . . . this lowly people who had so long kept silent and now suddenly wished to speak, to cry out [*PP*, pp. 200–201; see a shorter version of the same passage in *The Emergent Gospel*, p. 247].

As this eloquent statement makes clear, when all is said and done, what is said is not as important as what is done. It is not enough to have a new metaphysics that takes the subtleties of modernity into account, and perhaps even includes a kind word or two about "nonpersons." What matters, Gustavo insists, is *entering into solidarity with nonpersons* as they struggle to attain personhood.

So the "break" between the two positions is not simply theological; it is also political. Or to be more precise, theology is authentic only to the degree that it is also political (see *Emergent*, p. 241). Theology, as well as philosophy, has often thought it was sufficient to interpret the world, whereas the important thing is to change it. The circle always comes back to action. It is not enough to reread history, or even reread the Bible. Such activity will remain academic unless the *rereading leads to a redoing*.

Liberation theology, then, stands with the losers and insists that they need not remain losers. This sounds like a lonely spot to be until it is recognized that most of the human family already dwells there. And there have been moments, too few of them, when Christians have stood there too — certain members and groups within the early church before it became "successful," medieval and Reformation "sectarians" whom we today conveniently write off as wild-eyed or naive; Bartolomé de Las Casas, who became a "traitor to his class" in order to side with the exploited Amerindians; and the "anonymous" ones today who, across the face of the globe, undergo risks of a dimension unknown to the rest of us. "They tap into a stream of living water," Gustavo rejoices, "welling up periodically in the desert of academic theology" (in *Emergent*, p. 249).

Recognizing that oversimplification lurks within any such endeavor, we can characterize the two forms of theology as follows:

Dominant Theology	Liberation Theology
1. responds to the *nonbeliever* whose faith is threatened by modernity	1. responds to the *nonperson* whose faith is threatened by forces of destruction
2. begins with the world of modernity and remains thought-oriented	2. begins with the world of oppression and becomes action-oriented
3. is developed "from above" — from the position of the privileged, the affluent, the bourgeois	3. is developed "from below" — from the "underside of history," the position of the oppressed, the marginated, the exploited
4. largely written by "those with white hand," the "winners"	4. only beginning to be written; must be articulated by those with dark-skinned, gnarled hands, the "losers"
5. focuses attention on a "religious" world that needs to be reinforced	5. focuses attention on a political world that needs to be replaced
6. linked to Western culture, the white race, the male sex, the bourgeois class	6. linked to "the wretched of the earth," the marginated races, despised cultures and sex, the exploited classes
7. affirms the achievements of culture — individualism, rationalism, capitalism, the bourgeois spirit	7. insists that the "achievements" of culture have been used to exploit the poor
8. wants to work gradually, reforming existing structures by "superversion"	8. demands to work rapidly through liberation from existing structures by "subversion"

A person at the top of a high tower can see a ship still hidden from a second observer on the beach, and two different accounts of what is "out there" will result. Just as there are different geographical perspectives, so there are different theological perspectives that affect our vision in similar fashion. Having tried to clarify two such perspectives, we can now illustrate how differently they evaluate an event experienced by them both.

The event is the document from Vatican II, "The Church and the World Today" (*Gaudium et Spes*), the most forward-looking council document, hailed in Latin America for opening new doors, both for its *method* (starting with the human situation rather than immutable principles) and its *content* (affirming the duty of the church to engage in the struggle for justice). Hugo Assmann, not one to overpraise establishmentarianism, felt that the document represented "a first sign that the secular sciences were being taken seriously as providing data for theological reflection" (*Theology for a Nomad Church*, p. 63).

Adherents of both dominant theology and liberation theology share a perception that *Gaudium et Spes* indicated new stirrings within the Roman Catholic Church that responded to Pope John's plea "to shake off the imperial dust," emerge from its Catholic ghetto, and enter the contemporary world. They would also agree that the document did begin a dialogue with "modernity" and that certain questions confronting the contemporary world were taken seriously. Gustavo notes some of them: human rights, subjective values, freedom, social equality, the nature of human progress, and so on (*PP*, p. 181).

But once such points have been made, the shared perceptions begin to fade. For "the modern world" with which Vatican II decided to engage, was almost exclusively the European-northern hemisphere world, the world of the upper middle class. If the document "broke new ground," it was mainly ground lived on and owned by those same Europeans and North Americans. From the perspective of Latin Americans, the council did not really hear the cries of "the wretched of the earth," cries that sound day and night in the ears of all Third World peoples. The true interlocutors to whom the council was responding were the nonbelievers rather than the nonpersons.

So while it enunciated the *virtues* of a portion of the modern world with new openness and frankness, the document was guilty of ignoring its *defects*: "poverty, injustice, inequality, and class conflict were barely touched upon" (*Emergent*, p. 234). Not only were such defects virtually ignored, but causes of their remaining alive and well in modern society were not explored:

> Social conflicts are touched upon only in general terms. . . . There is no serious criticism of the implications of the monopolistic domination of the popular classes, especially the poor, by capitalism [*PP*, p. 182].

Furthermore, the council failed to challenge the perpetuation of such ills in the future: "Nor is there any clear realization of the new forms of oppression and exploitation perpetrated in the name of those modern world values" (Greinacher and Müller, eds., *The Poor and the Church*, p. 12).

Such concerns were sidestepped, Gustavo feels, because the council (after decades of Catholic condemnation of "modernity") wanted at last to enter into creative dialogue with the modern world. What flawed the performance, however, was that "the modern world" is not some homogenous unity, but a diversity deeply "divided into conflicting social classes." In sum, the world with which the council wanted to initiate dialogue was the world of the rich, not the world of the poor.

With all its shortcomings, however, the creation of the document was an event of singular importance, and its impact should not be downplayed. After all, it paved the way for Medellín.

Theology and the Social Sciences[5]

During the busy months of 1984, when Gustavo was under constant attack by Rome, he wrote an important article, "Theology and the Social Sciences." In addition to its significance in the ongoing struggle with Rome, the essay provides insights into Gustavo's overall theological method.

The topic is important because Gustavo feels that theology must relate itself to the language and thought-patterns of its time. In the face of an increasing acknowledgment of the presence of the poor and oppressed—an "irruption" of those who have hitherto been "absent" from the making of history—theology needs to draw on the social sciences to gain "a more accurate knowledge of society as it really is," so that it can "articulate with greater precision the challenges [society] poses for the proclamation of the gospel and thus for theological reflection as well" (*Truth*, p. 55).

After restating his conviction that language about God must combine prophetic and contemplative speech, Gustavo asks how such language can make use of the social sciences. The answer is that they can help us understand the reality of widespread poverty more adequately than we can without them. Their task is to acquaint us with the nature of the world to which theology must speak. Such sociological constructs must always be subjected to "critical discernment" by theologians. The theory of "dependency"—that poor nations remain poor because of their "dependency" on the policies of rich nations—is a case in point. While the theory originally introduced theologians to the play of economic forces, its usefulness was limited and it soon became a subordinate instrument of social measurement. Gustavo, in fact, was criticizing it as early as 1974, and it is infrequently used by liberation theologians today (see *Diálogos en al CELAM*, pp. 228–29).[6]

The example is useful not only to indicate the tentativeness with which any social theory must be employed, but also to illustrate the complexity of relating the social sciences to Marxism. Those who accuse liberation theology of overreliance on Marxist analysis, and simultaneously criticize its use of dependency theory, cannot have it both ways, for Marxist thinkers almost universally assert that it is antithetical to a Marxist outlook.

When Gustavo turns directly to the impact of Marxist analysis, he makes a number of important points usually overlooked by stock-in-trade right-wing critics. To use certain contributions of Marxist analysis does *not* "mean an acceptance of Marxism, especially insofar as Marxism embodies an all-embracing view of life" that "excludes the Christian faith and its requirements" (p. 61):

> There is no question at all of a possible acceptance of an atheistic ideology. Were we to accept this possibility, we would already be separated from the Christian faith and no longer dealing with a properly theological issue. Nor is there any question of agreement with a totalitarian version of history that denies the freedom of the human person. These two options—an atheistic ideology and a totalitarian vision—are to be discarded and rejected [ibid.].

Gustavo argues (1) that a distinction not only can but must be made between "the ideological aspects of Marxism" and a "Marxist social analysis," and (2) that any contribution of the latter must be *critically* situated within the broader framework of the other social sciences. His clarity on this point belies a host of conservative critics.

Marxist insights may have some utilitarian value in assessing forces in modern society, but their significance should not be magnified out of proportion. Gustavo has never tried, for example, to foster a "Christian-Marxist dialogue" in Latin America, after the fashion of many European theologians, in the hope that a "synthesis" could be achieved. Because he is dealing chiefly with the pastoral concerns of poverty and marginalization, he has different concerns. Indeed, his attention is not focused on the relatively narrow matter of "theology and Marxist analysis," but on the broader concern of relating "theology and the social sciences," of which Marxism is only one instance.

Even the latter endeavor must be properly circumscribed. One should not try "to deduce political programs or actions from the gospel or from reflections on the gospel."[7] It is not the function of theology to offer specific political programs. The "theology of revolution" (to use an example to which he frequently adverts) ends up "baptizing" revolution and thus fails to acknowledge "the autonomy proper to the political sphere" (p. 65).

It *is* the task of theology to ensure that "a comprehensive vision of a given historical process" is not reduced solely "to its political dimensions" (p. 65). Theology must issue a constant reminder that economic and social and political structures are not panaceas that solve all human problems, and that "deeper changes" need to take place in human beings as part of the total process. Sociologists, for example, cannot see from within the boundaries of their own discipline that sin is at the heart of unjust situations; theologians, on the other hand, must make that point, and failure to do so is a default of theological responsibility. So although faith cannot "provide strategies," it can call attention to aspects of the human situation that other disciplines fail to recognize.

Gustavo also deals with the reality of *conflict* in history, a theme to which we shall return later in this chapter. Christians cannot pretend that conflict does not exist. They live in its midst, whether they like it or not, and what makes this a special challenge to Christians is that "there are no situations, however difficult, that amount to an exception or a parenthesis in the universal demands of love" (p. 69). How do we exercise love of neighbor in the midst of conflict? It is the task of theology to listen to what the social sciences say descriptively in order to deal with the question: How are Christians to live their faith, their hope, and their love amid a conflict that takes the form of class struggle? (p. 70). If social analysis in the future were to determine that class struggle is no longer a dominant reality, Christians would still have to find ways to love in a new situation.

Gustavo intentionally refers to multiple aspects of conflict—"races discriminated against, despised cultures, exploited classes, and the condition of women" (p. 70)—to ensure that noneconomic factors will always be taken into account, lest history be "reduced" exclusively to class struggle. He also distances liberation theology from attempts to explain class struggle solely on the basis of economic determinism. Sometimes Marxists turn class struggle into "the driving force of history" or "a law of history." But this approach, Gustavo responds, "does not reflect my own thinking and. . . I have never used such expressions." He further strengthens his case (as we will see in the next section of this chapter) by numerous citations from the magisterium of the church, where the reality of class struggle is clearly acknowledged.

What, then, does Christian love demand in a world of conflict? Neutrality is not possible: "passivity or indifference would be neither ethical nor Christian" (p. 75). But, Gustavo continues, "this does not mean that the alternative is to promote conflict" (p. 75). As he had pointed out in the first edition of *A Theology of Liberation*, "those who speak of class struggle do not 'advocate' it" (p. 75; see *TheoLib*, p. 274). What they do is "recognize a fact" and seek "to get rid of it by attacking its causes" (p. 76). John Paul II's encyclical *Laborem Exercens* is cited to support the notion that there is "real conflict" that is not reducible to class struggle. What is needed in such situations is solidarity with the oppressed, for "it is not possible to remain neutral in face of the situation of poverty and the justice of the claims made by the poor" (p. 76). This, he argues, is exactly the pope's position.

Amid the taking of sides, of opting for the poor, and of disavowing neutrality, there is "a permanent demand of Christian love" that is not easy, because in conflict situations this means a love of enemies: "a painful situation that may cause us to regard others as our adversaries does not dispense us from loving them" (p. 79).

"Class Struggle" Revisited

In the initial edition of *A Theology of Liberation*, Gustavo concluded his chapter on the church with a section on "Christian Brotherhood and Class Struggle" (pp. 272–79). When the fifteenth anniversary edition was published in 1988, the original text remained intact save for this section, which, as Gustavo noted, "gave rise to misunderstandings that I want to clear up" (p. 156). As a result, he rewrote the section and gave it a new title, "Faith and Social Conflict" (pp. 156–61).

Those who compare the two texts looking for evidence that Gustavo has "backed down," succumbed to pressure, or recanted, will look in vain. The revision does not represent a retreat but a restatement. Nothing in the earlier edition has been retracted or suppressed; the themes have simply grown deeper and changed their manner of expression. Whatever fence-mending there is, is undertaken not to duck controversy, but to clarify implications of the earlier text, and buttress their positions by citations from bishops, popes, and councils. The result must persuade all but the most hardened that Gustavo's position is a faithful expression of Catholic teaching.

To clear the air, Gustavo interpolates occasional comments to forestall hungry critics from drawing false conclusions. Samples: "The claim that conflict is a social fact does not imply an unqualified acceptance of it as something beyond discussion" (p. 157). "Our active participation on the side of justice . . . does not mean that we are encouraging conflict" (p. 159). "I am obviously not identifying the preferential option for the poor with any ideology or specific program" (p. 160). "The determinist approach [of Marxism] based on economic factors is completely alien to the kind of social analysis that supplies a framework for the theology of liberation" (p. 249, n. 51). "'Real conflict' is one thing, its ideological transformation into 'a systematic class struggle' as the sole political strategy is quite another. *In my approach I refer to the former, not to the latter*" (p. 250, n. 59, italics added).

More important than rear guard actions, however, are the positive themes of the section, in which Gustavo supports his concerns by examples from official church teaching, much of it promulgated since the first edition of his work—suggesting to me that in the interval the church had been simultaneously trying to catch up with Gustavo as well as keeping him under wraps. In addition to references to *Quadragesimo Anno* (to which he had not appealed in the earlier recension) with its papal acknowledgment of the reality of class struggle, Gustavo calls upon the following authorities: the French Episcopal Commission on the Working Class; John Paul II's encyclical on work, *Laborem Exercens*, which he quotes more frequently than any other document; Paul VI and Medellín, referred to jointly; the Vatican Council; the Peruvian episcopate; the auxiliary bishop of Lyons;

and the Puebla Conference of the Latin American bishops. The purpose of this arsenal of resources is to convince the reader that the material being presented is part of the ongoing development of Catholic social teaching. The evidence is persuasive.

The section provides a further gift that, because it is buried in a footnote, deserves upgrading here, and can serve as a recapitulation of some of the concerns of "Theology and the Social Sciences." Responding to a question at meetings of CELAM 1973 about "class struggle," Gustavo said:

> The problem facing theology is not to determine whether or not social classes are in opposition. That is in principle a matter for the sciences, and theology must pay careful attention to them if it wishes to be *au courant* with the effort being made to understand the social dimensions of the human person. The question, therefore, that theology must answer is this: if there is a class struggle (as one, but not the only, form of historical conflict), how are we to respond to it as Christians? A theological question is always one that is prompted by the content of the faith—that is, by love. The specifically Christian question is both theological and pastoral: How are Christians to live their faith, their hope, and their love amid a conflict that takes the form of class struggle? Suppose that analysis were to tell us one day: "The class struggle is not as important as you used to think." We as theologians would continue to say that love is the important thing, even amid conflict as described for us by social analysis. If I want to be faithful to the gospel I cannot disregard reality, however, harsh and conflictual it may be. And the reality of Latin America is indeed harsh and conflictual! [in *Diálogos en el CELAM*, pp. 89–90; translated in *TheoLib*, p. 249, n. 52].

What, then, about "Faith and Social Conflict"? Since the discussion takes place in the context of the church's life, Gustavo notes that the Vatican Council opened up the church to the modern world and its conflictual nature, and that Medellín affirmed that the church could not remain neutral but must make the choice of a preferential option for the poor. How does the church affirm its unity in the face of crises that demand taking sides and thereby threaten to split its ranks?

Gustavo offers a two-part answer. The first task is to "see the real world without evasion," the second task is to change it.

1. Conflict is a *social fact*, and inequality and injustice are at the heart of it. We live in the midst of—and Gustavo does not flinch from using the term—"class struggle." But he is not alone in using the term. Pius XI had already acknowledged its reality in *Quadragesimo Anno* (1931), and so Gustavo concludes, with papal support, that "class struggle is a fact that Christians cannot dodge" (p. 157). The French bishops on the Commission on the Working Class argue that the ones most responsible for class struggle

"are those who deliberately keep the working class in an unjust situation" (p. 158). Pope John Paul II, in *Laborem Exercens*, describes the struggle as one between "capital" and "labor," but takes the discussion beyond the realm of social theory and inserts it into the realm of "living, actual persons." The reality, Gustavo summarizes, is "an opposition of *persons* and not a conflict between abstract concepts or impersonal forces" (p. 158, italics in original). *The issue is not "Marxist analysis" but the plight of human beings.*

2. Inasmuch as the fact of social conflict cannot be ignored, Christians must seek to *overcome it*, refusing to accept its legitimacy and attacking its root causes. The task is to establish peace and justice, which cannot be separated. Christians are called to love everyone; the reality of social conflict means not only affirming some persons, but opposing others and taking sides — all in the name of love:

> Our active participation on the side of justice and in defense of the weakest members of society does not mean that we are encouraging conflict; it means rather that we are trying to eliminate its deepest root, which is the absence of love [p. 159].

Pope John Paul II, in the face of such realities, strongly supports the solidarity of the church with workers movements in their struggle for justice, and affirms that this is part of the task of "the church of the poor." In the light of things to come, let us note that here is one place where Gustavo and the pope agree.

Gustavo concludes from this discussion that "the universality of Christian love is . . . incompatible with the exclusion of any persons, but it is not incompatible with a preferential option for the poor and most oppressed" (p. 160). God does not exclude any from the divine love, nor can Christians exclude any from their human love; the gospel, after all, requires us to love even our enemies. We will have adversaries and we must love them — such is the difficult but unavoidable Christian task.

This creates many problems for the church, particularly in Latin America where church and society are virtually coextensive. The church proclaims unity, and in the face of the increasing divisions within society the search for unity becomes more important than ever. But, as Vatican II pointed out, "unity among human beings is possible only if there is real justice for all" (*Lumen Gentium*, I). So to work for the eradication of injustice is not at odds with concern for unity, but a primary step toward the creation of unity, not only within the church but within the entire human family.

A Basic Unity: Spirituality and Methodology

To write of spirituality and methodology in the same sentence appears to many like mixing apples and oranges. Spirituality, they claim, is about intangibles, methodology about the nitty-gritty. But the implied division is false. Gustavo insists that "our spirituality *is* our methodology," and in the interview with Elsa Tamez cited at the beginning of this chapter, he comments that his study of Job persuaded him afresh that the great themes in Job — suffering, gratuitousness, justice — revolve around the relationship of spirituality and methodology.

A similar charge is lodged when Gustavo talks about spirituality and liberation in the same breath. This juxtaposition also seems alien to the outsider, or at best a recent novelty introduced in liberation theology to protect its adherents from the charge of being "too political." The charge is false. Gustavo's earliest book, *Líneas pastorales de la Iglesia en América latina*, based on talks going back to 1968, was about the *pastoral* tasks of the church, and the interrelationship of spirituality and liberation is set forth prominently, if succinctly, in *A Theology of Liberation* as the climax to a chapter "Encountering God in History" (pp. 116–20 [203–8]).

The extensive treatment of spirituality in *We Drink from Our Own Wells*, published a full decade after *A Theology of Liberation*, is simply a long-planned elaboration of earlier material. The three themes stressed in the section of *A Theology of Liberation* on spirituality — conversion, gratuitousness, and joy — are the first three major points of part 3 of *We Drink from Our Own Wells*, and its other two main points — spiritual childhood and community — are implicit in the earlier work. What we have is a continuity, in which themes are deepened with the passing of time, rather than representing a new departure.

This relation of spirituality to both the methodology and content of liberation theology deserves special attention in light of never-ending allegations about its presumed "political" preoccupation. We can restore an appropriate balance by walking briefly through *We Drink from Our Own Wells*, so that Gustavo can guide us on what he calls "the Spiritual Journey of a People."

The title, from Bernard of Clairvaux's *De Consideratione*, sets the theme. Bernard writes that the place from which our spiritual nourishment must come is the place where we ourselves think, pray, and work. For Latin Americans, the "wells" from which they must drink are located within the liberation process to which they are committed. It is there and not elsewhere that they receive living water "from the Spirit" that purifies and energizes them.

The life of spirituality is located in the midst of the world's turmoil rather than in a safe haven of retreat, and the overall structure of the book reinforces this claim. Part 1, "How Shall We Sing to the Lord in a Foreign Land?," sets out the Latin American context, which is one of hostility and death, and in which the Christian response must be an affirmation of life.

Gustavo distinguishes between true and false spirituality. The latter, he feels, becomes either a spirituality "for the few" (leading to two different classes of Christians) or an individualistic spirituality that turns away from the world. As the subtitle, "The Spiritual Journey of a People," indicates, spirituality must be *communal*, involving solidarity among all people as they engage in struggle. The theme of struggle is a characteristic of human living that permeates not only contemporary life on the firing line, but the psalms, prophets, gospels, and epistles as well.

Having established the life of spirituality in the immediate situation, Gustavo goes on in part 2, "Here There is No Longer Any Way," to examine biblical materials that provide sustenance for the journey. The title is from St. John of the Cross at that point in the ascent of Mount Carmel where the pilgrim has moved beyond the confines of the law, is released from external coercion, and can begin to live more freely in the light of liberating faith. The section is saturated with material from the synoptic gospels, the Johannine literature, and the epistles, as well as offering examples of how these resources are used by John of the Cross and Teresa of Avila. Karl Marx is never mentioned.

This biblical section is followed by part 3, entitled "Free to Love," in which Gustavo develops a spirituality growing out of the immediate situation and the biblical heritage (parts 1 and 2), "embracing all aspects of life and . . . done in community." The section represents a lasting contribution to the literature on spirituality. Five interconnected marks are distinguished.

The first of these is *Conversion: A Requirement for Solidarity.* Conversion means a break with the past, a setting out on a new path. There must be an acknowledgment not only of individual sin, but of the fact that we live in a sinful situation, creating structural causes of injustice. Conversion involves the possibility for a new life, lived in solidarity rather than isolation. Within it there is no longer a cleavage between the "material" and the "spiritual"; hunger for God and hunger for bread, especially bread for the neighbor, are forever interrelated.

A second characteristic of the new spirituality is *Gratuitousness: The Atmosphere for Efficacy,* which we might less cumbersomely translate as "Grace: The Power for Action." God's gracious love is the source of everything else, and our own ability to love and act flows from this. Efficacious love starts with the concrete need of the other, not with a "duty" to practice love. To live the gratuitous love of God is to be committed to "a liberative undertaking." Gustavo notes that grace provides beauty for our lives, "without which even the struggle for justice would be crippled." Prayer expresses our faith and trust in God, "a living dialogue" that becomes a touchstone of life. There is always "a twofold moment," as the parable of the last judgment (Matt. 25:31–46) makes clear: a full encounter with the neighbor presupposes the experience of gratuitousness, and Christ, as our way to God, is also our way to the neighbor.

The third note of the new spirituality is *Joy: Victory over Suffering.* While he does not gloss over the reality of suffering, Gustavo insists that it is not the last word. The last word is "joy born of the conviction that unjust mistreatment and suffering will be overcome." Such a paschal joy can be found even in times of martyrdom—which is a description of the Latin American scene—even though Christians are meant to stay alive and work for justice. (It is ironic that those who say such things are often the ones to die.) In the face of this, the only joy that can finally sustain is what Gustavo calls "Easter joy, joy springing from hope that death is not the final word of history," and that those who encounter crucifixion can likewise experience resurrection. God's activity can be seen in movements for justice, and human involvement in such movements makes the life of joy possible.

The fourth mark is *Spiritual Childhood: A Requirement for Commitment to the Poor.* The task, as Gustavo points out here and elsewhere, is to be "with the poor and against poverty." This double posture characterizes "spiritual childhood." The demands are severe: one must assume "voluntarily and lovingly the condition of the needy . . . in order to give testimony to the evil it represents." This will provoke opposition from the privileged, who are not enchanted with those who "disassociate themselves from the injustices of the prevailing system."

Gustavo is not settling for lip service here: commitment to the poor means accepting the world of the poor "as a place of residence and not simply of work"; sharing in exploitation and inadequate health care; but it also means making new friends, experiencing a new kind of love, and developing "a new realization of the Lord's fidelity." He acknowledges that the "real identification" he is calling for will elude most of us. Nevertheless, it is in such commitment that true "spiritual childhood" is nurtured.

The fifth mark of a new spirituality is *Community: Out of Solitude.* To be with the poor may initially mean lonesome travel through "the dark night of injustice," enduring ostracism, fear, weariness, cowardice, despair, and the need to make decisions when "nothing is clear." Such situations will often leave us feeling forsaken. But these are the times when (in a reversal of the section heading) we move "out of solitude" and into "community." God does not call us to remain in the desert alone, but only to pass through it on our way to the promised land, where we are drawn deeper into community.

In the Latin American experience, the *comunidades de base* have been providing foretastes of the promised land amid the desert. They are places where the death and resurrection of Christ are experienced, and where the eucharist becomes a point of departure and arrival. Joy enters once again, and "celebration" is the only adequate description of the new quality of life:

> Spirituality is a community enterprise. It is a passage of a people through the solitude and dangers of the desert, as it carves out its own way in the following of Jesus Christ. *This spiritual experience is the well from which we must drink.* Through it we draw the promise of resurrection [*Wells*, p. 137, italics added].

CHAPTER 5

Act Two, Scene Two:
Theology in the Light
of the Word of God (Content)

Theology is a love letter to the church.
— Gustavo, in conversation

The doctrinal riches of the gospel contain a revolutionary thrust.
— *Between Honesty and Hope,* p.74

*The political commitment to liberation [is placed] in the perspective of
the free gift of the total liberation brought by Christ.*
— *Liberation and Change,* p. 84

Gustavo's theology arises out of the "first act" of the Christian, which is
commitment to working with the poor for human liberation. This engagement gives rise to the "second act," which is "critical reflection on praxis
in the light of the Word of God." Having examined the first half of this
definition, "critical reflection on praxis," we can now look at the latter half,
"in the light of the Word of God."

In doing so, we move from *method* to *content.* Having explored *how*
Gustavo affirms, we now examine *what* he affirms. The division, we must
repeat, is artificial: how we affirm and what we affirm are interdependent.
The Second Act still has two scenes, and neither can be understood without
the other.

"Expanding the View"

When the fifteenth anniversary edition of *A Theology of Liberation* was
published, Gustavo felt able to preserve the text intact, save for the exception noted in the previous chapter. But in order to position his 1971 text
in 1988, he added a lengthy introduction, entitled "Expanding the View."[1]

This introduction represents Gustavo's position as of February 1988, affirming new nuances, rebutting old charges, and providing a comprehensive framework for reexamining the content of his faith. But the task of "expanding the view" did not end in February 1988, and the conclusions there presented are simultaneously an "introduction" to further expanding—a point to which we shall return at the conclusion of this chapter.

In what ways, then, has the view "expanded" during the decade and a half between the two editions? Gustavo's answer is organized around three realities that have marked liberation theology's ongoing development: (1) the viewpoint of the poor, and the consequent need for solidarity; (2) theological work, and the need for reflection; and (3) the proclamation of the kingdom of life in the face of increasing martyrdoms. These are not theoretical conclusions; they grow out of "a direct, real-life setting" (p. xx) and present the Latin American church with a *kairos*, a "special time" in which the demands and promises of God must be heard with increased intensity.

1. *"A new presence" is noted in the "irruption of the poor,"* the presence of those who have always been "absent." The poor are now being heard, and the church is one of the few places where they are taken seriously. It is not enough to "describe" the situation of the poor; "its causes must also be determined" (p. xxiii). Structural analysis and other tools of the social sciences have been helpful in this regard.

A "preferential option for the poor" is the result of this new engagement, a concept Gustavo carefully refines against persistent attacks, noting the care with which John XXIII, John Paul II, Medellín, Puebla, and even the second "Instruction on Liberation Theology" from the Congregation of the Doctrine of the Faith, endorse this approach. Conclusion: "the option [for the poor] is now an essential element in the understanding that the church as a whole has of its task in the present world" (p. xxviii).

2. *The role of reflection* has been deepened. A new theological perspective became possible as the result of close contact with the "nonpersons" who do not count on the conventional scales of social measurement. Authentic theological reflection must now be identified with the poor, in both a celebratory and contemplative fashion, in order to forge shalom—a rich biblical word that refers not only to "peace" but to the *whole* of life—that is, to "the establishment of justice and peace."

Gustavo does not temporize about the need for close identification with the poor:

> Being part of the life of our people, sharing their sufferings and joys, their concerns and their struggles, as well as the faith and hope that they live as a Christian community—all this is not a formality required if one is to do theology; it is a requirement for being a Christian [pp. xxxii-xxxiii].

It is out of this lived reality that Gustavo repeats his frequent insistence about theology being the "second act," including a recognition that "second" does not mean "secondary." Reflection has an irreplaceable role, but always in conjunction with action. "Any attempt to focus on only one means the loss of both" (p. xxxiv). It is always a challenge to see whether we can really do theology "while Ayacucho lasts"—that is, while there is misery and exploitation and death. But only from *within* Ayacucho and its all-too-numerous counterparts can liberation theology be authentic.

3. Christians are *"friends of life"* who, in witnessing to the risen Christ, realize that "life and not death has the final say about history," and that joy is therefore possible (p. xxxvi). Theology is reflection on this reality. "To liberate" is specifically "to give life," and all three levels of liberation—from oppressive social situations, from fate, and from personal sin and guilt—must be simultaneously affirmed. Liberation theology is a theology of salvation for the *whole* person.

But there is a serious downside that was only beginning to be felt when the first edition was published. Those with power will not tolerate a message of new life and hope for those whom they have always been able to sub-jugate and consign to death. The price attached to preaching the gospel of life is the likelihood of death. To live—and die—in a new era of martyrdom has become the everyday experience of those who proclaim that liberation *in this world* is the rightful birthright of all. The murder of Archbishop Romero for siding with the poor in El Salvador has become "a milestone in the life of the Latin American church" (p. xliii), for it witnesses both to the heavy cost of discipleship and to the courage with which believers can face death. Only when nourished by such biblical realism can theology be authentic.

Three Levels of Liberation: Clearing the Air

We have used the word "liberation" frequently in preceding chapters, and we must now clarify what Gustavo means by it. His main point is that there are three levels of meaning for liberation, and that *no one of them is properly understood unless the other two are simultaneously affirmed.*[2]

1. The first level is *liberation from unjust social structures* that destroy people. This is where everything starts. The structures may be political, economic, or cultural; they may grow out of warped attitudes based on race, class, nation, or sex; they may also be embodied in church structures. Gus-tavo has naturally given much attention to this first level, for it is the immediate barrier to full personhood in his situation, and is the aspect of liberation to which the church has given least attention in the past. Time for remedial work.

2. The second level is more subtle but no less important. It is *liberation from the power of fate,* from a sense that one's situation in life has been foreordained, and that there is nothing that can be done about it. If one is born poor, that is the way it was meant to be; if one is born rich, that, too, is the way it was meant to be. Good news to the rich, bad news to the poor.

Result: apathy or despair among the poor, exhilaration among the rich, who are determined to keep things that way. An appeal to fate is a magnificent justification for the status quo—a fact not lost on its beneficiaries.

For centuries the church played a major role in supporting this position by the simple device of substituting "providence" or "the will of God" for "fate." Accept the lot God assigns you without complaint, the sermons went, and you will be rewarded in the afterlife.

The liberation message on this level is that things need not remain the way they are, that the biblical God is working actively for justice, and seeks to enlist all people in the struggle. The operative word is *hope*.

3. The third level of liberation is *liberation from personal sin and guilt*.[3] More is involved than simply being liberated from evil structures:

> Modern human aspirations include not only liberation from *exterior* pressures which prevent fulfillment as a member of a certain social class, country, or society. Persons seek likewise an *interior* liberation not only on a social plane but also on a psychological [*TheoLib*, p. 20 (30)].

There is no doubt where this liberation comes from:

> Christ is presented as the one who brings in liberation. Christ the Savior liberates from sin, which is the ultimate root of all disruption of friendship and of all injustice and oppression. Christ makes humankind truly free, that is to say, he enables us to live in communion with him; and this is the basis for all human fellowship [p. 25 (37)].

Having begun by separating the three levels of liberation, it is necessary to conclude by rejoining them. "This is not a matter of three parallel or chronologically successive processes," Gustavo reminds us (p. 25 [37]). They are interrelated and interdependent, and "a comprehensive view of the matter presupposes that all three aspects be considered together" (ibid.). One is not present without the other, even though they are distinct. Bearing this in mind will save us from the temptation to take a "spiritualistic" approach that will simply deny the harsh realities of the world, or to offer shallow analyses or agendas that will claim to meet immediate needs but will not have staying power.

The gospel is not only liberation *from* but liberation *for*, and we can easily discern the positive counterparts to the three levels:

Liberation *from* unjust social structures = liberation *for* participation in creating a just society; liberation *from* fate = liberation *for* responsible action; liberation *from* sin and guilt = liberation *for* a grace-filled life, the "gratuitousness" of which Gustavo speaks so often.

Stated thus, the three levels correspond closely to the summation in

Micah 6:8: "And what does the Lord require of you but to act justly, to love tenderly, and to walk humbly with God."

To act justly = to participate in creating a just society

To love tenderly = responsible action

To walk humbly with God = a grace-filled life

It is not clear whether or not this resonance with Micah played a part in Gustavo's formulation. What *is* clear is that Gustavo and Micah are both plugged into the same source.

A Touchstone: The "Preferential Option for the Poor" and the Fact of "Gratuitousness"

It would be misleading to distill an "organizing principle" for liberation theology, giving the impression that liberation theology is believing in certain things rather than living in certain ways. But if we bear the warning in mind, we can acknowledge coherence as a theological virtue that becomes a vice only when too much is claimed for it.

So a proposal is offered: as an ongoing reminder of liberation theology's immersion in the real world, let us use "the preferential option for the poor" as a touchstone, and examine how Christian faith looks when it is the plumb line in relation to which all else is measured. The theological equivalent of "the preferential option" is surely the fact of "gratuitousness," a concern that we have found central in Gustavo's writings from the beginning. When, in his introduction to the fifteenth anniversary edition of *A Theology of Liberation*, Gustavo seeks to draw the biblical themes together, these are the two that are finally one: "the entire Bible . . . mirrors God's predilection for the weak and abused of human history. This *preference* brings out the *gratuitousness* or unmerited character of God's love" (p. xxvii, italics added). The option, he goes on, "is now an essential element in the understanding that the church as a whole has of its task in the present world" (p. xxviii).

Another way to show the connection is to emphasize that God does not love the poor because they are good (sometimes they can be very evil), but *because they are poor.* God's love is lavished on "the least of these," quite apart from merit or demerit. It is thus "gratuitous" love — grace-filled love — that is not dependent on good works or correct theology, but is continually offered no matter what human barriers are erected against it.

It is tempting to connect those portions of Gustavo's message dealing with traditional doctrines, and demonstrate, in effect, how orthodox he really is. This is doubly tempting in the face of continual attempts by Gustavo's foes to derail him on charges of heterodoxy. The maneuver could be successfully accomplished. But while this might serve the ancillary purpose of getting some of Gustavo's opponents off his back (a worthy end in itself), it would not serve the primary purpose of highlighting the radical convictions that are at the heart of Gustavo's theology *precisely because they are at the heart of biblical theology and church theology when viewed through the eyes of the poor.* There can be "no ease in Zion" when we confront Gustavo on his own terms, or, more properly, when he confronts us on his.

Gustavo *does* reappropriate the "great themes" of classic Christianity, but he does so by stripping away the tame, comfortable efflorescences we have created around them, and getting to their root. The result is that we are forced to reexamine them in their original naked and alarming power. The words are often the same, but the realities to which they point—Bible, God, Christ, Holy Spirit, church—are now viewed "from below" rather than "from above," and consequently carry different messages from the ones to which we have become accustomed. The new messages are not Gustavo's inventions; they are his recovery of the gospel writers' intentions.[4]

The Bible—and a "Militant Reading"

Only recently has the Bible begun to play an important role in Roman Catholic theology. Claims about the nature and truth of Christian faith have been formed by tradition: the church fathers, the councils, the popes. But the gradual discovery of scripture by contemporary Catholics, and the unleashing of the dynamics of its disturbing message, has shattered a complacency that always seems to dwell near the mainstream of Christian thought, whether Catholic, Protestant or Orthodox. The Second Vatican Council, perhaps more than it realized, gave fresh impetus to the study *and application* of the biblical message in the contemporary world, and no one has been more assiduous than Gustavo in responding to the opening thus provided.[5]

Biblical interpretation is notorious for the degree to which readers highlight passages that buttress their own point of view and filter out passages that challenge it. One could almost conclude that the Bible read by liberation theologians and the Bible read by middle-class Christians are different books, so diverse are the messages derived from such readings. North Americans, encountering Third World biblical interpreters for the first time, are likely to react, "These people are biased. Their own situation conditions their reading of scripture." Such a charge is appropriate only if it continues, ". . . and so does our situation condition our reading of scripture." No one approaches scripture de novo; we bring things *to* our reading as well as draw things *from* our reading.

But it is not enough to note the fact that they read one way and we another, as though that were the end of the discussion. For *one way of reading the Bible may be closer to its actual meaning than another.* Liberation theologians sometimes talk (in a jaw-breaking phrase) about "the epistemological privilege of the struggling poor" in reading scripture. By this they mean that a "privileged" or advantageous way of understanding the Bible is granted to the struggling poor because they are closer to the situation of the biblical writers than are the nonpoor. Most—not all—of the biblical writers were themselves oppressed, writing to people who were similarly oppressed. As a result, those in similar situations of oppression today are likely to have a better grasp of the biblical message than those in comfortable situations.

Gustavo's own writings are saturated with biblical material, as we have already seen.[6] His use of scripture is not a matter of "proof-texting" conclusions already reached by other means, but of employing scripture as a basic source of faith. He sees the Bible as "an ensemble of books that tell the history of a people" in different literary modes that are tied together because "they all tell of a people's faith." For Latin Americans, the Bible has become "our prayerbook par excellence," the place where "we rediscover the deep meaning of our life and our commitments."

But people who are reinforced by reading the Bible are sometimes intimidated by its complexity. The scholars are not much help at this point, for the scholars have always been "members of a very exclusive, expensive club," grounded in Western cultural values. So Gustavo and his friends have begun to reread and reinterpret the Bible from within their own situation, and he offers four insights that have emerged from this communal experience:

1. Since the biblical story centers on Christ, the reading will be *christological*, designed to penetrate as fully as possible into his meaning for our lives.

2. The reading will be a reading *in faith*. While it will not be centrally assisted by trained specialists, it will be engaged in by a community that conceives itself as participating in the story, and finding itself directly addressed.

3. The reading will be *historical*. The God of the Bible is found within the ancient history of a people who believed in God, and their story speaks to the contemporary history of those who also believe in God. Because both ancient and contemporary history are "crisscrossed by confrontation and conflict," the reading is not as innocuous as it sounds: true entry into the biblical story can be made only from involvement "in the popular struggles for liberation."

4. So the reading will be *a militant reading*. "It is time," Gustavo insists, "to open the Bible and read it from the perspective of 'those who are persecuted in the cause of right' (Matt. 5:10), from the perspective of the condemned human beings of the earth—for, after all, theirs is the kingdom of heaven." The message is destined for all such persons, and "it is to them that the gospel is preferentially addressed."

From the perspective of such "a militant reading," Gustavo finds the Bible bursting with claims about a God who is partial to the cause of the poor, seeks to enlist the children of earth in the ongoing struggle for justice, and promises a kingdom that will fulfill the divine purposes, not just for a few but for all. Those who continue to do injustice indicate that they do not know this God (Jer. 22:13-17); those who fail to respond to Christ present in the sick, the poor, the naked, and the hungry, indicate that they do not know Christ (Matt. 25:31-46); whereas those who acknowledge God truly, know God as one who works for the liberation of the oppressed (Luke 1:46-55), a work in which all who believe in God must enlist.

Interwoven in all the subsequent biblical stories is an ongoing retelling of the exodus story, with its recognition that God takes sides, acting *for* the slaves and *against* the oppressive rulers. But Gustavo strongly disputes the charge that liberation theology is fixated on the early chapters of Exodus. Of course those chapters are important, but the story compressed in them is the same story found throughout the Bible—in the prophets, the gospels, the epistles—the story of a liberating God and a people whom God desires to liberate.

God—and a Challenge to All Other Gods

Classic theology stresses an omnipotent God who is set over against finite human beings. Contemporary theology emphasizes the "weakness" or "suffering" of a God who identifies with weak and suffering persons. (Dietrich Bonhoeffer and Jürgen Moltmann have been important articulators of this position.) Liberation theology has a different emphasis. The poor and oppressed talk about a God of the poor and oppressed, God as liberator, Lord of life rather than death. Such affirmations are not intellectual expressions so much as the consequence of "lived experiences" that create "the subversive joy of the poor," who know that they will rejoice tomorrow even though they weep today. In the words of José María Arguedas, "the God of the masters is not the same God as the God of the poor."

Such, in capsule form is Gustavo's theological positioning of belief in God.[7] None of this is "new"; it is simply a recovery of something "old," the biblical witness to a God whom subsequent tradition consistently tries to sideline. But such is the power of God, and the power of the biblical text over its manipulators, and the power of the poor now engaging in an "irruption" into contemporary life, that the good news of the liberating God who can no longer be identified with "the god of the masters," is being heard with new power.

Most of this is implicit in the preceding chapters, so a brief consideration of some of the biblical passages to which Gustavo refers in "God's Revelation and Proclamation in History," in *The Power of the Poor in History*, will suffice:

> Father of orphans, defender of widows,
> such is God in [God's] holy dwelling;
> God gives the lonely a permanent home,
> makes prisoners happy by setting them free,
> but rebels must live in an arid land
> [Ps. 68:5-6].

The least privileged in ancient society, the widows and orphans, are special objects of God's concern—a theme prevalent throughout the

Hebrew scriptures. The lonely, the strangers, and the prisoners are also objects of special care by this God of the dispossessed. Such concerns not only describe God's relationship to the world, but all that God is in the fullness of the divine majesty: "Such is God in [God's] holy dwelling."

God's actions are the exacting standard by which human actions are measured:

> You must not pervert justice in dealing with a stranger or an orphan, nor take a widow's garment in pledge. Remember that you were a slave in Egypt and that Jahweh your God redeemed you from there. That is why I lay this charge on you [Deut. 24:17-18].

God, having freed Israel from bondage, demands that Israel free others from bondage. To be treated in a certain way by God has the disturbing consequence that one must treat others in the same fashion.

The acid test of belief in God is how one treats one's neighbor, who is anyone in need. Gustavo cites a celebrated passage in Jeremiah (perhaps after Luke 4:16-30 the most widely cited biblical passage in the literature of liberation theology):

> Doom for the man who founds his palace on anything but
>   integrity,
> his upstairs rooms on anything but honesty,
> who makes his fellow man work for nothing,
> without paying him his wages,
> who says, "I will build myself an imposing palace
> with spacious rooms upstairs,"
> who pierces lights in it,
> panels it with cedar,
> and paints it vermillion.
> Are you more of a king
> for outrivaling others in cedar?
> Your father ate and drank, like you,
> but he practiced honesty and integrity,
> so all went well for him.
> He used to examine the cases of poor and needy,
> then all went well.
> Is not that what it means to know me?
> —It is Jahweh who speaks [Jer. 22:13-16].

The king is living unjustly, a charge catalogued with detailed instances of exploiting the poor. His beautiful, if garish, palace has no merit, for its construction is based on exploitation. His father, however, concerned himself with the poor and needy, and did so from a stance of honesty and integrity. "Is not *that* what it means to know me?" Jahweh asks, and the question will bear only one answer: "Of course." The message is clear: *to know God is to do justice*, and to do injustice is to demonstrate that one does not know God.

The life God asks, then, is a life in which love for God and love for the oppressed are inseparable—a theme encapsulated in the biblical notion of *covenant*. In simplest form it goes: "I shall be your God, and you shall be my people" (see Jer. 7:23). But the living out of this agreement is far from simple, for the reciprocal relationship is not only between God and humanity, but *within* humanity as well: "To be faithful to the covenant," as Gustavo sums it up, "means to practice the justice implied in God's liberating activity on behalf of the oppressed" (p. 10).

Citing the Protestant theologian Karl Barth, Gustavo shows how this understanding cuts across all confessional lines and becomes an ecumenical platform on which all can stand:

> A great twentieth-century theologian, Karl Barth, whose central concern was the transcendence of God, said that God has always been on the side of the poorest, the most despised, the most oppressed. And I believe that this truly reflects what we read in the gospel. Throughout the entire Bible, God manifests himself as the defender of the weak in the face of the powerful, the one who upholds the human worth of those scorned by this world, the One who affirms the right of life of the poor who are dominated by the forces of death. The God we Christians believe in is a God who prefers the poor because they are the poor, because they are living in an inhuman situation that is against God's will. This is the meaning of "Blessed are the poor;" It is a gospel expression that is first of all a revelation about who God is: love for all and especially for the outcast and the oppressed [*Latinamerica Press,* May 10, 1984, p. 4].

Such a vision enables us to see God as the *gō'ēl*, the "defender and vindicator of the poor and oppressed" (Torres and Eagleson, eds., *The Challenge of Basic Christian Communities*, p. 122).

To attempt to separate this God from the kingdom of God, which is justice and light, is to fall into idolatry. This temptation to idolatry, to the worship of a false god, is one into which people easily fall, either because belief in a true God is so demanding, or because the attractions of the alternate deity are so enticing. Among all the false gods vying for human allegiance today, "national security" is surely the one most blatantly worshiped in Latin America and most subtly worshiped in North America. The choice could not be clearer: to serve this god means to deny the God of the Bible, whereas to serve the God of the Bible means to repudiate the god of national security. It is either/or, not both/and.

When we recall the reprisals that have been visited on lay persons, priests, peasants, sisters, and sometimes even bishops, because of their commitment to the *gōʾēl* who is "the defender and vindicator of the poor and oppressed," we discover that the matter is far from academic. Belief in the God of the Bible is never a private matter; it immediately thrusts one into political, social, and economic controversy. The battle is between the God of life and the god of death, and Joshua's admonition remains central: "Choose you this day whom you will serve."

What are the characteristics of this rival deity, this god of death? National security is a consistent ideology claiming that we are in the midst of never-ending war between the forces of "the West," which are held to coincide with "Christian civilization," and the forces of communism. Church and state must enter alliance to see that communism does not prevail. So pervasive and subtle is the latter's influence that anything that suggests "change" is by definition "communist." This applies to soup kitchens, farmer cooperatives, day-care centers, rival political parties, and Bible study groups, all of which share an implicit if not explicit challenge to the status quo.

Any means of thwarting them are appropriate, from banning the works of Paulo Freire to torturing prisoners. The latter practice is virtually pro forma; it not only silences opponents, but extracts information from them and warns others to remain docile. Even worse are the "disappearances." One day an individual is on hand and the next day he or she is gone. No explanation is ever given, no clue as to the whereabouts save that mutilated bodies sometimes turn up, mute reminders that the rule of survival under "national security" is "don't rock the boat, don't speak up, and (especially) don't challenge the authorities."

If the above paragraphs suddenly seem far removed from "belief in God," one of the enduring contributions of liberation theology will be to continue to lay that canard to rest, and make clear that "belief in God" is the center of the controversy. Before Puebla, Gustavo pointed out that one of the major shortcomings of the "Preliminary Document" was its virtual silence on this major alternative to Christian faith. Only because of the assiduous lobbying of Gustavo and his friends did the bishops finally deal with the threats posed by the god of "national security." Their conclusions are worth recording.

Commission I stated:

> In many instances the ideologies of National Security have helped to intensify the totalitarian or authoritarian character of governments based on the use of force, leading to the abuse of power and the violation of human rights. In some instances, they presume to justify their positions with a subjective profession of Christian faith [*Puebla*, §49].

Commission IV, in its section on "The View of Statism," had perhaps the strongest critique, cited on p. 18, above.

After condemning both "capitalistic liberalism" and "collectivist Marxism" for leading to an "idolatry of riches," the report of Commission VIII continues:

[National Security] suppresses the broad-based participation of the people in political decisions. In some countries of Latin America this doctrine justifies itself as the defender of the Christian civilization of the West. It elaborates a repressive system, which is in line with its concept of "permanent war." . . .

The doctrine of National Security, understood as an absolute ideology, would not be compatible with the Christian vision of the human being as responsible for carrying out a temporal project, and to its vision of the State as the administrator of the common good. It puts the people under the tutelage of military and political elites, who exercise authority and power; and it leads to increased inequality in sharing the benefits of development [ibid., §§547, 549].

The threats remain. The "disappearances" continue. But the spine of the people continually stiffens.

Jesus Christ—and a "God Become Poor"

The test of any Christian theology is the place it accords to Jesus of Nazareth. So central is the place accorded him in Gustavo's writings—"the full manifestation of the God who is love"—that it is difficult to limit, let alone organize, a brief synopsis. We will summarize one such attempt on his part:[8]

1. *Jesus is the Christ.* Christians do not first believe in a message, but in a person:

Having faith means believing that a certain human being of our own history, a Jew named Jesus, who was born of Mary, who proclaimed God's love, the gospel, to the poor, and liberation to those in captivity, who boldly confronted the great ones of his people and the representatives of the occupying power, who was executed as a subversive—is the Christ, the Messiah, the Annointed One [*PP*, p. 13].

In Jesus, God is not only revealed in history, God becomes history; that is to say, God "pitches a tent" in the midst of our human situation and shares it fully. (In chapter 6 we will examine the astonishing attempt of a curia official in Rome to transform this fully orthodox claim into a brand of Marxist Hegelianism.) Jesus leaves his mark on history as a full participant in the process, and Gustavo recounts in detail, for example, his involvement in the political conflicts of his own time (*TheoLib*, pp. 130-35 [225-32]).

But the claim is more sweeping, for Jesus, rather than bringing the historical process to completion and closing it off, opens it up in unexpected new directions. He becomes "the future of our history," which makes possible an "openness" of history to Christ not only in some far-off second coming but in the "today" of the church and the whole human family.

2. *Jesus Christ is the liberator.* Since the center of the biblical message is God's love for the poor, "Jesus Christ is precisely *God become poor*" (*PP*, p. 14, italics in original):

> He was poor indeed. He was born into a social milieu characterized by poverty. He chose to live with the poor. He addressed his gospel by preference to the poor. He lashed out with invective against the rich who oppressed the poor and despised them [ibid., p. 13].

His message is the kingdom of God—a theme that means "God reigns"—a kingdom of justice. Gustavo singles out the summary in Luke 4:16-21 as the heart of Jesus' message, a message of liberation drawn from Isaiah 61:1-2, words whose revolutionary import is often dulled by their too-frequent hearing on the part of persons who are not really listening:

> The spirit of the Lord has been given to me,
> for God has annointed me.
> God has sent me to bring good news to the poor,
> to proclaim liberty to captives
> and to the blind new sight,
> to set the downtrodden free,
> to proclaim the year of the Lord's favor
>   [Luke 4:16-18].

Gustavo's summary: "[Jesus] is proclaiming a kingdom of justice and liberation to be established in favor of the poor, the oppressed, and the marginalized of history" (ibid., p. 14).

This is not a message calculated to win friends and influence persons in high places, and his unwillingness to mince words "leads Jesus to his death." To preach and embody justice means to get to the root of injustice, to assault all expressions of injustice, and to build an alternative amid "our conflict-filled history, a kingdom in which God's love will be present and exploitation abolished" (ibid.).

In other contexts, Gustavo develops the notion that Christ does not just liberate us from the consequences of individual sin, but from the power of social sin, or, as it is now often called, "systemic evil." This is what he describes as "integral liberation," liberation of the *whole person*, which makes full human reality possible for us. "This fulfillment embraces every aspect of humanity; body and spirit, individual and society, person and cosmos, time and eternity. . . . [He] takes on all the dimensions of human existence" (*TheoLib*, p. 85 [151-52]; see also pp. 97-105 [168-78]).

No wonder the principalities and powers of the ancient world realized very early in Jesus' ministry that the world was not large enough to hold them both.

3. *Jesus Christ is the new covenant.* God's new "agreement," or bonding with all humankind, foreshadowed in Jeremiah 31:31-34, is embodied in Jesus. "In him God becomes the God of all nations, and all men and women see that they are his children and one anothers' sisters and brothers" (*PP*, p. 15). The yes to all of God's promises, as St. Paul puts it, is in him. There is a circle of interpretation here that is reciprocal and all-encompassing:

> From the human being to God and from God to the human being, from history to faith and from faith to history, from love of our brothers and sisters to the love of God and from the love of God to the love of our brothers and sisters, from human justice to God's holiness and from God's holiness to human justice, from the poor person to God and from God to the poor person [ibid., p. 15].

Here we have "a new creation," whose norm will remain "Love one another as I have loved you" (John 15:12). The death of Jesus "is the consequence of his struggle for justice," but it broke open the limitations of his contemporaries' understanding of him, so that the resurrection could give a qualitatively new insight into "the universality of the status of the children of God, and the community of brothers and sisters that he announced" (ibid., p. 15).

Everything is to be reread in the light of Easter.

4. *The Lord's Supper.* The eucharist is "couched in the context of the passover supper that celebrates Jahweh's liberating deed in rescuing the Jewish people from Egypt" (ibid., p. 16). It is thus a thank-offering for all the events in which God's love has been revealed. But it is more than that. It celebrates an openness to the future built on trust and joy, that "presupposes a communion and solidarity with the poor in history" (ibid., p. 16). For without this solidarity, Gustavo insists, we fail to understand either Jesus' death or his resurrection.

The implications are far-reaching:

> To believe in the God who is revealed in history and whose tent is pitched in its midst, *means to live in this tent* — in Christ Jesus — and to proclaim from there the liberating love of God [ibid., p. 16, italics added].

"Christology" is not a matter of doctrinal correctness. It is a way of proclaiming God's love by enlisting in the struggle for liberation.

The approach we have been examining is sometimes called "christology from below," an apt posture for those who view life from "the underside of history." The term is neither demeaning nor reductionist. It is simply a proposal that the route for discovering who Jesus really is must resemble that of his first friends and followers.

They encountered a first-century Jew, a rabbi or "teacher," who shared their lot, got hungry, discouraged, had a tremendous ability to be *simpático* with the poor since he was one of them, and enlisted their involvement in a very risky vision called the kingdom of God. Even though the state authorities could not abide the vision and brutally destroyed its initiator, the friends and followers of Jesus had a series of encounters that persuaded them that he was still alive.

As they shared the whole remarkable story with others, they found that they could not adequately describe the central character solely in human terms. He outstripped all their categories. He was—somehow—God in their midst. They employed many titles trying to share his unique import: Messiah or Christ (meaning in Hebrew and Greek "God's annointed one"), Son of God, Son of Man, eternal Logos, Savior, "very God of very God." By the fourth century their explorations coalesced in a widely shared confession that he was not only "true humanity" but "true God" as well—as much of God as could be contained within a fully human life. Exaltation came last in the sequence, not first.

The mistake of many later Christians has been to *start* where the early Christians *finished*—namely, with Jesus as "God." And it is difficult, if not impossible, to move from that starting point—a "christology from above"—to an affirmation of the *full* humanity of Jesus of Nazareth, Jeshua bar Josef, "tempted at all points like as we are."

A "christology from below," then, allows Christians to affirm that in one they already know as a fully human being, God has not only approached, but has shared their life to the full. They are hungry? So was he. They are poor? So was he. They are tortured? So was he. They are killed? So was he. They are empowered to live lives of love? So was he. Wherever they go, whatever they do, God has already been there in this Jesus.

And that is the stuff out of which contemporary risk-takers for the kingdom of God are born.

The Holy Spirit—and the "Base Communities"

No part of Christian faith is more difficult to define or contain than the Holy Spirit. This is because what the Spirit means precludes "defining" or "containing" God within any human construct. Every human statement about the Holy Spirit will have an uncontrollable "remainder." The infinite God cannot be defined by finite persons; the power of God will escape every humanly erected boundary designed to tame or domesticate that power.

From earliest times Christians have talked about "the *koinonia* [the fellowship or community] of the Holy Spirit" (cf. 2 Cor. 13-14) but they have never been able to limit the ways in which that communal power might manifest itself. One of the last places anyone would have anticipated new life in the Spirit in our time would have been in the traditional, conservative, culture-bound Latin American church. And yet that is precisely where the most unexpected onrush of new power has taken place — the emergence of the base communities.[9]

Underlying our exploration of this strange development must be a clear recognition that *the base communities do not represent a "rival church," breaking off from the "institutional" church, but a movement within the church through which the participants share more fully in the ongoing life of the church as a whole.* Italics are needed, since the favorite, if threadbare, charge against the base communities is that they force people to choose between the "institutional church" and the "popular church." Not so.

What are the base communities and what do they do? Two vignettes follow.

• The room is almost dark because fuel for the oil lamps is hard to get, and too expensive anyhow. Fifteen or twenty campesinos are discussing the biblical passage in Matthew 2:16-18 on the slaughter of the innocents (Christmas is just over) under the leadership of a Delegate of the Word, a lay person trained in Bible, catechesis, and pastoral counseling. The story is an ancient and ugly one: soldiers go from house to house methodically killing all children under the age of two, and bayoneting and raping mothers who will not surrender their children for slaughter.

"But that's just what happened last week in Ocotal!" a young woman says in startled and anguished tones. "The contras went from house to house killing the babies and raping the women. My sister lost her child, and her husband was killed trying to defend them." References in the biblical text to "Rachel weeping for her children" and "refusing to be consoled" take on new meaning. The old story has become a current event, and those in the room see themselves in a new way; they are part of the ongoing Christian story. They go on to discuss how to deal with those who want to kill, and whether there are any other ways to deal with them besides killing in return. A few begin to share ideas about what kind of society would make such killings unnecessary.[10]

• Sometimes the gatherings are very practical. Where do we get more beans for the soup kitchen so the children will not go hungry? Why does the gospel tell us we are supposed to love our enemies? Bartoloméo has "disappeared." We need ten people to go to the police station to make inquiries, for the *jefe* will not pay any attention to just one of us. Rafael's widow has no wood for her stove. Who will cut some for her? "The body of our Lord Jesus Christ, broken for you. . . . Take and eat." We know there is an informer in the group tonight, so be careful not to say anything that might cast suspicion on someone else. Marta has just heard that her brother died in prison. Let us pray for her and for him.

While Gustavo has not written as extensively about the base communities as about many other topics, his own writings grow out of, and are nurtured by, his participation in them. He describes those in the base communities as "the uninvited," similar to the parable of Jesus in which the master of the house, rebuffed when the invited do not show up, sends his servants to bring in the lame, the halt, and the blind—the poor, in other words, who are invited not because they are good but simply because they are poor. Of such is the kingdom of heaven, and of such are the base communities.

Here is a vision of what Gustavo hopes they will bring to the church:

> We shall have to create Christian communities in which the private proprietors of the goods of this world are no longer the owners of the gospel too. . . . They will be communities in which the dispossessed will be able to carry out a social appropriation of the gospel. . . .
>
> Only by striking root at the marginalized and exploited segments of society—or rather, only by rising up out of these segments, out of their yearnings, interests, struggles, and cultural categories—will a people be forged that will be a church of the people, a church that will make the gospel message heard by all human beings, a church that will be a sign of the liberation wrought by the Lord of history. . . .
>
> These Christian communities spring up from every growing involvement with the Latin American liberation process. Workers, professional persons, farmhands, bishops, students, priests have all begun to "get involved" [*PP*, p. 71].

No one knows exactly how or where the base communities started.[11] There were antecedents in the Catholic Actions groups in the 1950s, started for working-class Catholics by the Belgian priest Cardinal Cardijn. These groups had a threefold approach: "observe, judge, act"; see what is going on, evaluate it in the light of the gospel, and then take appropriate action.

In Latin America, an increasing shortage of priests meant that lay leadership was increasingly needed in forming groups to relate the gospel to the world. Two further problems contributed to the need for catalysts for change: the expropriation of land in the rural areas through large seizures by already wealthy landowners, and the exploitation of workers in the cities by denying them fair wages, the right to bargain collectively, and so forth (cf. Betto, *¿Que es la comunidad eclesial de base?*, p.11). This meant that the poor were the main constituencies of the resulting base communities.

With such concerns already in place, the controlling image at Vatican II of the church as "the people of God" rather than only the hierarchy gave further impetus to the growth of such groups. And by the time Medellín gave episcopal blessing to the movement three years later, it was already spreading across Latin America.

It is impossible to make sense of liberation theology without seeing it as a response to reflection on the people's situation by the people themselves, "in the light of the Word of God." What happened as the experience of the poor and the biblical story of the poor meshed was that an incipient movement for change was transformed from potentiality to actuality, creating what Frei Betto calls "a voice for those who had no voice." Four fundamental orientations, Guillermo Cook asserts, began to crystalize: (1) a new way of seeing reality, (2) a new way of being the church, (3) a new way of approaching scripture, and (4) a new way of doing mission (Cook, *The Expectation of the Poor*, pp. 89-107).

The new model for the church, Leonardo Boff asserts, is "a church of the poor," and the base communities are an example of the poor taking control over their lives by organizing within the church for their own reflection, action, Bible study, mutual support, and liturgical sharing. Boff speaks of "ecclesiogenesis," by which he means the birth or beginning of a new church,

> but one that is not apart from the Church of the apostles and tradition, taking place . . . in the grassroots of society, that is, among the lower classes who are religiously as well as socially deprived of power [Boff, *Church: Charism and Power*, p. 116].

Chiefly comprised of lay persons from among the poor, the base communities meet in groups of ten to twenty families once or twice a week, "to hear the Word of God, to share their problems in common, and to solve those problems through the inspiration of the gospel" (p. 125). The gospel is "the calling card" of the base communities, and the gospel and life are in incessant interplay, whether the issue is the need for a clinic, the lack of drinking water, or the "disappearance" of a political activist. Whatever the issue, the social commitment is based on a vision that comes from a biblically-oriented faith.

Base communities are not covert or "underground." They are open manifestations to the world of new hope for the human family. People are conscientized by participation and work together for liberation in "group projects, community activities, neighborhood credit unions, efforts to resist land takeover," and so on (p. 129). The fact that their concerns threaten the status quo does not seem to diminish their strength. Indeed, they seem to deepen in the midst of adversity, partly because they gather to affirm and celebrate as well as strategize. They believe that there is good news no matter how bleak things may appear:

> A people that knows how to celebrate is a people with hope. They are no longer a wholly oppressed people but a people who march toward their liberation [ibid., p. 130].

One would think that such manifestations of new life would be eagerly supported by the authorities, but this is far from true. While the "official" position is one of qualified support, many church functionaries still look nervously at the increasing influence of the base communities. There is never an easy truce between hierarchies and the Holy Spirit, for no hierarchy, be it ever so exalted (or humble) can finally control the Holy Spirit, even though it is the self-perception of many hierarchial authorities that they are meant to do precisely that.

We can see the ambivalence of the church authorities in the documents that came from the Puebla Conference. On the one hand, there are words of high praise. The base communities "are one of the causes for joy and hope in the Church" (§96). "The vitality of the experiences [of the base communities] will be recognized and their further growth in communion with their pastors will be fostered" (§156). In the crucial report on the laity the bishops write, "We are happy to single out the multiplication of small communities as an important ecclesial event that is peculiarly ours, and as such the hope of the church" (§629). Most important, perhaps, is a clear acknowledgment that the base communities are an expression of the church's "preferential love for the common people" (§643).

But the bishops are also uneasy. They allege that some communities have become "purely lay institutions or have been turned into ideological radicals" (§630). Again (rather archly): "The impact of the secularized milieu has sometimes produced centrifugal tendencies in the community and the loss of an authentic ecclesial sense" (§627). In certain places, "it is regrettable that . . . clearly political interests try to manipulate them" (§98).

So there must be more clerical control: the base communities can, indeed, be "centers of evangelization," but only "in communion with their bishops" (§96). Development of new base communities is to proceed "in communion with their pastors" (§156; see also §648). The laity cannot be trusted to act on its own, and must be more carefully watched.

A decade after Puebla, however, it is fair to say that the mandate for clerical control has largely gone by default. It is unlikely that the base communities of the future will become arms of the episcopate. Leadership will increasingly come "from below," and signs of new life will not be initiated in chancery offices.

The Church—and the "View from Below"

The base communities are part of the church, but the church is more than the base communities. Gustavo's commitment to both the base communities and the whole church is patent. While he has taken much abuse from ecclesiastical authorities, as we shall see in chapter 6, his devotion to the church, and especially the poor within the church, is unstinting. He devotes two chapters in *A Theology of Liberation* explicitly to the church: the first (chapter 7) is a summary report on "The Church in the Process of Liberation;" the second (chapter 12) is a theological consideration of "The Church: Sacrament of History."

While much has happened to "the church in the process of liberation" since the publication of *A Theology of Liberation* in 1971, the main lines of the process could be observed even then. The Latin American church was rising out of its ghetto mentality and becoming more politically involved; theological thinking was emerging more powerfully from groups committed to liberation than from traditional theological centers; it was becoming increasingly clear that liberation "implies a break with the status quo, that it calls for a social revolution" (*TheoLib*, p. 59 [102]). This was true not only of lay people, whose faith led them to increasing politicization, but also of priests and religious, who began to take political positions that earned them the charge of "subversives." It was even true (though less frequently) of bishops, who because of their place in society were immediately vulnerable but potentially powerful. Such bishops not only individually supported movements for change, but corporately began to produce documents that became rallying points for more radical church engagement.

One such group of documents was directed at establishing "the solidarity of the church with the Latin American reality" (p. 63 [108]). Analyses of church complicity in evil, and descriptions of such forces as "institutionalized violence," dependency, neocolonialism, and the rights of the poor, provided conscientizing instruments throughout Latin America. Openness to socialism, and a recognition that "it is the poor who must be the protagonists of their own liberation" (p. 67 [113]) engendered widespread controversy as well as empowerment.

A second group of statements sought to establish "a new presence of the church in Latin America" (pp. 68-71 [114-19). Gustavo cites five main emphases:

1. an acknowledgment of the need for ongoing prophetic denunciation of grave injustices—the prevailing theme of the texts;

2. a recognition of the urgent need for "a conscientizing evangelization," a theme stated more bluntly in Gustavo's comment that "the doctrinal riches of the gospel contain a revolutionary thrust";

3. an acknowledgment that poverty is the most pressing demand on the church, and that Christians will have to stop talking about "the church of the poor" and begin living as "a poor church";

4. a recognition that present church structures are inadequate to deal with today's world;

5. a commitment to change the current lifestyle of the clergy, perhaps by permitting them to take secular jobs in the real world, and sharing previously guarded clerical prerogatives with lay people.

The climax of the cumulative argument in *A Theology of Liberation* is a consideration of "the Christian community" in chapters 12 and 13. It is consistent with this design that the second of these chapters is an extended treatment of poverty (summarized in chapter 3, above), since the task of the church is to make "a preferential option for the poor."

In treating the church as a "sacrament of history" (pp. 141-61 [255-85]) Gustavo notes that there has been a historical "uncentering" of the church from seeing itself as the exclusive place of salvation "toward a new and radical service of people" (p. 144 [256]). "Salvation" is no longer a guarantee of heaven through church membership, but the experience of a reality that takes place here and now. A historical sketch traces the shift from the early church, conscious of the work of Christ beyond its boundaries, to the later church as an exclusive channel of salvation (pp. 143-45 [256-58]). It has taken centuries to break this imperialistic model, centuries that Gustavo describes as "a long and laborious learning experience" (p. 145 [258]).

A new ecclesiological perspective is emerging, set in motion (though by no means unambiguously) by Vatican II, that sees the church as a sacrament — an "efficacious sign of grace" through which there can be "an effective personal encounter between God and the human person" (ibid., p. 146 [260]), as well as a unity between persons.

The implications of this shift are tremendous. The church no longer exists "for itself" but "for others." Consequently, it must turn toward the world, and even "allow itself to be inhabited and evangelized by the world" (p. 147 [261]). For the sake of that world, the church must not only proclaim, but *embody in its own inner life*, the salvation of which it speaks. Since the message is liberation, the church must itself be "a place of liberation." There must be congruence between the church's message and its structures, for "a sign," Gustavo reminds his readers, "should be clear and understandable" (p. 147 [261]).

Two things follow: "the break with an unjust social order and the search for new ecclesiastical structures" (p. 148 [261]). Whatever time is spent on intraecclesial problems must grow out of an attempt to relate more compellingly to the world's needs. Anything else misses the point, which is "not to survive but to serve" (p. 148 [262]).

The double emphasis is encapsulated in a section, "Eucharist and Human Fellowship" (pp. 148-56 [262-72]), arguing that the two are inseparable. The first task of the church — Gustavo is very clear about this — is "to celebrate with joy the gift of the salvific action of God in humanity accomplished through the death and resurrection of Christ" (p. 148 [262]). The eucharist is both memorial and thanksgiving, and God's work therein "gives the church its reason for being" (p. 149 [263]). But (in the words of the title of this section of the book) "the eucharist" is also the establishment of "human fellowship" — through a means that recalls, in addition to the liberating work of Christ, the divine action at the passover on behalf of the Jews for political liberation, and the ongoing promise that God's liberative acts continue to the present. The theme of "human fellowship" as integral to the "eucharist" and to all worship is further exemplified in the fourth gospel, where foot-washing replaces the eucharistic meal recounted in the synoptic Gospels, making the connection to the building up of human fellowship very clear, and in the admonition in Matthew's Gospel:

> If, when you bring your gift to the altar you suddenly remember that your brother [or sister] has a grievance against you, leave your gift

where it is before the altar. First go and make peace with your brother,
[or sister] and only then come back and offer your gift [Matt. 5:23-
24].

We take something *from* the eucharist, of course, but we also bring
something *to* it: "Without a real commitment against exploitation and alienation and for a society of solidarity and justice, the Eucharistic celebration
is an empty action, lacking any genuine endorsement by those who participate in it" (p. 150 [265]).

The interweaving of eucharist and human fellowship is further underlined in Gustavo's treatment of the task of the church as "denunciation
and annunciation"—a theme he develops here and elsewhere out of the
writings of Paulo Freire (see pp. 150-56 [265-72]; also pp. 66ff., 114ff. [pp.
136, 233]). This is the only context in which the political concerns of the
church can be properly understood. Starting point: the church is *already
political*, whether it perceives the fact or not, because of being "tied to the
prevailing social system that rewards greed and perpetuates injustice." Such
ties must be broken:

We believe that the best way to achieve this divestment of power is
precisely by resolutely casting our lot with the oppressed and exploited
in the struggle for a more just society [ibid., p. 151 (266)].

Such a move will be costly, since "the groups that control economic and
political power will not forgive the church for this. They will withdraw their
support" (p. 151 [266]). But any claim to noninvolvement "is nothing but
a subterfuge to keep things as they are" (ibid). The church has two choices:
it can be either for or against the established order. It must be against.

So the initial task is *denunciation*, a "radical critique of the present
order" (p. 152 [267]), getting to the root causes of trouble. The critique
cannot only be verbal, it must be enacted from within the struggle by those
who have already chosen sides. Truth is not spoken, it is "done."

But true denunciation is completed only in *annunciation*, an announcement of the good news that other possibilities are available, and that the
love of God is already present for healing and new beginnings. Such an
annunciation has both a "conscientizing function" and a "politicizing function" (p. 153 [269]). The real "announcement" is not word but deed, coming
"from within a commitment to liberation, only in concrete, effective solidarity with people and exploited social classes" (p. 153 [269]).

Blueprints for carrying out this task cannot be supplied in advance. They
will come only out of careful *reflection* and *action* in specific situations with
tactics that may sometimes be right, sometimes wrong. The fact that human
actions are always provisional and incomplete cannot be used as a loophole
"to disregard the urgency and necessity of taking stands" (p. 155 [272]):

Every attempt to evade the struggle against alienation and the violence of the powerful and for a more just and more human world is
the greatest infidelity to God. To know God is to work for justice. There
is no other path to reach God [ibid., p. 156 (272), italics added].[12]

History, Creation, Eschatology—and Politics[13]

Gustavo points out in a footnote that the structure of part 4, "Perspectives," in *A Theology of Liberation* follows the sequence of the three great
questions posed by Immanuel Kant—one part of Gustavo's European formation he has not entirely repudiated. Chapter 9 on "Liberation and Salvation" asks about the meaning of the human struggle (What can I *know*?);
chapter 10 on "Encountering God in History" explores our responses
(What ought I to *do*?); while chapter 11 on "Eschatology and Politics"
discusses human and divine fulfillment (What may I *hope*?). Knowing Gustavo's delight in "three-point analyses," we may note further that the three
questions have their biblical counterparts in the Pauline virtues of faith,
love, and hope, in that order.[14]

What is the relationship between the divine gift of salvation and the
process of human liberation? Are they coextensive? Does one lead to the
other? Or are they necessarily separate?

For many centuries, salvation was viewed in *quantitative* terms: "how
many are saved?" The assumption was that many, perhaps most, were not.
But Gustavo believes that the Pauline idea of "the universality of the salvific
will of God . . . has been established" (*TheoLib*, p. 84 [140]). As the scope
of salvation has widened, the emphasis has shifted to a *qualitative* view:
"persons are saved if they open themselves to God and to others, even if
they are not clearly aware that they are doing so" (p. 84 [151]). Salvation
is not something "otherworldly," but something that "embraces all human
reality," since Christ has shared all human reality. Old dualisms are gone;
fulfillment involves "body and spirit, individual and society, person and
cosmos, time and eternity" (p. 85 [151-52]). Such a view of salvation gives
new meaning to the here and now.

Another way to make the point is to stress that *history is one*. "There
are not two histories, one profane and one sacred"; rather, "the salvific
action of God underlies all human existence." (p. 86 [153]). Biblically, this
is expressed by linking creation and salvation. Creation is not a preliminary
act of God that has to be completed by a subsequent salvific act; creation
is itself part of the process of salvation. God is both creator *and* redeemer.

The liberation from bondage in Egypt is part of this one story: salvation
and liberation (in this case, political liberation) cannot be separated. But
there is more: the God who creates is not only the God who liberates, but
the God who lays upon human persons the task of completing the liberation
of all who are being dehumanized. The work of Christ is central to this
story; he represents a "re-creation" into new human possibilities for all.
"Building the temporal city," Gustavo affirms, is "part of a saving process

which embraces the whole of humanity and all human history" (p. 91 [160]).

But in addition to the theme of creation, the Bible develops the theme of the eschatological promises: "God's promise is *already* fulfilled in historical events, but *not yet* completely; it incessantly projects itself into the future, creating a permanent historical mobility" (p. 92 [161]). Rather than being an appendix to theological manuals, the "promises" become a driving force; their orientation to the future bears incessantly on the present, with a call not only to break with the past but to conform the present reality to the future hope. "This tension toward the future lends meaning to and is expressed in the present" (p. 95 [164]). God's name, rather than being understood in a static sense ("I am who I am") is better understood in a dynamic sense ("I will be who I will be," or even "I am here ready to act" [p. 95 (164-65)], which contains a full linguistic discussion).

Gustavo points out that what is at stake is not inner, spiritual "peace" for the individual, but peace as an outward and tangible reality that presupposes the establishment of justice. "The Kingdom and social injustice are incompatible," Gustavo asserts, supporting his assertion with a host of biblical references (p. 97 [167-68]).

What is the relationship, then, between "temporal progress" and "the growth of the kingdom?" Vatican II, after much debate, concluded that there was a close relationship. Paul VI's subsequent encyclical *Populorum Progressio* was more explicit: Christians must be committed to move society from "less human conditions" (characterized by sin and injustice) to "more human conditions" (characterized by the possession of necessities for all, overcoming social ills, and cooperating for the common good). The text indicates that "what is human" and "the grace and communion with God" share much in common.

But Gustavo argues that such texts do not go far enough. They fail to issue a radical challenge to the unjust systems on which so-called temporal progress is based. Many creative relationships can be established, for example, in the faith-science axis. But when it comes to the "social injustice-justice axis," or the "oppression-liberation axis," the task is not to adapt to, but to reject, present relationships as "fundamentally unjust and dehumanizing" (p. 101-2 [174]).

This means viewing sin not simply as an individual or private reality, but as "a social historical fact," which is evident in oppressive structures, exploitation, domination and other concrete manifestations. "Sin demands a radical liberation, which in turn necessarily implies a political liberation" (p. 103 [176]).

How, then, does the theme of "Christ the liberator" speak to this situation? "This radical liberation," Gustavo claims, "is the gift which Christ offers us." He cited Medellín:

It is the same God who, in the fullness of time, sends [God's] Son in the flesh, so that he might come to liberate all [people] from all slavery

to which sin has subjected them; hunger, misery, oppression, and ignorance, in a word that injustice and hatred which have their origin in
human selfishness [p. 103 (176); Medellín "Justice," §3].

"Human history . . . is the location of our encounter with God in Christ"
(p. 106 [189]). Gustavo traces various "locations" of God in the Hebrew
scriptures: a mountain, a tent, an ark, a temple, and finally a recognition
that God's presence cannot be limited to such places. In the Christian
scriptures, the process continues in the incarnation of God in Jesus of
Nazareth, so that Christ is the "temple of the Lord." But the process continues even further in new directions: *the Christian* is also the temple of the
Lord, and finally *every person* is the temple of the Lord. There is no longer
any place that is "pro-fane," outside the temple:

> The modes of God's presence determine the form of our encounter
> with God. *If humanity, each person, is the living temple of God, we meet
> God in our encounter with others*; we encounter God in the commit-
> ment to the historical process of humankind [p. 110 (194), italics
> added].

Such a conclusion lands us in familiar territory: *to know God is to do
justice.* Here the theme is developed positively in the widely used text of
Jeremiah 22:13-16, and in a passage from Arguedas's novel *Todas las
sangres*; and negatively in another passage from the Medellín documents:
"Where . . . social peace does not exist there will we find social, political,
economic, and cultural inequalities, there will we find the rejection of the
peace of the Lord, and a rejection of the Lord himself" (p. 111 [195],
Medellín "Peace," §14).

We love God, then, by loving the neighbor, by acts of justice rather than
sacrifices (and their modern counterparts), and by extending the concept
of "neighbor" to include strangers, widows and orphans—who stand for
the most oppressed and powerless in our society. This conclusion is fleshed
out by a careful exegesis of Jesus' parable of the last judgment (Matt. 25:31-
46, see pp. 112-16 [196-203]), and a consideration of certain pitfalls into
which naive applications can drift. The story promises, Gustavo concludes,
that "we will find the Lord in our encounter with others, especially the
poor, marginated, and exploited ones" (p. 115 [201]). The story is not
dealing with individual acts of charity but with the demands placed on "the
nations"—on society as a whole—to deal with hunger, imprisonment, sick-
ness, lack of shelter, in ways that lead to political engagement.[15]

What of the future? The commitment to a just society presupposes confidence in the future. Christians committed to this process must offer an
eschatological perspective "as the driving force of a future-oriented history," that will have "clear and strong implications for the political sphere,
for social praxis" (p. 122 [215]). This will involve three things:

1. *An ability to account for the hope that is in us.* Christians can even draw on non-Christian thinkers like Ernst Bloch to be reminded that "an active hope subverts the existing order" (p.123 [216]). It is hope for change that transforms the present. Christians, however, must not replace a "Christianity of the Beyond" (all will be well in heaven after we die), with a "Christianity of the Future" (all will be well here and now as soon as we get a new social order). For Gustavo, hope is not *knowing* the future but *being open* to it, and accepting it as a gift by struggling to negate injustice. Hope mobilizes and liberates its proponents to work for change.

2. *A clear articulation of the political dimensions of the gospel.* After considering the contributions of Johann Baptist Metz to a new political theology for our time, Gustavo tackles the prickly question of the relation of Jesus to the political work of *his* time. This area of scholarship is in flux, and Gustavo wends his way skillfully through potential minefields. As for Jesus' relationship to the Zealots (the militant revolutionaries of his time), Gustavo acknowledges that some of Jesus' associates were Zealots, and that there is significant overlap between his views and theirs. But he insists that "Jesus kept his distance from the Zealot movement" (p. 131 [227]), especially in relation to the universality of his message and the narrow nationalism of theirs, and his opposition to the politico-religious messianism they espoused.

Such differentiations, however, do not establish that Jesus' teaching was devoid of political concern. Indeed, there was head-on opposition between Jesus' "radical option for the poor" and the vested interests of the rich and powerful, who viewed him as a dangerous rival. The placard on the cross, "king of the Jews," indicates that they saw him as a political challenger. (One of the paintings of the crucifixion from the Solentiname community of Nicaragua renders the inscription on the placard as *Subversivo* — an accurate summation of Herod's and Pilate's fears about Jesus.)

Gustavo draws certain conclusions about Jesus and the political world of his time: the leaders were correct in believing that Jesus' message threatened them on every level; they were incorrect in thinking that to dispose of him would dispose of his ideas or influence. The impact of his message is lasting because it is not directed to only one set of historical circumstances, but goes to the root of human existence: "The Gospel does not get its political dimension from one or another particular option, but from the very nucleus of its message. If this message is subversive, it is because it takes on Israel's hope" (p. 134 [231]).

The political dimension does not detract from the gospel's message; instead, "it enriches the political sphere:"

[Jesus'] testimony and his message acquire this political dimension precisely because of the radicalness of their salvific character: *to preach the universal love of [God] is inevitably to go against all injustice, privilege, oppression, or narrow nationalism* [p. 135 (232), italics added].

3. *An analysis of the relation of the gospel to human utopias.* This is an issue around which liberation theologians have been much maligned, and yet, paradoxically, one to which they have made important contributions. A "utopia" was originally an imaginative plan offered as a challenge for change, but in our time the term has become pejorative, signaling "illusion, lack of reason and irrationality" (p. 135 [232]). Elsewhere, however, and particularly among radicalized Christians, the term has been regaining currency.

Any projection of a new order will employ two strategies we have already encountered: denunciation of the present social order (as people finally become "discontent with their discontent"), and annunciation of a new order, achieved by the use of "creative imagination which proposes . . . alternative values to those rejected" (p. 136 [233]). But it must be more than talk. "If utopia does not lead to action in the present, it is an evasion of reality" (p. 136 [234]).

The dynamic for change will come not from centers of established power (where the motivation is always to resist change) but from those previously excluded from creating their own destinies. "In today's world only the oppressed person, only the oppressed class, only oppressed people, can denounce and announce" (p. 137 [235]).

The question for Christians, then, is how this utopian vision, achieved by human effort, and the kingdom of God, given by divine grace, relate to each other. On the one hand, there are important connections:

> Faith proclaims that the fellowship which is sought through the abolition of exploitation is something possible, that efforts to bring it about are not in vain, that God calls us to it and assures us of its complete fulfillment, and that the definitive reality is being built on what is transitory. Faith reveals to us the deep meaning of the history which we fashion with our own hands: it teaches us that every human act which is oriented towards the construction of a more just society has value in terms of communion with God—in terms of salvation; inversely it teaches that all injustice is a breach with God [p. 139 (237)].

But on the other hand, there are important differences that "prevent these manifestations from becoming translated into any kind of Christian ideology of political action or a politico-religious messianism" (p. 139 [238]). Gustavo is crystal clear about the danger of equating the final gift of God's kingdom with *any* human construct:

> Christian hope opens us, in an attitude of spiritual childhood, to the gift of the future promised by God. *It keeps us from any confusion of the Kingdom with any one historical stage, from any idolatry toward unavoidably ambiguous human achievement, from any absolutizing of*

revolution. In this way hope makes us radically free to commit ourselves to social praxis, motivated by a liberating utopia and with the
means which the scientific analysis of reality provides for us. And
our hope not only frees us for this commitment; it simultaneously
demands *and judges* it [p. 139 (238), italics added].

It is not the task of the gospel to provide a utopia; that is something
people do. "But the gospel is not alien to the historical plan; on the contrary, the human plan and the gift of God imply each other" (p. 139 [238]).

Whole books of imprecations of liberation theology would have been
unnecessary if their authors had absorbed these pages that are so central
to Gustavo's writing.

"Expanding the View" Once More

It is not the case that we have completed an exposition of liberation
theology and can now examine or admire or critique a finished product. As
we learned earlier, the "praxis situation" is never finished—reflection and
action will continue to need mutual refinement. The same is true of the
theological venture. One reason for this is that it arises out of the praxis
situation and shares its characteristics. But because of the nature of the
subject matter of theology—the infinite mystery of God—no human statement about God will ever do justice to it. So Christians will always be
"expanding the view." If that is the beginning of their task, it is also its
conclusion; every "conclusion" is only an "introduction" to what comes
next.

We never know ahead of time where the new expansion will be located.
Who would have thought in the 1950s that the greatest new vitality for
Christian faith would spring from formalistic, largely irrelevant, Latin
American Catholicism, or that Vatican II would spawn Medellín (along
with help from the local folk), or that an unpretentious parish priest in
Lima, Peru, would be more significant in articulating the faith today than
the combined faculties of Tübingen, Oxford, and Rome?

Gustavo (who might be embarrassed by the last claim) reminds us of
how the view keeps "expanding," in the *spatial extension* of liberation concerns. It has spread to include "Black, Hispanic, and Amerindian theologies
in the United States, theologies arising out of the complex contexts of
Africa, Asia, and the south Pacific, and the especially fruitful thinking of
those who adopted the feminist perspective" (p. xix). This spatial extension,
with which we will deal in chapter 7, is a dramatic reminder that the whole
story on human liberation has not yet been told, and never will be.

The perpetually "unfinished" nature of the theological task is acknowledged by Gustavo in a more personal way. Two things have happened, he
notes, in the creation of liberation theology. One of these is *the freshness*
or newness that comes through the first-time-ever appearance of a consis-

tent "theology from below." The other, complementary rather than conflictual, is a recognition of the *continuity* that leads it to sink its roots deep in scripture, tradition, and the magisterium. As a basis for keeping these two concerns in creative tension, Gustavo cites Pope John XXIII's comment that "it is not that the Gospel is changed; it is that we have begun to understand it better," from which Pope John concluded "that the moment has come to discern the signs of the times, to seize the opportunity, and to expand the view" (pp. xlv-xlvi).

Gustavo responded as follows to a journalist who asked whether today he would write *A Theology of Liberation* the same way he did two decades earlier:

> I said that though the years passed by, the book remained the same, whereas I was alive and therefore changing and moving forward thanks to experiences, to observations made on the book, and to lectures and discussions. When he persisted, I asked whether in a love letter to his wife today he would use the same language he used twenty years ago; he said he would not, but he acknowledged that his love perdured. My book is a love letter to God, to the church, and to the people to which I belong. Love remains alive, but it grows deeper and changes its manner of expression [p. xlvi].

CHAPTER 6

The Plot Thickens: Some Unscripted Entrances, or Gustavo under Attack

[Gutiérrez's language is] language on the homiletical rather than the theological level. We are hearing a Christian, not a theologian, speaking.
— Alfredo Fierro, *The Militant Gospel*, p. 326

Is better to be Christian than theologian.
— Gustavo, in conversation

Liberation theology has been welcomed with sympathy and hope by many and has contributed to the vitality of numerous undertakings in the service of Christian witness. At the same time it has stimulated an interest in reflection on the Christian faith. . . . The years have also brought serious and relevant critiques that have helped this theological thinking to reach maturity.

On the other hand, the theology of liberation has also stirred facile enthusiasms that have interpreted it in a simplistic or erroneous way by ignoring the integral demands of the Christian faith as lived in the communion of the church. Finally, there has been the foreseeable resistance of some.
— *A Theology of Liberation*, p. xviii

Any drama intent on holding attention will have conflict; two men competing for the hand of the same woman or, perhaps two women competing for the hand of the same man; Robin Hood challenging the Sheriff of Nottingham; the White House and Congress trying to negotiate agreements on the basis of different agendas; a powerless majority in a Third World country confronting a powerful minority backed by First World military might.

Authors do not, as a rule, introduce into their script characters who are trying to demolish the drama itself. The rule seems to read: critique, yes; annihilation, no. And yet there have been various unscripted entrances onto the stage of liberation theology's endeavors that range from trivial annoyance to acts with deadly intent, posed by a variety of individuals and groups, and culminating in serious charges of theological malfeasance by the Congregation for the Doctrine of the Faith. Any examination of liberation theology must take some, though not all, of these charges seriously.

Criticism is a two-edged sword. Those who wield it should be aware that their own presuppositions are also under scrutiny, and that they may inflict more damage on themselves than on those they seek to discredit. If Gustavo is to be held accountable by the critics, the critics can also be held accountable by Gustavo. Many of the attacks on liberation theology are more damaging to the viewpoints of their adherents than to their intended targets.

Lesser Critiques[1]

As a prelude to dealing with Rome's attacks, which are the most important, we can dispose of a number of lesser critiques.

1. *Misrepresentations.* The least significant critique, no matter what the subject, is one that (either maliciously or out of ignorance) misrepresents its subject and then demolished a creature of its own making.

Ernest Lefever, for example, asserts that liberation theology attracts only those eager "to embrace novelty and the radical chic shibboleths of the past two decades." He defines liberation theology as "a utopian heresy because it sanctifies class violence" and utopianism as "an escape from responsibility." So much for the integrity of thousands of martyrs in the liberation struggle.

He complains that attention to a "preferential option for the poor" negates "concern for every man, woman, and child," since we are "all in need of liberation and redemption," totally ignoring Gustavo's clear distinction between a "preferential option" and an "exclusive option." Lefever further claims that a preferential option for the poor "pits class against class and encourages enmity," a stale version of the canard that liberation theologians exalt violence. He argues that liberation theology "stresses novelty at the expense of the tried and true," although "the tried and true" has been responsible for centuries of Third World oppression. The charges pile up: liberation theology fosters "economic determinism," "a new materialism," and implies (along with Karl Marx) that freedom, culture, music, and love are all "economically determined."

Such charges need not be dignified by serious comment, and are mentioned here only to illustrate that persons who ought to know better frequently do not.

Dennis McCann, in a review of the fifteenth anniversary edition of *A Theology of Liberation*, is closer to the target but still wide of the mark. He tells us, for example, that "Gutiérrez now finds it necessary to emphasize caution against reductive and purely 'immanentist' understandings of praxis and liberation," and that "though liberating praxis still 'endeavors to transform history,' this transformation is not reducible to changes in socioeconomic structures."

Although McCann elsewhere stresses that the shift is one of emphasis rather than a new direction, he leaves the impression that in the earlier edition Gustavo *did* advocate reductionist understanding, and felt that liberating praxis *could* be "reducible to changes in socioeconomic structures," inferences that are incorrect.

McCann acknowledges that while the clarifications in the new edition do not contradict Gustavo's earlier statements, "the shifts of emphasis do seem to amount to a very large practical difference" — namely, that Gustavo is now "repudiating the attempt to identify the option for the poor with an ideology or specific political program." McCann concludes that Gustavo's theology "can *no longer* be understood *primarily* as a form of political theology." But it could never be so understood, and the italicized words only strengthen a misunderstanding: that until the new edition, Gustavo's position *was* to be understood "primarily as a form of political theology."

2. A second dismissal of liberation theology employs the tactic of *trivialization*. Significant issues of life and death are transformed into intellectual games. Michael Novak, for example, states that liberation theology "gains its excitement from flirting with Marxist thought and speech," an assessment credible only to those who want to cerebralize the entire position. To those in the midst of the struggle, however, liberation theology "gains its excitement" *not* because it flirts with Marxism, but because it offers hope to otherwise hopeless persons; because it reminds them that things need not stay the way they are; because it proclaims a God who has not abandoned the poor but has a special concern for them; because it empowers those who have been trodden upon to stand up and reclaim their human dignity; because it creates community among those who have been isolated by cruel economic and political structures; because (most "exciting" of all) in the midst of ongoing death it proclaims the good news of life.

Sinister intent is read into simple statements of fact. Enrique Dussel (the foremost Latin American church historian) insists that any analysis of the Latin American situation must start with the fact that oppression is a patent reality that needs to be overcome. But to Novak, this insistence is not a *cri de coeur* from someone who (like Dussel himself) has been the target of assassination attempts; it is simply an indication that Dussel and people like him are Marxists: "Once their first self-defining act is to declare themselves 'oppressed,' they have sided with Marx and Lenin."

Surely it is not fanciful to insist that such people did not learn that they were oppressed by reading *Das Kapital* or *The Communist Manifesto*. They learned that they were oppressed because they woke up hungry every morning, or could not sleep at night for the same reason; because they ended up in prison cells for engaging in demonstrations against their governments; because they had friends who were thrown into ditches with slit throats after days and nights of being tortured; because they walked with grieving parents to primitive cemeteries where the children of neighbors were being buried after starving to death. To claim otherwise is to trivialize their life and death struggle.

3. If some critics cannot enter sufficiently into the experience of Third World living to be taken seriously, other critics have only too clear an understanding of the threat liberation theology poses for the status quo, even if their understanding of it is flawed. This instinctive *reflex against change* is well illustrated in the 1980 Santa Fe Document, prepared by Latin American "experts" within the Republican Party to help their new president, Ronald Reagan, set a course for dealing with Latin America:

> The foreign policy of the United States must start to confront (and not simply respond after the facts) the theology of liberation as it is used in Latin America by the clergy of the "liberation theology."

This will be more difficult to effect than to prescribe, because of the way in which proponents of liberation theology have been duped:

> In Latin America, the role of the Church is vital for the concept of political freedom. Regretfully, the Marxist-Leninist forces have used the Church as a political weapon against private property and the capitalist system of production, by infiltrating the religious community with ideas which are more Communist than Christian.

The explicit proposal of the Santa Fe Document is that liberation theology be opposed, discredited, and attacked. The reason for the proposal is likewise explicit: liberation theology is infected with Marxist-Leninist ideology, and that is inimical to U.S. interests overseas. Even if not all Christians are "Marxist-Leninists," they have been duped by those who are, and have become accomplices, willing or unwilling, in schemes within the church that "are more communist than Christian."

Other critics are less generous: the Marxist bias has not been smuggled in but consciously built in. So Richard John Neuhaus:

> "Liberation theology" is largely a Latin American phenomenon associated with the writings of men such as Gustavo Gutiérrez and Juan Luis Segundo, and with the revolutionary activities (praxis) of priests, some of whom have taken up arms in guerilla movements. It is conventionally based upon *an explicitly Marxist analysis of class struggle* which its proponents believe should be *normative* for the Christian Church's teaching and life [italics added].

Both the notion that priests are rather routinely enamored of firearms, and the notion that liberation theology makes Marxist analysis "normative," suggest the degree to which truth can be bent for polemical purposes. Fortunately, as we have already seen and will continue to see, the reality does not match the rhetoric.

4. A fourth critique, more subtle than the others, accepts the fact that liberation theology is here to stay (however much the fact may be deplored), and proposes a tactic of *co-option and domestication*. Advocates of this approach affirm that they, too, support liberation theology, only they want an "authentic" and "full" liberation theology. By this they mean a theology that gives *more* attention to the personal or "spiritual" liberation that Gustavo allegedly underemphasizes, and a theology that gives *less* attention to the political/social/economic issues that Gustavo allegedly overemphasizes. "Political" and "spiritual" are defined so that the former collapses without remainder into the latter, resulting in a message that what we really need is a "spiritual liberation," devoid of political content. And since we *all* need "spiritual liberation," whether we are rich or poor, distinctions between rich and poor are likewise collapsed, and the need for structural change disappears; the status quo will do just fine.

Gustavo is well aware of efforts to complete the "domestication" of liberation theology. "People are using its terminology," he records, "but emptying it of any real meaning." He is justifiably impatient with middle-class attempts to tone down a radical position. Liberation theology must be based, he insists, on "a concrete historical praxis," which in this instance means identifying with the poor in the midst of their poverty:

> This is the difference between a theology of liberation and any attempts to apply the cosmetic vocabulary of "social concern," or even "liberation," to old pastoral and theological stances. Facile attitudes, coupled with a certain "trendiness," or penchant for the newest vogue, have encouraged some persons simply to tack on the word "liberation" to whatever they have always been saying anyway and go on saying it, hoping to update a sluggish old inventory by slapping a new label on obsolete goods [*PP*, p. 64].

A variant on this position has been popular among certain Latin American bishops who argue that neither "capitalism" nor "socialism" presents an adequate model for society, and that a "third way" between them (*tercerismo*) must be found. The difficulty, as Gustavo wryly points out on the basis of long experiences, is that when real choices have to be made, proponents of *tercerismo* inevitably tilt to the right rather than the left.

The common thread in these critiques is that Gustavo and his friends are advocating that "the church take sides." Earlier we noted Gustavo's response to this charge: the church has *always* "taken sides," almost always with the rich, and what is now needed is for the church to "change sides," switching from a subtle but thoroughgoing option for the rich to an overt and thoroughgoing option for the poor. The real fear is not "political involvement" but "political involvement *from the left.*" The quasi paranoia about "Marxist influence" is only one surface manifestation of a deeper fear: *radical change is inevitable if liberation theology is taken seriously.*

Whether that is good news or bad news depends on who is talking.

The Struggle with Rome Heats Up

When Rome speaks, people listen, particularly if their own right to speak is the subject of the conversation. We recall from chapters 1 and 2 that shortly after the Medellín Conference, Gustavo began to find himself in trouble, and that his troubles mounted to a crescendo in the years after Puebla. We must now discern some of the milestones on his painful journey.

Medellín unleashed powerful forces within the Latin American church that had been building momentum in the wings before assuming center stage. Conservative bishops, forced to read with fresh eyes the documents they had signed, discovered that they had unwittingly endorsed an impetus for far-reaching change, running the gamut from base communities, new kinds of social analysis, a preferential option for the poor, Paulo Freire methods of education, and "liberation theology" (even though the phrase was not used), to recommendations for toned-down episcopal lifestyles and numerous other causes for discomfort. Nor was their inquietude diminished by the alacrity with which lay persons, priests, sisters, and even some fellow bishops, began using the Medellín documents, in tandem with the Vatican II document "The Church and the Modern World," as leverage for change within society and within the church.

A natural lightning rod for grounding such episcopal agitation was Gustavo, who, as a "theological expert" at Medellín, had played a central role in drafting the most controversial documents, notably "Peace" and "Justice," and whose *A Theology of Liberation*, published less than three years after Medellín, became the major rallying point for socially concerned post-Medellín Catholics, and an object of opprobrium to the rest. A flurry of reviews, articles, and interviews attacking Gustavo and his writings began to appear, orchestrated by those in high places. The fact that the new leader of CELAM, Archibshop López Trujillo, was a committed conservative, made it possible for CELAM to authorize and circulate strong counter-vailing literature in the decade between Medellín and Puebla.

Attempts to stack the deck at Puebla (through an ultraconservative "Preliminary Document," the exclusion of targeted "liberation theologians" from the Puebla meetings, and last-minute appointments of conservative bishops from Rome) backfired, with the result that the Puebla documents, while convoluted and prolix, were consistent with, rather than at variance with, those of Medellín. A seemingly powerless little David, holding in his hands only a stone labeled *A Theology of Liberation* (to borrow Henri Nou-

wen's imagery), had, if not quite demolished the curial Goliath, nevertheless inflicted significant rebuffs by offering new directions for the life of the
church.

The "Ten Observations"

Goliaths, whether curial or otherwise, do not suffer rebuffs gladly, and
rather than advancing down the new directions Puebla charted, those with
power in Rome felt a need to stem the tide of change before it engulfed
them, as they clearly feared it might. Consequently, the Congregation for
the Doctrine of the Faith, charged with upholding orthodoxy and confound-
ing heresy, embarked on an intensive scrutiny of all Gustavo's writings,
which came to a head in March 1983, with the release of a document
entitled "Ten Observations on the Theology of Gustavo Gutiérrez."[2] From
1983 through most of 1985, Gustavo had to devote most of his time to
replying to these and subsequent charges, frequently by going to Rome (at
his own expense) to defend himself in person and clarify from his own
writings what he actually meant. (We may recall again Gustavo's comment:
"The Sacred Congregation invented a new torture for me. They forced me
to read many times my own books.")

Here is a paraphrased summary of the charges:

The church, while affirming the good news of liberation, must also protect this message from "all reductionism and all ambiguity." This makes it
necessary to examine the theology of "one of its principal adherents, Gustavo Gutiérrez."

1. Gutiérrez's theology, because of its "uncritical acceptance of a Marxist interpretation," is guilty of "seductiveness" and "extreme ambiguity."

2. "The determining principle" by means of which Gutiérrez reinter-
prets the Christian message is "the Marxist conception of history, structured
around class struggle."

3. This leads to a selective rereading of the Bible, especially in relation
to poverty and Yahweh as the God of the poor. This allows Gutiérrez to
advocate revolutionary commitment against capitalism.

4. Other examples of a selective reading of texts, to give them "an
exclusively political meaning," are the exodus story, the Magnificat, and
the treatment of themes in Genesis.

5. This leads to "a temporal messianism and reduces the growth of the
Kingdom of God to the increase of justice . . . in society."

6. Sin is reduced to "merely the bias of political alienation in the socio-
political sphere." For Gutiérrez, there is no sin "except 'social sin.'"

7. "The influence of Marxism is clear both in the understanding of truth
and the notion of theology. Orthodoxy is replaced by orthopraxy, for truth
does not exist except within praxis, that is, in commitment to the revolution." A number of consequences follow:

a. because truth comes from within the struggle for liberation, the
"transcendence of revelation" is denied;

b. the formula "God becomes history" leads to relativism;

c. the conviction that human beings can "make history" illustrates the heresy of Pelagianism;

d. theology is a reflection of class interests, so a "class theology" opposes "dominant theology" in order to discredit the latter as a tool of the rich;

e. class interests determine truth, and so the functions of the church and Vatican II in determining truth are disregarded.

8. The Kingdom of God is the result of human struggle [rather than a gift of divine grace] and so the "structures" of the church are changeable. Some consequences:

a. the church must be involved in class struggle;

b. this challenges Christ's once-for-all redemptive work, and "transcendent grace within the mystery of the church is not recognized";

c. the concept of class struggle leads to struggle *within the church* between "a church collaborating with power [and] a church of the poor";

d. the church of the poor is being realized through the base communities;

e. the meaning of the eucharist is attenuated.

9. Gutiérrez "never examines the beatitudes in their true meaning," nor does he engage in "a theological reflection on violence." Class struggle is simply presented "as a fact."

10. Summary conclusion: "Therefore, the objective is to make of Christianity a means of mobilizing for the sake of revolution. By its recourse to Marxism, this theology can pervert an inspiration that is evangelical: the consciousness and the hopes of the poor."

More Challenges

We will later give Gustavo his own day in court, and discover what degree of accuracy or inaccuracy he found in the Sacred Congregation's charges. But before doing so, we must take the outward events several steps further, starting with a document about which it is impossible to remain dispassionate.

The year 1984 was crucial in the proceedings against Gustavo—the symbolism of which, in the light of George Orwell's novel of the same name, could provide a rich vein for ecclesiastical satire about the watchfulness of "Big Brother." In April of that year, Cardinal Ratzinger, hoping to bring matters to a head, visited Peru and met with the entire Peruvian hierarchy for a formal discussion of liberation theology. It is no secret that the intention behind the visit was to secure, if possible, a letter from the Peruvian bishops condemning liberation theology in general and Gustavo in particular. But at the conclusion of the visit no such letter appeared. The vote to condemn Gustavo had ended in a tie, which, for the moment, translated into no condemnation.[3]

This was not the end of the matter, however. For their further edification, the bishops were supplied by Rome with an unsigned 50-page single-spaced attack on Gustavo, "La Théologie de la libération de Gustavo Gutiérrez,"[4] dealing almost exclusively with presumed instances of Marxist bias in *The Power of the Poor in History*. The document deserves attention, not because of any intrinsic merit (in which it is singularly lacking), but because it reveals the lengths to which those in the curia were prepared to go in order to discredit Gustavo. The only way to provide a rationale for its composition is to assume that someone in Rome was instructed to go through one of Gustavo's books and extract every possible hint of Marxist influence and infection. While there are a few references toward the end of the document to *A Theology of Liberation*, there is not even a mention of two of Gustavo's subsequent books, *El Diós de la vida*, a series of Bible studies, or *We Drink from Our Own Wells*, a study of liberation spirituality, both of which were available when the attack was written and would have invalidated all its premises. A bias was apparent before a word was put on paper.

Attempts by the author to demonstrate a Marxist slant in Gustavo's writings are extraordinary. Three examples will suffice: (1) Twice Gustavo is chided for asserting that "God becomes history" — a phrase that the critic, writing in French, extracted from the Italian translation of Gustavo's Spanish text. The phrase is cited to demonstrate that Gustavo is really a Hegelian who thus "reduces" God to the historical process and thereby equates the two. And since it is well known that Marx, too, was a Hegelian, the use of the phrase indicates that Gustavo's thought and Marx's thought are virtually interchangeable.

When one checks out the passage in question, however, one discovers that Gustavo is simply making the impeccably orthodox assertion that in Jesus Christ God has entered the historical process; in Johannine terms, that "the Word became flesh and dwelt among us," a theme that Gustavo reiterates throughout his writings.

(2) In similar fashion, Gustavo is charged with being a Pelagian, and on the theory that as is the father so are the children, the entire theology of liberation fathered by him can be tarred with the same brush. (The Pelagian theme is also raised by the Sacred Congregation; we can dispose of both assertions in the present context.) This novel conclusion is arrived at by setting out as contradictory the notions of grace and works, and then implying that by stressing the importance of human activity, as all Marxists do, Gustavo is denying the reality of grace. This is the most wildly inaccurate of all the charges lodged against Gustavo, whose central insistence, from his first book to his last, is on "gratuitousness." In a book available to the critic, *We Drink from Our Own Wells*, the theme is particularly strong, and there is an entire section on "Gratuitousness: The Atmosphere for Efficacy," in which Gustavo affirms among other things that "the gift of God's love is the source of our being and puts its impress on our lives. . . . God's love for us is gratuitous; we do not merit it, it is a gift we receive before

we exist, or, to be more accurate, a gift in view of which we have been created" (pp. 109–10). So much for the accuracy of the Pelagian charge.

(3) Another charge against Gustavo is that because he writes so much about "conflict" and "struggle" he must be a Marxist. Critics residing in the safe confines of the Vatican need to be reminded that conflict and struggle are not "concepts" that Gustavo imposes upon the Latin American scene for Marxist reasons, but the everyday reality, the inescapable fact, of Latin American life. Christians in Gustavo's situation are not theoreticians trying to insinuate alien philosophical categories; they are persons who breathe every breath realizing that their friends are being imprisoned, tortured, and martyred, and that their own turn may come next. They do not impose a "theory of conflict" where no conflict exists; they try to work out modes of survival and creative response in situations where conflict is a given.

So it goes through fifty pages. Asked by Gustavo to provide a theological critique of the document as a whole, eight members of the faculty of the Pacific School of Religion, an affiliate of the Graduate Theological Union in Berkeley, California, concluded as follows:

> It seems clear to us that the Sacred Congregation has not been well-served by the document. The theology that is described and critiqued in the paper is not the position of Gutiérrez, and his own spirit and theological commitments are not discernible in it. Based on limited and wholly inadequate appeal to sources, it proceeds by selective quotation, and arrives at what can only appear to be predetermined conclusions. It insists on seeing everything in terms of a Marxist perspective, whereas a less biased reading of the material cannot help but lead to different conclusions.

Outside Support

The impression should not be left that during these trying years Gustavo was without support. Not only were there many within the Latin American church who stood with him (including at least half of his own Peruvian espiscopate and his archbishop Cardinal Landázuri Ricketts), but strong affirmations emerged from elsewhere as well. Letters on his behalf flooded the Sacred Congregation in Rome and the chancery office in Lima. The University of Tübingen awarded him an honorary degree. He returned to the University of Lyons, presented the corpus of his writings in lieu of a dissertation, as we have already noted, was examined by the faculty, and awarded the doctorate in theology with highest honors.

A group of prominent Catholic theologians associated with the publishing venture *Concilium* likewise came to Gustavo's defense.[5] The group included such prominent Catholic theologians as Edward Schillebeeckx, David Tracy, Elisabeth Schüssler Fiorenza, Hans Küng, and John Coleman. After asserting the importance of the contribution of liberation movements and theologies to the church, particularly in their message of hope to the poor, the theologians concluded:

> As these movements are a sign of hope for the whole church, any premature intervention from higher authorities risks stifling the spirit, which animates and guides local churches. We express our strong solidarity with these movements of liberation and with their theology. We protest against the suspicious and unjust criticism registered against them. We firmly believe that the future of the church, the coming of the kingdom, and the judgment of God on the world are tied up with these movements.

Just two weeks before his death, Karl Rahner, the most eminent Roman Catholic theologian of modern times, wrote a strong letter of support for Gustavo, commending him not only for the scope of his theology, but also for recognizing that "the voice of the poor must be listened to in theology," and that "theology can never prescind from the cultural and social context in which it takes place in the life situation of those to whom it is directed." And then, speaking without equivocation, Rahner continued:

> I am fully convinced that a condemnation of Gustavo Gutiérrez would have extremely unfortunate consequences for the whole climate that is necessary today for the very existence of a theology that is alive and serving the task of evangelization. . . . A legitimate pluralism in Catholic theology existed even in the Middle Ages and the Baroque period. It would be deplorable, then, if such a legitimate pluralism were to be excessively restricted by means of administrative measures.

Nor was support limited to the Roman Catholic world. At the conclusion of their appraisal of the essay circulated by the Sacred Congregation, described above, the Protestant theologians at the Pacific School of Religion gave their own testimonial:

> We find Gutiérrez important for our day not only in carrying out the tradition of the Catholic church, but informing the faith of non-Catholics as well, especially by his deep dependence on Scripture. We grieve that he and others like him must be deflected from their ongoing tasks of mercy and empowerment to others, to rebut charges so far off the mark as these. And we count on the wisdom of the Sacred Congregation of the Doctrine of the Faith to clear him and free him to continue the theological and practical work that has placed so many of us, from all over the Christian world, in his debt.

The First "Instruction" — Still More Challenges[6]

After its queries about Gustavo's theology, Rome next cast a wider net by attempting to snare liberation theology as a whole. Dated on the Feast of the Transfiguration, August 6, 1984, and released on September 3, 1984, the Sacred Congregation for the Doctrine of the Faith issued an "Instruction on Certain Aspects of the 'Theology of Liberation,' " signed by Joseph Cardinal Ratzinger, the prefect of the Congregation, with the approval of the pope. A second document was also promised that would deal positively with "the vast theme of Christian freedom and liberation in its own right." This document did not appear until twenty months later, and will be considered in due course.

The "Instruction" begins with support for a *true* theology of liberation, after which it expresses strong misgivings about "misinterpretations" of this concept. At no point does it name names, cite sources, employ direct quotations, or announce condemnations. The affirmative early sections were not part of Cardinal Ratzinger's original document, but were added at the insistence of the pope. They contain clear and prophetic words:

> [Humankind] will no longer passively submit to crushing poverty. . . . The scandal of the shocking inequality between the rich and the poor—whether between rich and poor countries, or between social classes in a single nation—is no longer tolerated. . . . The aspiration for liberation, as the term itself suggests, repeats a theme which is fundamental to the Old and New Testaments. In itself, the expression "theology of liberation" is a thoroughly valid term; it designates a theological reflection centered on the biblical theme of liberation and freedom, and on the urgency of its practical realization [I, 4, 6; III, 4].

Documents are cited that locate this concern for liberation centrally within the life of the Roman Catholic Church. There is utter realism in facing what is going on in Latin America today:

> the seizure of the vast majority of the wealth by an oligarchy of owners bereft of social consciousness, the practical absence or the shortcomings of a rule of law, military dictators making a mockery of elementary human rights, the corruption of certain powerful officials, the savage practices of some foreign capital interests [VII, 12].

The "Instruction" acknowledges that such factors "nourish a passion for revolt among those who thus consider themselves the powerless victims of a new colonialism in the technological, financial, monetary or economic order" (VII, 12). And the document states unequivocally that its issuance "should in no way be interpreted as a disavowal of all those who want to respond generously and with an authentic evangelical spirit to the 'preferential option for the poor.' "

With enemies like this, liberation theologians might have wondered, who needs friends? In the face of such enconiums, why issue a warning? But the tone abruptly changes, and Cardinal Ratzinger, as though anticipating such questions, calls stern attention to "the deviations and risks of deviation, damaging to the faith and to Christian living, that are brought about by certain forms of liberation theology which use, in an insufficiently critical manner, concepts borrowed from various currents of Marxist thought."

That single sentence sums up the substance of curial concern: in an otherwise praiseworthy concern for the poor, certain forms of liberation theology betray the cause of the poor by employing Marxist categories. To give force to this claim, the "Instruction" claims that if one adopts any single part of the Marxist analysis (for example, "class struggle") one will *inevitably* end up embracing the Marxist ideology as a whole. "No separation of the parts of this epistemologically unique complex [i.e., Marxism] is possible," the "Instruction" declares (VII, 6).

This is a head-on challenge to almost all liberation theologians, who claim that while they use portions of a Marxist social analysis to understand the dynamics of the world around them, they do *not* go on to adopt dialectical materialism, atheism, the necessity of violence, the theory of "surplus value," and so on, as components of their own perspective. Not so, replies the Sacred Congregation: start with class analysis, end up a total Marxist.

This deeply entrenched fear is intimately related to a second major critique of liberation theology in the "Instruction." If the structures of the church are examined from the perspective of "class struggle," the result will be a church in which two classes are pitted against each other. Liberation theologians, the "Instruction" argues, claims that truth resides with the oppressed class and its "church of the base," and in conflict with the church of the "other" class, aligned with the hierarchy. Hence the establishment's fear of structures independent of the hierarchy: insights emerging from the "peoples' church" will rend the seamless robe of Christ, and "temporal messianism" (an exclusively political reading of the scriptures) will be invoked to deny the legitimacy of other interpretations.

The "Instruction," then, manifests apprehension about the fate of existing church structures in a new situation. The danger is that there will be "a challenge to the sacramental and hierarchical structure of the church, which was willed by the Lord himself. There is a denunciation of the members of the hierarchy and the magisterium, as objective representations of the ruling class which has to be opposed" (IX, 13).

Underlying both of these points of contentions is a third cause for curial alarm, the implicit and sometimes explicit honoring of violence in seeking social change:

> The class struggle is presented as an objective, necessary law. Upon entering this process on behalf of the oppressed, one "makes" truth, one acts "scientifically." Consequently, the conception of the truth goes hand in hand with *the affirmation of necessary violence, and so, of a political amorality*. Within this perspective, any reference to ethical

requirements calling for courageous and radical institutional and structural reforms makes no sense [VIII, 7; italics added].

Once the first step down this road has been taken, the "Instruction" warns, one has surrendered any distinctively ethical, let alone Christian, position. "In fact," the text continues, "it is the transcendent character of the distinction between good and evil, the principle of morality, which is implicitly denied in the perspective of the class struggle" (VIII, 9).

Within these major areas of concern are a variety of further reasons for curial apprehension worth cataloguing (even at the cost of repetition of earlier specific charges against Gustavo) in order to clarify the depth of Rome's concerns. One must, of course, play a very coy game of theological cat-and-mouse with the text of the "Instruction," since it never cites a single name, but refers only to "certain forms of liberation theology," "certain of the writings of 'theologies of liberation,' " "some liberation theologians," "theologians of liberation of which we are speaking," "serious deviations of some 'theologies of liberation,' " and so on. Even so, we can highlight ten further charges in the "Instruction" that share at least the distinction that not one of them can appropriately be applied to Gustavo:

1. Liberation theologians "localize evil principally *or uniquely* in bad social, political or economic structures" (IV, 15; italics added).

2. Some liberation theologians "demand first of all a radical revolution in social relations and . . . criticize the search for personal perfection" (IV, 15).

3. Some liberation theologians claim that "the necessary struggle for human justice and freedom in the economic and political sense constitutes the *whole essence of salvation*" (VI, 4, italics added).

4. Some liberation theologians rely on "concepts *uncritically borrowed* from Marxist ideology and [have] recourse to theses of a biblical hermeneutic marked by *rationalism*" (VI, 10, italics added).

5. Liberation theologians fail to realize that "*a critical consciousness* has to accompany the use of any working hypotheses" (VII, 13, italics added).

6. "The theory of class struggle as *the fundamental law of history* . . . has been accepted by these 'theologies of liberation' as a principle. . . . According to this conception, the class struggle is *the driving force of history*" (IX, 2, 3, italics added).

7. "Some go so far as to *identify God with history*" (IX, 4, italics added).

8. "The new hermeneutic inherent in the 'theologies of liberation' leads to an *essentially* political reading of the scriptures. Thus a major importance is given to the exodus event inasmuch as it is *liberation from political servitude*" (X, 5, italics added).

9. "Liberation theologians harbor the "fatal illusion . . . that these new structures will *of themselves* give birth to a 'new person' " (XI, 9, italics added).

10. Finally, a list is compiled of further "essential aspects which the

'theologies of liberation' *especially* tend to misunderstand or *eliminate,* namely: the transcendence and gratuity of liberation in Jesus Christ, true God and true man; the sovereignty of grace; and the true na⁺ure of the means of salvation, especially of the church and sacraments. One should also keep in mind the true meaning of ethics, in which the distinction between good and evil is not relativized, the real meaning of sin, the necessity for conversion and the universality of the law of fraternal love" (XI, 17, italics added).

Only three weeks after the publication of this document, which immediately became a widely debated item in the public domain, the Sacred Congregation summoned the entire Peruvian hierarchy to Rome for another series of closed-session discussions of liberation theology. Having failed to secure a repudiation of Gustavo on his home turf, those in Rome must have hoped that the adage "when in Rome, do as the Romans do," would be persuasive to the Peruvian episcopate, and that the desired condemnation would have more chance of success inside the walls of Vatican City than it had had within earshot of the insistent cries of the poor back home.

The sessions lasted for several days and the exchanges of opinion, according to informed sources, were frank and open. But once again, the condemnation desired by the Sacred Congregation was not forthcoming—which says something both about the stiffened spines of the Peruvian bishops and also about the degree of persuasiveness of the "charges" accumulated by the Sacred Congregation's researchers.

What *was* forthcoming was a statement about liberation theology signed by the Peruvian hierarchy and released in October 1984.[7] In substance it did no more than indicate the bishops' willingness to abide by the recent "Instruction" and offered their own comments about liberation theology. While the document plows no new furrows, it does say something about the lay of the land in episcopal minds. Much familiar territory is recultivated: the expression "theology of liberation" is fully valid; there are some "deviations and distortions," however; God is "in solidarity with all who are miserable"; Marxism is no answer—such themes, the bishops declare, deserve the support of the church and are fully consistent with scripture. The message of *authentic* liberation is "a sign of hope and salvation, especially among the poorest and marginated in society" (§10).

There is clear acknowledgment of the Peruvian reality—violence, repression, drug trafficking—and the need to get to the root of such problems. But discernment is needed in order "to realize a true synthesis between the vertical and the horizontal, the divine and the human" (§23). A section on discernment urges a clear commitment to the poor, but cautions against those who want to go an exclusively "social sciences" and Marxist route; more attention must be given to the church's magisterium and especially to the recent "Instruction." Three themes are highlighted: (1) the need for a clear vision of history and society, (2) a clarification between the claims of praxis and truth, and (3) a reexamination of the relationship between the kingdom of God and human endeavor. After dealing with these well-trodden paths, the bishops conclude that the task is "to affirm simultaneously the implications of the gospel in all life, the world, and human history, *and* the ineradicable distinction between the order of nature and the order of grace—a difficult position, but one indispensable for our faith" (§53).

The closing section deals with pastoral applications of the document, in relation to publications, religious formation, etc. Among the tasks laid at the theologians' doors are the need to remain in conformity with canon law, to continue fruitful dialogue with the magisterium of the church, to deepen their own understanding of essential biblical themes without "for a single moment" forgetting the situations of misery of the poor, to help all the faithful distinguish clearly between authentic and inauthentic versions of liberation theology, to evaluate their own studies and publications in the light of the "Instruction" and the present document, and to be sensitive to the repercussions of their theological work in pastoral situations.

Inasmuch as support of Vatican documents by Roman Catholic bishops is strictly pro forma, the pyrrhic victory represented by this document, which gives something to everybody, is not a great deal for the Sacred Congregation to have salvaged from the meetings, particularly when Gustavo and his friends and supporters indicated that they could live comfortably within the bishops' admonitions.

The Second "Instruction"—Change of Mood[8]

Rome, however, still possessed the right of acting unilaterally, quite apart from national hierarchies. In the interval between the first "Instruction" and its successor, Leonardo Boff, a Brazilian Franciscan who had undergone similar scrutiny because of his views on the power of the Holy Spirit in relation to the hierarchy and the base communities, was formally "silenced" for what turned out to be a period of eleven months. If Boff had been chastised, could Gustavo's fate be far behind?

The second "Instruction," entitled "Instruction on Christian Freedom and Liberation," issued on April 5, 1986, did not, however, substantiate such fears. Although it has its share of negative comments about liberation theology, the overall tone is surprisingly irenic, and, at least in its first three chapters, almost bland. The initial portions of the "Instruction" give an overview of Catholic social teaching as it has developed out of the Vatican II document "The Church in the Modern World," and reiterate well-established emphases, such as the claim that "there is no gap between love of neighbor and desire for justice." The heart of the message is found in chapters 4 and 5, and some of the emphases, as they bear on liberation theology, can be briefly noted.

1. Salvation must be "integral" — that is, involving the whole person, body and soul. The Beatitudes are proposed as a way to keep "the grace of divine life" and "temporal good" together, as well as uniting "evangelization and the promotion of justice" — a consistent liberation theme.

2. The document lays great stress on concern for the poor, although (in a deliberate attempt to undercut the Puebla phrase "a preferential option for the poor") an awkward phrase, "a love of preference for the poor," is occasionally substituted. A warning is issued against "reductive sociological and ideological categories" that would make "the option for the poor" (the phrase returns unchallenged) a "partisan choice and a source of conflict." This "reductionist" critique, so frequently used against liberation theology, has no detectable dwelling place in the life and work of living, breathing liberation theologians.

3. The base communities receive support, provided "they really live in union with the local Church and the universal Church" — an admirable statement of the intention of Leonardo Boff and his friends.

4. Theologians are admonished to be careful to interpret the experience from which they begin "in the light of the experience of the church" — almost an echo of Gustavo's definition of theology as "critical reflection on praxis *in the light of the Word of God.*"

5. Church teaching on matters relating to action "develops in accordance with the changing circumstances of history." There can be no "closed system," since "contingent judgments" will always be involved. *"Critical* reflection on praxis" would be another way of making the point.

6. After appearing to give primacy to the "conversion of the heart" as a basis for social change, the document asserts that this perspective "in no way eliminates the need for unjust structures to be changed." A few sentences later the point is even more explicit: "It is therefore necessary to work *simultaneously* for the conversion of hearts and for the improvement of structures" (italics added) — as tidy a summary as one could desire of a basic liberation recognition that sin has both social and individual dimensions.

7. There is a fresh repudiation of class-struggle theory as an "alleged law of history," since action sanctioned by the church "is not the struggle of one class against another in order to eliminate the foe. . . . Liberation in the spirit of the Gospel is therefore incompatible with hatred of others . . . and this includes hatred of one's enemy." Gustavo could hardly have said it better; his treatment of class struggle specifies that the task is not to "eliminate the foe," but to get rid of the social stratification that makes struggle necessary. He goes further, recalling that the gospel message is to love, not hate, enemies.

There are further admirable sections on work, repeating claims in John Paul II's encyclical *Laborem Exercens,* and the "Instruction" closes with extended reference to the Magnificat, one of the most widely used biblical passages in the liberation struggle, although the radical and revolutionary themes of Mary's song, so central to liberation concern, have either been missed or muted in the Ratzinger exegesis.

The Struggle with Rome Subsides

The second "Instruction" represents a clear change of perspective over its harsh and illogical predecessor. Its strictures are mild by comparison, and its overall ambiance is positive. By its tone, it gives a signal, one hopes, that the Vatican had reconsidered its earlier decision to throw down the gauntlet to liberation theology; by its content, particularly in its later portions, it suggests that rather than excluding liberation insights in the future, the church will incorporate them into its own formulation of Catholic social teaching, and open the way for new degrees of collaboration.

At the same time, if the lessons of recent history are any guide, liberation theologians will not fully lower their guard. Rome's ways are past finding out, and even if overt pressures from the Sacred Congregation diminish, there are other pressures, both overt and covert, that can be exercised. In Gustavo's case, future difficulties are likely to be initiated more from Lima than from Rome. To replace each retiring bishop who was a supporter of Gustavo, Rome routinely designates a conservative successor, sure to be unfriendly to him, so that the even balance of a few years ago has already been replaced by a tilt against him. In addition, as we have already seen, the successor of Cardinal Landázuri, who had been a supporter of Gustavo, is an adamant foe, author before his elevation of two books attacking Gustavo directly. One must hope that the Peruvian episcopate will be wise enough not to exert its potential power for divisiveness, and will recognize that if the Sacred Congregation could not construct a convincing case against Gustavo, others are not likely to succeed where Rome failed.

Gustavo's Response: *The Truth Shall Make You Free*

After this recital, it may seem redundant to offer Gustavo's response to charges made against him, because we know that the curial case did not stand up under scrutiny, and we have a well-grounded suspicion that most if not all the charges were wide of the mark from the start. As Gustavo put it in an interview with Fred Herzog after the first "Instruction:"

> The response from some liberation theologians in Latin America like Sobrino or myself was this: in our works it is not possible to find the points criticized by the "Instruction." [The "Instruction"] may be useful. But it is not a description of present Latin American liberation theology.

It would almost be sufficient to ask the reader to reexamine chapters 3–5 above, where Gustavo's theology is set forth, confident that such an exercise would dispose of the curial distortions once and for all.

Nevertheless, it is important to allot space to him, not only for the sake of the record, but also because charges (no matter by whom or against whom) have an unfortunate ability to outlast their refutations; the battle of truth against error is never fully over. In addition, Gustavo himself has provided a long essay in which he clarifies his own beliefs in light of all the controversy.

In 1986, after some of the dust had settled, the immediate pressures from Rome had relaxed, and both "Instructions" had been issued, Gustavo wrote a long essay, "The Truth Shall Make You Free," using materials that constituted parts of his "defense" when he was being questioned in Rome. In serene and irenic fashion, he offers "a stocktaking and a review" of the controverted issues.[9]

As an example of the degree to which Gustavo's teachings, far from being heretical, exemplify the best in the Catholic tradition, the essay is a masterpiece. But one can hardly finish it without reflecting that a conscientious reading of his texts by the Sacred Congregation would have obviated the need for its issuance, and one realizes why Cardinal Ratzinger was unable to secure a condemnation: there was nothing to condemn.

This does not reduce Gustavo to a pale centrist, parroting the teaching of the past, but demonstrates that thinking and living the central mysteries of the faith in company with the poor provide new and often bold perceptions from the heritage that had previously been overlooked. Although new perspectives always threaten those with closed minds, they challenge those with open hearts. As Gustavo says in the penultimate paragraph:

> As I reach the end, it becomes clear that the task is an open-ended one. ... One of the great joys of theological work, and indeed of Christian life generally, is undoubtedly the realization that *the gospel always has new things to say to us* [*Truth*, p. 174, italics added].

There can be no quarrel with Gustavo's starting point in *The Truth Shall Make You Free,* that "the primordial, and in a certain sense unique, source of revealed truth is Jesus the Christ" (88); it is when he asserts that theology "must be a dialogue with the culture of its age" (89) that differences begin. Europeans may feel that the problem of contemporary society is "secularization" (as was proposed in the discredited "Preliminary Document" for Puebla), but for Gustavo the major problem is the widespread presence of "unjust suffering." Those who ignore this "cannot speak of God and expect to be heard" (90).

Knowledge, from such a perspective, cannot be separated from action — a dangerous notion to those who like a tidy universe. But (as Gustavo's accompanying historical survey shows) the relation of theory and practice is not some fly-by-night import by a twentieth-century Marxist, but an ancient tradition of Western philosophy. Within that tradition, the church has usually lined up with the Greeks, viewing truth as residing "in the essence of things" (94), whereas the Bible, to which Gustavo here appeals, discovers truth in the world of the interpersonal, something that is *done* rather than something that simply *is*. Truth is found "not between things and concepts but between promise and fulfillment" (94–95). The promises of God are found within the historical process, *already* fulfilled but *not yet* completely fulfilled, in the coming of one who said, "I am the Truth."

What we can know of God (even in Jesus Christ) is not the *fullness* of God, but only *what we can know of God from our limited perspective*. "God is irreducible to our manner of understanding," Gustavo had earlier argued in *The Power of the Poor in History* (p. 19). We have "access" to God, but the "transcendent mystery" of God is hidden from us. This is a crucial point in rebutting the charge that Gustavo loses the "vertical" dimension and flattens out Christianity into nothing but a "horizontal" ethic devoid of deity.

The Christian, then, is not so much one who "knows" the truth as one who "does" the truth, by engaging in the "following of Jesus" (*Truth*, pp. 97ff.). One verifies the truth by praxis, the integration of reflection and action. Gustavo demonstrates that this is the position of Pope John Paul II in *Laborem Exercens*, where the pope writes about "verifying," "checking," and even "proving" one's faith in concrete action. *Faith is not reduced to works, but faith will have its fruits in works.*

The praxis of liberation "is ultimately a praxis of love—real love, effective and concrete, for real, concrete human beings" (100, citing *PP*, p. 50). Such action has its roots "in the gratuitous and free love of the Father" (*Truth*, ibid.). Contrary to the charges of the Sacred Congregation, Gustavo does not preach "works-righteousness," or Pelagianism, or a denial of the priority of grace. Everything flows from grace. As he writes later in the essay, discussing the task of the church in relation to divine grace and human action, "testimony to the Lord's resurrection is situated between the acceptance of the grace of the kingdom and the historical demands that this grace makes" (159). Grace is promise, but it is also demand.

In this life of engagement in the world, "the ultimate criteria come from revealed truth, which we accept in faith and not from praxis itself" (101). Gustavo explicitly rejects what the Peruvian bishops call "another aspect of Marxist thought"—namely, that praxis "becomes the fundamental criterion of truth" (181).

The challenge is not to set belief against action and make action the sole criterion for belief, but "to be able to preserve the circular relationship between orthodoxy [right belief] and orthopraxis [right action] and the nourishment of each by the other" (104). In a passage he uses so frequently in his writings that we may be excused for quoting it a second time, Gustavo elaborates the point:

> This, then, is the fundamental hermeneutical circle: from humanity to God and from God to humanity, from history to faith and from

faith to history, from the human word to the word of the Lord and from the word of the Lord to the human word, from the love of one's brothers and sisters to the love of the Father and from the love of the Father to love of one's brothers and sisters, from human justice to God's holiness and from God's holiness to human justice [105; see also inter alia *TheoLib*, p. 83; "Praxis of Liberation and Christian Faith;" Eigo, ed., *Living with Change, Experience, Faith*, p. 41, *PP*, p. 61].

What keeps the circle from becoming a vicious circle is a recognition that the one who says, "I am the Truth," is also the one who says, "the truth shall make you free." This Johannine claim, from which Gustavo derives the title for his essay, is the linchpin of his argument:

Christ is the *truth*, a truth that *sets us free*. The liberation he gives is an integral one that embraces all dimensions of human existence and brings us to full communion with God and one another [105, italics added].

A difference of outlook emerges between liberation theology and its European critics (114). Their concern for "freedom" comes out of such movements as the rise of individualism and the Enlightment, whereas the Latin American concern for liberation grows out of living on "the underside of history." Much of the polemical struggle into which Gustavo has been drawn stems from the fact that many of his critics are formed by what R. Marlé calls "Eurocentrism." European "progressives," Gustavo notes, tend to call liberation theology " 'traditional,' and 'spiritual,' and excessively 'church-centered,' " while European " 'conservatives' ... pass a different judgment; they see us as reducing everything to the political, and as standing to the left of the 'progressivism' they are used to fighting against" (185). Gustavo appropriately complains that "these European approaches imprison us in categories which are not ours." The only way out of this dilemma is to acknowledge—as Gustavo does aggressively—"the right of the poor to think," and to think for themselves, a right that the classic theological tradition has been singularly loathe to grant (115ff.).

Gustavo next turns to a central point of dispute: the relationship of the kingdom of God to human achievement, and the corollary claim that God bestows liberation and yet human beings must work for it. Picking up on material in both "Instructions," Gustavo reexamines the exodus story, a paradigm account of the way that religion and politics are both present without either one negating the other. There is a "religious" element, the keeping of covenant with Yahweh, but also "a social and political liberation, the deliverance from slavery."

In describing the exodus event, Gustavo uses the word "paradigm," not in the sense of a story that is repeated again and again in scripture, but to affirm that "the deeper meaning of the event—the liberating intervention of God—is permanently valid" (119). It is the whole biblical story *in nuce*.

Within this "liberating intervention of God," human beings have a crucial role to play in creating transitions "from less human conditions" to "more human conditions"—a theme Gustavo appropriates from Paul VI's encyclical *Populorum Progressio*. Divine and human interactions together create new conditions, and these transitions finally include all levels of the human condition—passing, as the pope puts it, *from "less human conditions,"* such as lack of material necessities, oppressive social structures, and exploitation of workers, *to "more human conditions,"* such as the passage from misery to victory over social scourges, to growth of knowledge, to esteem for the dignity of others, to cooperation and good will, to the desire for peace, to faith in God, and finally to unity in Christ. The key point is that "liberation" includes *all* these things—not just gaining material necessities (without regard for union with Christ) but also not just union with Christ (apart from gaining material necessities).

Out of this papal approach, Gustavo formulates the three levels of liberation we have earlier noted, but this time he explains their interrelationship by employing the "Chalcedonian principle." (The phrase refers to the attempt by the Council of Chalcedon to describe the person of Christ in ways that *distinguish between* but *do not separate* his divine and human natures.) Although we have encountered these three levels before, a fuller exposition is important as a reminder of how inaccurate most criticisms of Gustavo's theology turn out to be.

The three levels must be "distinguished" from one another, but then "conjoined" as parts of "a single, complex process"—"complex" because otherwise there might be "confusions and simplistic identifications" (121). The levels are "interdependent"—that is, they are "different ways that are nonetheless connected with one another." They are "distinguished" *only in order that they may be united,* not so that they can be separated.

Such terminology may seem hopelessly abstract on first reading, but Gustavo wants to show the unity of the three levels:

> Christ the Savior liberates from sin, which is the ultimate root of all disruption of friendship and of all injustice and oppression [first level]. Christ makes humankind truly free [second level]—that is to say he enables us to live in communion with him, and this is the basis for all human fellowship [third level] [cf. also *TheoLib,* p. 25 (37)].

None of the levels can be isolated from the others. Much criticism of liberation theology comes from those who argue that Gustavo deals only with the political/social level. A brief review of the interrelation of the three will reveal the inaccuracy such charges.

1. *Social liberation* is the first level, dealing with political, social, and economic conflict; the task is to eliminate "the proximate causes of poverty

and injustice" (130). The goal is a "qualitatively different society," the basic characteristic of which Gustavo captures in a memorable phrase: *"a society in which the needs of the poor are more important than the power of the privileged"* (131, italics added). This is not the whole of liberation, but it is an indispensable part.

2. *The freedom of the human person.* Liberation on this second level means that persons themselves must assume conscious responsibility for their own destiny. They need interior as well as exterior liberation, for "new social structures are not enough" by themselves. "Society must be based not only on justice, but also on freedom" (133). Although change in social structures can help achieve such realizations, change "does not automatically bring it about" (133). This cuts both ways: *If structural changes do not automatically create a new humanity, neither do personal changes ensure social transformations.* The emphasis in both cases on individual human freedom is utterly antithetical to any "historical analysis based on economic determinism" (133). So much for Gustavo's "dependence" on Marx.

Like the first level, this second level demands human effort, and it relates to the first level, for it is the place where plans for a new society, utopias, and human aspirations are initiated. It deals with deeper human realities than the first level can do by itself, but neither one is fulfilled unless integrated within a third.

3. *Toward full communion.* The third level—without which the other two are inadequately understood, and which is inadequately understood without the other two—is primarily the liberation from sin that Christ offers, which in turn enables human beings to live in full communion with one another and with God. Sin is present *both* in the individual human hearts (a claim liberation theology fully acknowledges), and also within social structures (a claim liberation theology has forced a reluctant Christian world to rediscover). The latter claim does not negate the former, as Gustavo's opponents frequently insinuate, and inasmuch as sin is "a rejection of the gift of God's love" (136), the overcoming of sin by the power of God's grace will lead beyond separation by restoring communion both with God and with God's children.

So the three levels can be "distinguished" (as the above summary endeavors to do), but they must not be "separated" (as any summary is in danger of appearing to do). They are not "parallel" or "chronologically successive." *They are three levels of meaning of a single, complex process.*

The final section of *The Truth Shall Make You Free* moves outward to consider "The Liberating Mission of the Church." Those who have been liberated must share what has happened to them, and since liberation is "integral," meaning that *no* part of life is untouched by it, in addition to sharing in the grace of the divine life, those in the church must also "pursue [the peoples'] temporal good" (143).

To establish this connection, Gustavo adopts the Vatican II imagery of

the church as "sacrament," which means "an efficacious sign [that] transforms the life of human beings" (144). The church both proclaims and is
meant to embody the present reality of the kingdom of God, but it also
works for the historical realization of a just society. Liberating events enable
the growth of the kingdom, but the kingdom is more than liberating events.
The kingdom cannot be "reduced" to a historical embodiment, nor can any
historical achievement be interpreted as an unambiguous sign of the kingdom's presence.

There are two gifts in particular that the Latin American church can
offer the rest of the church: (1) the fact that *the poor have the gospel preached
to them,* which has not been a notable part of the church's life elsewhere;
and (2) a recognition of *the evangelizing potential of the poor,* since the poor
are not only the recipients of the gospel message, but also its bearers. The
base communities are signs of this new vitality within the church, for "they
reveal the presence in the church of the 'nobodies' of history" (152).

As the church reaches out in its "liberating mission," it discovers that
"the deepest meaning of praxis is love and justice" (152). But the exercise
of praxis always "involves contingent judgments" (153). Historically, for
example, there have been changing attitudes on the matter of private property, although within a recognition that, in Pope John Paul II's words, "a
social mortgage has been placed on all private property." The church always
has to safeguard against "an individualistic conception that regards profit
as the driving force of the economy," and "a totalitarian vision that disregards the freedom of each person" (154). Balancing private ownership,
social ownership, and state ownership involves "contingent" judgments,
since no single formula is appropriate to all times and places.

Treatment of "the preferential option for the poor" reiterates themes
we have already encountered, save that here Gustavo particularly stresses
christological aspects of the theme. Commenting on a Lucan passage, he
writes: "Christ makes himself present precisely through those who are
'absent' from history, those who are not invited to the banquet" (157). "The
poor," he continues, "are not a 'category,' but "real persons" in concrete
situations.

After a lengthy treatment of the Beatitudes (and a rehabilitation of the
Matthean version from charges that it has falsely "spiritualized" the text
of Luke), Gustavo turns in conclusion to further reflection on how "the
church of the poor" can be the church of all. He points to two interventions
by Cardinal Lercaro at Vatican II stressing the need for the whole church
to embrace a life of poverty. This raises "the great question" the council
put to many Latin American Christians: "What is required of the church
if it is to be a universal sacrament of salvation in a world stamped by poverty
and injustice?" The church, instead of just being "the church of the poor,"
will have to become a poor church, as Medellín said in response to Vatican
II. Puebla seven times picked up the theme of "a preferential option of
the poor," and as Gustavo comments, "What the phrase calls for is *a radical*

change of outlook" that will involve a new degree of "solidarity with the poor." This will always be in creative tension with the universality of God's love.

Is this too much to work for? Gustavo reminds his readers that the notion of "the church of the poor" is not a new notion, but one that goes back to the New Testament, and has surfaced sporadically in subsequent Christian history. In reclaiming this vision, the church will not be losing its identity but recovering it.

But, Gustavo warns, "we must pay a price in order to be the church of the poor" (173). And when all is said and done, this is probably the biggest single reason for outcries against Gustavo's theology. The church can suffer fools gladly, but it has a harder time with prophets, particularly when they threaten to interfere with profits.

Residuals

In many cases directly, and in some cases indirectly, the essay we have just considered lays to rest the charges against Gustavo that have emanated from Rome and elsewhere. Within our discussion of the first "Instruction," we noted ten charges that (whether they apply to other liberation theologians or not) clearly cannot be laid at Gustavo's theological doorstep, and in dealing with the second "Instruction" we discovered seven examples of liberation themes of Gustavo's that are embraced by the "Instruction" as part of authentic Catholic teaching. In light of all that, it is almost embarrassing to return to the Sacred Congregation's original ten charges against Gustavo and propose that they can still be taken seriously or that they any longer deserve to be dignified by extensive rebuttal. Claims, for example, that Gustavo denies the transcendence of revelation, or the centrality of grace, or disregards Vatican II, or equates social utopias with the kingdom of God, or deals only with the social dimension of sin to the exclusion of the personal dimension, or gives an "exclusively" political interpretation to biblical passages, or "uncritically" accepts Marxism—simply cannot be sustained.

Since, however, the common underlying theme of all the accusations is one form or another of "reductionism" of the gospel (to Marxism, or "horizontalism," or "temporal messianism," or revolution, or Pelagianism, or relativism, or whatever), let us observe Gustavo as he turns the charge of "reductionism" back on his accusers. If he can (wrongfully) be accused of "reducing" the gospel to a political instrument, his attackers can (appropriately) be accused of "reducing" the gospel to an unearthly "spiritualism" that is equally "political" since it sanctifies the status quo, and puts "the gospel to ideological use so that it may justify a situation which is contrary to its most elemental demands."

In that context, Gustavo delivers himself of a powerful series of assertions:

Are we, then, talking about reducing the gospel to purely political terms? Are we advocating a "political reductionism"? Yes, in the case of those who use it to serve the interests of those in power; no, in the case of those who denounce that usage on the basis of the message of liberation and gratuitous divine love. Yes, in the case of those who place themselves and the gospel in the hands of the mighty of this world; no, in the case of those who identify themselves with the poor Christ and seek to establish solidarity with the dispossessed on this continent. Yes, in the case of those who keep it shackled to an ideology that serves the capitalist system; no, in the case of those who have been set free by the gospel message and then seek to liberate it from that same captivity. Yes, in the case of those who wish to neutralize Christ's liberation by restricting it or reducing it to a purely spiritual plane that has nothing to do with the concrete world of human beings; no, in the case of those who believe that Christ's salvation is so total and radical that nothing escapes it [in Gibellini, ed., *Frontiers of Theology in Latin America*, p. 28.].

Two can play the "reductionist" game.[10]

What Threatens One, Threatens All

In the preceding pages, it may appear that the author has abandoned any pretence at a "reportorial" role, and emerged as an unabashed partisan. The perception would be correct. What is at stake is not only a theological dispute, but the presence or absence of justice in the world. It is not enough to extol justice. One must be a partisan for justice. Anything else is a betrayal of Gustavo's commitments.

In the light of Gustavo's gifts, it is both dismaying and disheartening to have seen him subject to such attacks by heavy theological artillery from within his own church. What happened to him is not an exclusively Roman Catholic affair, but something that has repercussions for the rest of the Christian family, and indeed, for the poor and oppressed everywhere, who have found in Gustavo someone who not only speaks for them but—more importantly—stands with them.

All of us have been nurtured by this man, and our faith has been deepened by our encounters with his writing and his person. In our moments of doubt about the relevance of our faith in a parched world, he has encouraged us to keep working, praying, evangelizing, acting, and drinking "from our own wells" so that we, too, can draw living water. We need his help in finding wells whence the power of the Spirit can pour forth to us. It is a deprivation to everyone when he has to turn his energies from struggling with the poor in order to "defend himself" against attack. We must hope that there will be a respite from further attacks, so that he, and we, can turn with renewed commitment to the holy tasks of justice and love.

CHAPTER 7

Act Three: Some Scripted Entrances, or What Liberation Theology Means for Us

Liberation theologies are born not in books but in communities of resistance to deeply entrenched social relations of domination and subordination.
— Marvin Ellison, *Christianity and Crisis,*
June 12, 1989, p. 185

The Church of Jesus Christ is not called to be a bastion of caution and moderation. The Church should challenge, inspire, and motivate people. It has a message of the cross that inspires us to make sacrifices for justice and liberation. It has a message of hope that challenges us to wake up and to act with hope and confidence. The Church must preach this message not only in words and sermons and statements, but also through its actions, programs, campaigns, and divine services.
— *The Kairos Document*, South Africa, p. 30

The point is not to backtrack; new experiences, new demands have made heretofore familiar and comfortable paths impassible and have made us undertake new itineraries on which we hope it might be possible to say with Job to the Lord: "I knew of thee then only by report, but now I see thee with my own eyes" (Job 42:5).
— Gustavo, *A Theology of Liberation*, p. 119 (206)

Most of us like the idea of the drama ending after act two. We have gained some information, watched some of the characters grow (and others diminish), and observed interesting conflicts and unexpected twists and turns in the plot. We look forward to reading the reviews in the drama section of tomorrow's paper. But the hour is late, and it is time to return to our own world. . . .

157

On Trying To Leave the Theater— and Ending up on Stage

And here is where we make an important and unappealing discovery: in the course of the evening, whether we like it or not, we have been transformed from spectators into participants. The play does not end with act two. *There is an act three and we are participating in the action on stage.*

There are several ways to view this unexpected turn of events. One is to imagine ourselves leaving the theater through a door we are sure was marked *EXIT*, and discovering that the resultant passageway does not lead out of the theater but onto the stage.

Or, we imagine ourselves remaining in our seats, and discovering that the arena where the actors perform is moving out to surround us so that we are soon "on stage" ourselves. Or, after the conclusion of act two, we realize that the theater is so constructed that the entire area has been a stage all along and we were simply unaware of it.

We were never actually "spectators"; we only thought we were. Whether consciously on stage or not, we are actors who through our own lives are doing things that make a difference in the lives of those we are watching. We support policies that make life better (infrequently) or worse (frequently) for the poor two-thirds of the human family; we benefit materially by their poverty; we enjoy comforts bought at the price of their misery. We keep trying to get out of the theater, or at least off stage, to avoid such disturbing facts, but it is now too late to do so. We are not spectators, we are participants.

How will we adjust to our newly perceived role? This chapter will attempt to provide some stage directions, once we accustom ourselves to the glare of the lights and realize that they will be illuminating our actions more than we would wish. While that adjustment is taking place, here are some initial reflections to ponder:

1. We will not receive a script containing our lines, so that all we need to do is read them well. Nor will we be able to turn to lines already spoken by others, and make them our own. We will have to deliver lines of our own creating, and initiate actions of our own devising, based not only on what has happened in acts one and two, but on how we propose to move the direction of act three for the good of all.

2. We had better not speak too glibly or too soon. We still have a lot of listening to do. Our worst approach: "We know what is good for you people, so move over and let us take charge." At best we will have subordinate roles, based on a recognition that our leadership roles in the past are the reason things went awry.

3. If we are lucky, we will grow in the process, increasingly recognizing how our perceptions and consequent actions must change.

(I share an example of the need for growth. In the Foreword to an earlier book on liberation theology I mentioned the recent deaths of two friends, and indicated that I would not be dealing with such matters in a book on liberation theology. I thus gave the clear — and erroneous — impression that while liberation theology was concerned with political, economic, and social questions, it was not concerned with suffering, death, and the affirmation of life in the face of personal grief. This was a truncated understanding of liberation theology at best, and a distinct disservice to its "integral" message at worst. It has been one of my concerns in the present book to show that the liberating gospel speaks to *every* aspect of human experience.)

As we move into act three, we find (in faithfulness to Gustavo's three-point methodology) three things happening: (1) enlarging the cast, (2) intensifying the plot, and (3) joining the company.

1. Enlarging the Cast

As liberation theology began to command attention, it became clear that the impulses behind it, and the injustices that created it, were not confined to Latin America. If U.S. imperialism was evident in Brazil, it was equally evident in Korea; if the long arm of multinationals was choking the life of the Latin American poor, it was doing the same to Filipinos; if the relationship of capitalism to racism was a reality in Andean countries, it was equally evident in South Africa; if the effects of colonialism were still alive and well in El Salvador and Guatemala, they were likewise exhibiting vital life signs in India and southeast Asia. (In the northern hemisphere, as we shall presently see, oppressed groups were also becoming conscious of their need for liberation — blacks, Hispanics, Amerindians, women, gays and lesbians.) Although each group had its own specific problems to combat, the overall problems had enough in common to suggest that banding together would be the best way to overcome them. But before describing this colorful and expanding cast too euphorically, we must note that getting people of different races, classes, colors, genders, and backgrounds to work together is far from simple. Fortunately, there is a case study that dramatizes both the possibilities and the problems.

EATWOT[1]

The organizing impulse for the creation of an international group grew out of a number of meetings of Third World theologians attending various international church conferences. Its formal creation was aided and abetted by Oscar Bimweniji of Africa, François Houtart of Belgium, Sergio Torres of Chile, and Virginia Fabella of the Philippines. It soon became the Ecumenical Association of Third World Theologians. It is readily identified by the acronym EATWOT.

An initial gathering of twenty-two participants was held in Dar es Salaam, Tanzania, in August 1976, on "The Emergent Gospel: Theology from the Underside of History." Those who gave papers represented thirteen countries and three continents—Africa, Asia, and Latin America—along with one invited guest, a black from North America. The composition of the group became a point of intense debate, since Latin Americans did not initially feel that First World persons—even blacks—should be part of a Third World group. Black Africans, however, insisted that the need for liberation was not geographically determined, and that blacks from other parts of the world—even from the United States—should be included.

While the delegates agreed that theology in the future must come from "the underside of history," they also realized that the three continents represented had different social and cultural settings, different histories (particularly in relation to colonialism), and different situations vis-à-vis the presence and role of Christianity. Tensions were apparent whenever individual speakers appeared to be generalizing from their situation to the whole. Furthermore, since only one of the twenty-two delegates was a woman, the inherited sexism of Third World cultures was plainly exposed.

A second gathering was held in 1977 at Accra, Ghana, and long-felt militancies about theological imperialism were aired. As the convenor, Kofi Appiah-Kubi, put it:

> We demand to serve the Lord on our own terms and without being turned into Euro-American or Semitic bastards before we do so. . . . Our question must not be what Karl Barth or Karl Rahner, or any other Karl has to say, but rather what God would have us do in our living concrete condition [Appiah-Kubi and Torres, eds., *African Theology en Route*, p. viii].

Sergio Torres, in a powerful opening address, noted what a painful procedure it had been "to discover that the theology that our people of the Third World have received from the missionaries was not a universal theology, but a European theology, a white theology, a male theology" (pp. 3–4)—a theology, he went on, "linked to the dominant class of Europe and did not speak on behalf of the poor and the oppressed" (p. 4). Third World theologians must stress "the God of the poor," and the world not as something to be accepted uncritically, but as "an unfinished project being built" (p. 5). Torres also cited the representation of eleven black North Americans (including five women) at the conference as a symbol of further unity and hope.

The conference speakers presented a variety of "new perspectives" on the African scene, among them the perceptive comments of Gabriel Setiloane of Botswana about unresolved confusions over the relation of black theology to African theology, and there were several papers on liberation currents in South Africa, including contributions by Desmond Tutu (writing in the aftermath of Steve Biko's murder), and Allan Boesak, already emerging as a major theological voice in South Africa.

The issue of tensions between black theology and African theology was directly addressed by James Cone, a black from North America, in response to John Mbiti's complaint that "black theology hardly knows the situation of Christians living in Africa, and therefore its direct relevance for Africa is either nonexistent or only accidental" (cited on p. 176). Cone responded vigorously that black and African theologies are not as different as claimed, and that "their common concerns require a dialogue that is important to both" (p. 178). Cone urged his fellow black theologians to "enlarge the oneness of the Black World to include our solidarity with the world's poor" (p. 179) and urged African theologians to give attention not only to the need for cultural change but political change as well.

The conference also acknowledged that "the African situation requires a new theological methodology that is different from the approaches of the dominant theologies of the west. . . . Our task as theologians is to create a theology that arises from and is accountable to African people" (p. 193). Such a theology will be a contextual theology, a liberation theology, and a theology opposing sexism—an important new constituent, given substance at the conference by the presence of fifteen women.

A third gathering was held in Sri Lanka in 1979 in conjunction with the Asian Theological Conference. It challenged the "academic" approach of meeting only for papers and discussion, by assigning each delegate to live with a Sri Lankan family in the days before the meetings began—a procedure that drew mixed reactions but manifestly served to personalize the issues.

Both the second and third conferences attempted to break the centuries-long bondage that "Western" theology had imposed on Africa and Asia, and affirmed that indigenous contexts and experiences had to be the starting point for African and Asian theology. Unanswered questions were posed for later examination: For whom, and by whom, is theology done? If theology must "emerge from the life struggles of people," *which* life struggles are to be paramount in a continent as vast as Asia? Have the "struggling grassroots poor" really been part of the conference or was it too "academic"? Having to use English as the common language left the delegates with another question: Can an authentic "Asian theology" be done in the language of oppressors?

A larger conference on the challenge of the Christian base communities was held in São Paulo, Brazil, in early 1980, with representatives from forty-two countries. Cultural tensions were openly expressed. A delegate from Sri Lanka wondered if the poor were yet speaking for themselves, or whether others were still speaking on their behalf. Cornel West, an American black theologian who makes use of Marxist analysis, raised questions about too uncritical an appropriation of Marx, who does not speak with equal relevance to all cultures. Ruvimbo Tekere, from Zimbabwe, deplored the small number of Indians and blacks in the membership of the conference. Tissa Balasuriya of Sri Lanka reminded the delegates that "Asians live in poverty much worse than that of the average Latin American," and insisted that the traditional relationship of people to the land was more important in discussing development policies than was being acknowledged. Latin American anti-Asian immigration policies were challenged by many delegates.

James Cone described the tensions between Latin American liberation theologians and North American black theologians in ways that are instructive for all attempts at making common cause, citing the relation between *racial* oppression and *class* oppression as the source of difficulty. In their earliest contacts, he recalled, at a conference in Geneva in 1973, the two groups brought deep-seated suspicions of one another: Latin Americans saw blacks as captives of bourgeois capitalism because they did not deal with class, and blacks saw Latin Americans as captives of a white-dominated theology because they did not deal with race. They discovered at Geneva, however, that they needed to talk directly to one another, rather than through the mediation of Europeans who had convened the conference.

"Talk directly to one another" they did at a conference in Detroit in 1975, sponsored by "Theology of the Americas," but as Cone reports it, hostility between the two groups predominated, each side stereotyping the other for seemingly exclusive interest in either class or race. At a conference in Mexico City two years later, however, genuine dialogue between Latin Americans and blacks began—a breakthrough Cone attributes to the mediatorial endeavors of Gustavo, in whom blacks finally found a Latin American who seemed willing to listen and interpret. And at a conference later in 1977 in Atlanta, blacks acknowledged for the first time the importance of economic analysis in developing a theology, and even said some good words about Karl Marx.

An increasing openness on the part of EATWOT is symbolized by the fact that the sixth conference, held in Geneva in 1983, also included First World theologians, such as Georges Casalis, Johann Baptist Metz, Dorothee Sölle, Rosemary Ruether, Letty Russell, and Jim Wallis. It was discovered that First World theologians are no more homogeneous than their Third World counterparts: some still talk in abstractions, some do only formal "academic" theology, some are "liberals" in their own countries but insensitive to the injustices their countries perpetuate elsewhere, and only a small group are "in active opposition to the existing global injustices and the complicity of the churches and universities in relation to these" (Fabella and Torres, eds., *Doing Theology in a Divided World*, p. xi). First World theologians also discovered that not every person from the Third World is a revolutionary. The air, in other words, was cleared. An interesting device was used to begin the meetings: "storytelling." Case histories of struggle in five different countries (Holland, Nicaragua, Sri Lanka, Sweden, and Canada) were presented, as a way of entering into theological discussion by other than the traditional academic, cerebral route.

Other insights from the conference: Johann Baptist Metz, perhaps the European theologian most sensitive to Third World concerns, suggested that "we are standing at the end of the European-centered era of Christianity." The presence and power of women theologians was stronger than at any previous conference. A recognition that theology must be reconceived as "a theology at the service of the people" was strongly urged by Samuel Rayan of India. An attempt to join Christian spirituality and "the praxis of the prophets" was evident throughout.

Although his words were written before the Geneva conference, James Cone's hopeful appraisal is truer after Geneva than before:

> On the basis of Third World theologians' dialogue together, it is clear to us all that the future of each of our theologies is found in our struggles together. I am firmly convinced that black theology must not limit itself to the race struggle in the United States but must find ways to join in solidarity with the struggles of the poor in the Third World. The universal dimensions of the gospel message require that we struggle not only for ourselves but for all. For there can be no freedom for any one of us until all of us are free. Any theology that falls short of this universal vision is not Christian and thus cannot be identified with the Jesus who died on the cross and was resurrected so that everyone might be liberated in God's emerging Kingdom [Fabella and Torres, eds., *The Irruption of the Third World*, p. 244].

The emerging role of women in EATWOT has been noted in passing, and must now be made more precise. At the New Delhi conference in 1981, "Irruption of the Third World," there was an "irruption within the irruption" by women delegates. The flash point was the sexist language of the liturgies, and Marianne Katoppo of Indonesia, speaking for the women delegates, sternly warned the other delegates to watch their use of language "about God and before God." The language issue only exposed more deeply-seated issues such as the fact that—in 1981!—not a single formal paper for the conference had been assigned to a woman. Some male delegates even treated the internal "irruption" as a joke. But EATWOT, as Mercy Oduyoye insisted, must issue a challenge not only to the West's "dominant theology," but to "the maleness of Christian theology worldwide."

As a result, a woman's group was established within EATWOT, and held an international conference of its own at Oaxtepec, Mexico, in 1986, on the theme "Doing Theology from Third World Womens' Perspective," with twenty-six delegates from Asia, Africa, and Latin America. A summary of highlights from the "Final Document" will reveal the power and depth that Third World women were bringing to the concerns of EATWOT.

1. *The reality of the oppression and struggle of women.* This is a common experience on all three continents, and is economic, social, political, cultural, racial, sexual, religious, and often experienced within family units.

Withal, women's liberation is seen as part of the liberation promised all poor and oppressed peoples.

2. *Vital aspects of womens' experience of God in emerging spiritualities.* Women's theology comprises "spiritual experience rooted in action for justice . . . in common with all those who fight for life." The main elements of women's theology are compassion and solidarity expressed in action for the sake of life for all. "We as women feel called to do scientific theology passionately, a theology based on feeling as well as knowledge, on wisdom as well as on science, a theology made not only with the mind but also with the heart, the body, the womb."

3. *Women and the Bible.* There is a special problem in reading the Bible: "We women face the constant challenge of interpreting texts that are against us." Such texts must be seen as peripheral rather than normative. Instead of rejecting the Bible because of its oppressive and patriarchal elements, women must "mine" deeper into scripture, highlighting elements "that portray women as individuals in their own right."

4. *Women and the church.* Women keep the churches alive but are still powerless and voiceless within them. In most churches they are excluded from leadership and ordination. Women's leadership in the base communities is one sign of a new era, for both women and the church.

5. *Women and christology.* Women find their liberation from all discrimination grounded in the person and praxis of Jesus Christ. Christology everywhere must be contextualized:

> In Africa, Christology has to do with apartheid, racial discrimination, militarism, deficiency syndromes that come in foreign aid packages, and genocide perpetrated through family-planning programs. In Asia, with the massive poverty, sexual exploitation, and racial, ethnic, caste, and religious discrimination, Christology incorporates the efforts to draw out the humanizing elements in other religions. In Latin America, where poverty and oppression often give rise to a tendency to use religion to reinforce a passive and fatalistic attitude to life, Christology is necessarily connected with the preferential option for the poor. In short, to Christologize means to be committed to the struggle for a new society [Fabella and Oduyoye, eds., *With Passion and Compassion: Third World Women Doing Theology*, p. 188].

Women must not interpret Jesus' suffering in the wrong way however: "Suffering that is inflicted by the oppressor and is passively accepted does not lead to life; it is destructive and demonic." But suffering that is "part of the struggle for the sake of God's reign" is redeeming, and "evocative of the rhythm of pregnancy, delivery, and birth."

More Participants on Stage

In the light of the EATWOT story, we can distinguish other new participants on stage. Our first impression is of a dazzling array of characters, points of view, and special concerns, described by a variety of descriptive terms. We encounter proponents of a theology of development (fast being replaced by a theology of liberation); a theology of revolution (disavowed by Gustavo in a variety of places); a theology of "signs of the times" (growing out of Vatican II); a theology of exodus and, alternately, a theology of captivity; a theology of struggle, particularly articulated in the Philippines; Asian liberation theology, dealing with the fact that Christians in Asia are a tiny minority of the total population; *minjung* theology in Korea; and a Jewish theology of liberation as well.[2]

With their differing emphases, proponents are agreed that there is oppression worldwide and that those who are victims of oppression are now seeking to throw off the shackles of bondage, convinced that God is involved in the struggle with them, and that however long the struggle for liberation lasts, the final word *will* be liberation, not further bondage.

In addition to these global expressions, liberation movements have grown up in the United States. We confront not a single North American "theology of liberation," but a variety of *theologies* of liberation in various ways indigenous to the United States experience.[3]

The initial liberation theology on North American soil is *black theology*, which has grown directly out of the U.S. black experience of oppression, victimization, marginalization, and powerlessness. In one of those acts of prescience of which he was frequently capable, Dietrich Bonhoeffer prophesied back in 1931 that it might be the black churches that would save America. The new sense of concern for justice in American Christianity has sprung in significant measure from black theology and the black churches. And as we have seen in the discussion of EATWOT, affinities between the black experience in North America and the black experience in South Africa have been clarified, and representatives of the two continents are finding much in each others' theological reflection for mutual empowerment.

A second indigenous North American liberation theology is *feminist theology*. Feminist movements have become worldwide, but the contemporary articulation of theology from a feminist perspective had its origins in the United States. This movement, like black theology, has grown out of the experience of human beings who have undergone oppression, victimization, marginalization, and powerlessness. It is symptomatic of the widespread oppression of women that links with women elsewhere were quickly established by North American feminists; local realizations of outrage could be replicated globally with dreary ease.

Particularly distinctive has been a concern among *Amerindians* to create a theology springing from their situation of oppression. This theology, which has distinctively American geographical and cultural roots, also shares affinities with the black South African situation, where government policies disclose disturbing parallels to the treatment Amerindians continue to receive in the United States. Connections to Latin America are also clear, where Amerindian groups, often referred to as indigenes, are counterparts of Amerindians in the United States who were similarly displaced from their ancestral lands.

A fourth distinctive North American liberation theology has grown out of *gay and lesbian oppression*. While this issue is by no means uniquely North American, the most significant articulations of such a theology have again come from the United States.

Because the development of theology out of a specific context is so widely shared, further versions of liberation theology spread rapidly among other groups in the United States. Puerto Ricans, Hispanic-Americans, Asian-Americans, Filipino-Americans, all claim the right to be heard on their own cultural, economic, and class terms, rather than being forced to adopt the framework of an alien "Western" mode of doing theology.

While all these positions have distinctive emphases that must not be artificially conflated, they do share common characteristics already noted: they are responses to oppression, victimization, marginalization, and powerlessness. They have needed time and space to develop a sense of self-awareness and self-worth ("black is beautiful," "The Lord's my shepherd and he knows I'm gay," "Christ in a poncho," and so forth). They have usually been "separatist" at first, drawing apart in order that self-discovery and self-empowerment can be well internalized. In varying degrees, however, their advocates are drawing closer to one another, because of an overlapping of concerns, and also because together they can wield power for effecting change that they can never hope to wield individually.

2. Intensifying the Plot: The *Kairos* Factor

So there are now a great many participants on stage — the biblical phrase "cloud of witnesses" comes to mind — deeply committed to transforming the human situation from overwhelming oppression to at least rough-hewn justice. As the numbers increase, the challenges intensify. Three documents have already been inserted into the script from members of the cast in South Africa, Central America, and seven countries (the Philippines, South Korea, Namibia, South Africa, El Salvador, Nicaragua, and Guatemala), setting forth fresh options that force the rest to take sides.

All three challenges are built around a biblical word for time, the word *kairos*, which means a special time fraught with high consequences, a moment for decisive action that must be seized before the opportunity is lost, a time (as the South African document puts it) "when God visits people to offer them a unique opportunity for repentance and conversion, for change and decisive action. It is a moment of truth, a crisis" (*The Kairos Document*, p. 33). *Kairos* is to be distinguished from another biblical word *chronos* (from which we get "chron-ology"), which means clock-time, ordinary time, the sequence of moment after moment.

Are we in an "ordinary time" (*chronos*), in which nothing special happens, or are we in a "special" time (*kairos*), when great possibilities for transformation are present? All three documents affirm the latter, signaling that the plot will indeed intensify, and serious choices will have to be made. The documents are the product of lengthy involvement by "grassroots" persons living on "the underside of history," who start by examining their own situation and their commitment to struggle, and then move into the "second act," reflecting theologically about what this means for their future.

The Kairos Document: *South Africa*[4]

The South African document, issued in September 1985, has generated more discussion than any previous South African church document—which is saying a great deal. After acknowledging that the church in South Africa is divided (even though both oppressors and oppressed claim membership in the church), the signatories present critiques of "state theology" and "church theology," followed by a description of the needed "prophetic theology," and concluding with "a challenge to action." Denunciation, then annunciation.

"State theology" justifies "the status quo with its racism, capitalism, and totalitarianism," on theological grounds, and does so "by misusing theological concepts and biblical texts for its own political purposes" (p. 3). Romans 13 (the biblical bottom line for those who claim divine sanction for evil empires) is treated exegetically to show that it does *not* provide sanction for tyranny; the concept of "law and order" is examined in order to refute state actions that make national security more important than justice; the threat of "communism" is exposed as a fear tactic to buttress the status quo; and the god of the state is identified as an idol, "the god of superior weapons," the "god who exalts the proud and humbles the poor"—a god, in short, who is "the devil disguised as Almighty God—the antichrist." "State theology," in a word, is not only heretical but blasphemous (p. 8).

"Church theology" fares no better. While there is "cautious" criticism of apartheid within the English-speaking churches, criticism is superficial, since it does not rely on in-depth analysis but on three stock ideas that are easily distorted:

1. Premature pleas for *reconciliation* and peace become counterfeit, since "there can be no true reconciliation and no genuine peace *without justice*" (p. 9, italics in original). There are some conflicts in which one side is right and the other wrong, and Christians are not to "try to reconcile good and evil, God and the devil."

2. Nor can there be reconciliation without *repentance*, something singularly lacking in the upholders of apartheid. What is needed—and what "church theology" has failed to provide—is "a biblical theology of direct confrontation with the forces of evil rather than a theology of reconciliation with sin and the devil" (p. 11).

3. The same problem is faced in church appeals to *justice*. The "justice

of reform" is a sham for it is justice determined by oppressors, consisting of no more than small concessions here and there. Reforms cannot come from the white power structure at the top. "True justice, God's justice, demands a radical change of structures. This can only come from below, from the oppressed themselves" (p. 12).

Church theology also errs in the selectivity of its appeal to *nonviolence*. Violence is understood by "church theology" as throwing stones, burning cars, looting or rioting, with no recognition of "the structural, institutional, and unrepentant violence of the state, and especially the oppressive and naked violence of the police and the army" (p. 13). There is something deeply wrong with a position that counsels nonviolence to the oppressed, but accepts the violence of the oppressor as a legitimate instrument for upholding an evil state.

The fundamental problem with "church theology" is its superficiality and its lack of social analysis and political strategy. Believing that the real task of the church is in the private or individualistic sphere, it assumes that changing a few individuals will lead to changes in social structures. It fails to take account of the corporate arena where an evil system destroys all who challenge it.

Since state theology and church theology are inadequate, what would "prophetic theology" look like? Various characteristics are suggested: it would be biblical, reading the signs of the times, calling people to action, abounding in hope, confrontational, practical, and pastoral, naming the sins and evils of South Africa as "an offense against God," and announcing "the hopeful good news of future liberation, justice, and peace, as God's will and promise, naming the ways of bringing this about and encouraging people to take action" (p. 18).

There are two conflicting projects vying for control in South Africa, and no compromise is possible between them:

> The structural inequality (political, social, and economic) expressed in discriminatory laws, institutions, and practices has led the people of South Africa into a virtual civil war and rebellion against tyranny [p. 22].

Tyranny is an operative word. Tyranny is an *illegitimate* authority, and the response demanded of Christians is clear: it is a "Christian duty to refuse to cooperate with tyranny and to do whatever we can to remove it" (p. 22). The more that tyranny is opposed, the more tyrannical will be the attempt to crush the opposition. There is only one way out of this impasse:

> A regime that is in principle the enemy of the people cannot suddenly begin to rule in the interests of all the people. *It can only be replaced by another government* — one that has been elected by the majority of

the people with an explicit mandate to govern in the interests of all the people [p. 24, italics added].

But . . . to work for radical change does not justify hatred. Christians are called to love their enemies. How is this to be spelled out in South Africa today? "The most loving thing we can do for *both* the oppressed *and* for our enemies who are oppressors is to eliminate the repression, remove the tyrants from power, and establish a just government for the common good of *all the people*" (pp. 24–25, italics in original).

The treatment of "prophetic theology" closes with a ringing appeal to *hope*. The Bible not only describes oppression, but liberation from oppression, and does so in hopeful terms, for God is not neutral but "always on the side of the oppressed" (Ps. 103:6). Jesus' promise of "good news to the poor" and "liberation for the oppressed" is the word of annunciation for today. "The road to hope is going to be very hard and very painful. . . . But God is with us" (p. 27).

The final chapter of the *Kairos* Document offers a "Challenge to Action." Since God *does* "side with the oppressed," there are a number of directions in which Christians must go: (1) participation in the struggle—that is, no sideline Christianity; (2) transformation of church activities, so that "ordinary" events—worship, communion, baptisms, funerals, Bible study—are "reshaped to be more fully consistent with a prophetic faith;" (3) special campaigns in addition to regular church activities, carefully coordinated with the goals and activities of political organizations "that truly represent the grievances and demands of the people" (p. 29); (4) civil disobedience when necessary, as an enacted statement that "the church cannot collaborate with tyranny," as a way for all Christians to witness to the need for a change of government, and as a demonstration of taking responsibility seriously; and finally (5) moral guidance, through which the church not only makes its position clear, but joins with others in taking seriously "the *moral duty* of all who are oppressed to resist oppression and to struggle for liberation and justice" (p. 30, italics in original).

The concluding words are a cry for help:

Finally, we would also like to repeat our call to our Christian brothers and sisters throughout the world to give us the necessary support in this regard so that the daily loss of so many young lives may be brought to a speedy end [p. 31].

Kairos: Central America[5]

Partly in response to this call, Christians in Central America began a similar process of reflection, issuing a statement of their own in April 1988, *Kairos: Central America, a Challenge to the Churches of the World*, signed by more than one hundred priests, lay persons, women religious, evangelical Protestant pastors, theologians, and a few Roman Catholic bishops. As in the case of the South African document, there were further signatories who for reasons of personal safety could not be publicly listed.

Like its predecessor, this statement begins not with an outline of Christian faith or a succession of abstract principles, but with a description of life in Central America—a picture very different from the one routinely offered by the U.S. State Department.

The picture is stark. Some two hundred thousand persons, almost all of them poor, have died violently in the past twenty-five years, during an incessant war attributable to national oligarchies financed by the United States, which use military means to keep economic and political control over the region. The overall pattern is U.S. military support for tyrants, aimed at destroying people who want to take control of their own lives. In this situation, Central American churches, which used to support the repressive regimes, are now changing sides at great personal cost. So this portrayal is validated in the shed blood and broken lives of tens of thousands of victims, whose friends and children are now saying, "Enough! Our faith tells us not to accept this any longer."

The analysis is followed by a consideration, "Seeing This Historic Hour in Central America from a Perspective of Faith." What do the Bible and Christian tradition say about changing the situation?

The writers get at this question by asking another question: "Where are the signs of the kingdom in this situation?" Where, even in the tragedy and turmoil, is God already at work? For them, the major sign of the presence of the kingdom is that *"the poor become subjects of history"* (italics added). For centuries, the poor had no control over their lives; they were objects and pawns—regarded as subhuman and expendable, who were ordered about and destroyed at the whim of tiny minorities who held power.

That is now changing. Despite terrible ongoing repression, the poor are now organizing to acquire power. The document calls them "servants of Jahweh," those who redeem oppressive situations by their suffering and struggle. They join Mary in proclaiming that the mighty will be cast down from their thrones and the poor lifted up. They announce that God is on the side of the oppressed and will help them in their ongoing struggle. They remind others that Jesus himself was born and lived among the poor, and ministered to them. They recognize that in their case, as in Jesus' case, the price of siding with the poor is likely to be persecution, and their actions announce that they are willing to pay the price. The role call of their martyrs is humbling.

The "servants of Jahweh" are convinced that they are not alone in their struggle; they believe they are participants in the ongoing biblical story of God's opting for the poor. They believe furthermore that working for liberation is a pointer toward salvation, for although a social utopia on earth is not the equivalent of the kingdom of God, the two cannot be separated. They believe it matters to God whether we are creating just or unjust social structures short of the final consummation. So there are "signs of the kingdom" in the world today. Christians are to affirm them, identify with them, and help them spread.

But there are also signs of the "anti-kingdom," realities that are clearly opposed to God's will and must be opposed by God's children. The true sins against the Holy Spirit in Central America today include such things as the legitimization of conquest and genocide; the equation of faith with domination and oppression; puppet governments that falsely represent themselves as something other than what they are; forms of transnational capitalism that exploit rather than help the poor; and claims that Christians should be "above politics," which means in practical terms giving silent approval to tyrannical regimes.

We in the United States are included in the document's denunciation: we are seen as accomplices in sin against the Holy Spirit when we "remain entrenched in comforts," using distance and lack of clear information as excuses to remain uninvolved.

The document also acknowledges that not all sin is on the "other side." There is sin also "in the people's movements." It is hard for people working for social change to admit their own shortcomings, and it is a sign of integrity when they do. "Our fight against sin," the writers say, "is also directed against whatever sin there might be in the means that we use in our struggle on behalf of the kingdom." They pledge to keep a critical eye on their own activities, to denounce whatever in them is wrong, and to see themselves as "sinners who are called continually to conversion."

Things are clearer today than they have ever been in Central America, and this creates a kairos, a decisive hour calling for action. Never before have the churches been so engaged with the poor and the God of the poor. Never before has evil been so nakedly exposed. The time must be seized.

How is the time to be seized? The closing sections recommend that the *first* response must be "an option for the poor." Christians and churches must make clear choices:

> You are on the side of the people or you have become an accomplice of their oppressors; you are on the side of the poor or you are with the Empire: [you are] with the God of Life or with the idols of death.

A *second* response is for the churches to "nourish the people's hope." Christians especially are called to discern hope in the midst of hopelessness. Where one would expect discouragement and despair, Christians proclaim hope. This is a gift of the gospel: the awareness that the struggle, while real and lifelong, is finally going to lead to justice rather than injustice, and that there will be a future for "the least of these our brothers and sisters."

Third, and most important, the document calls on Christians to be "radical in our service of the kingdom." This may well mean taking a leftist political stance, but it means fundamentally getting to the *radix,* the root of things, and taking sides, recognizing that so-called neutrality ultimately advances repression, hunger, and death squads. In sum:

> We want to help our churches to overcome all dichotomies and reductionisms, to become incarnate in the people, to accept the people's prophetic and priestly roles, to abandon their supposed neutrality and overcome their internal division while taking an unequivocal stand for the poor.

Kairos International: "The Road to Damascus"[6]

A third *kairos* document was released on July 19, 1989, the tenth anniversary of the triumph of the Sandinistas in Nicaragua and the beginning of a new Latin American reality of repudiating subservience to tyrannical regimes sponsored and subsidized by the United States, "the giant of the North." This time there is a wider representation of voices, including Christians from the Philippines, South Korea, Namibia, South Africa, El Salvador, Nicaragua, and Guatemala, who share the fact that they all live in the midst of violent political conflict, and that within their churches are people on both sides of the conflict. They exemplify "two antagonistic forms of Christianity"—a variety of liberation theologies on the one hand, and right wing, conservative, "state theologies" on the other. The intent of the writers is to lay bare the historical and political roots of this conflict, to reaffirm the faith of the poor and oppressed, to condemn the sins of Christians on the right who oppress, exploit, and kill, to acknowledge their own sins and shortcomings, and to call to conversion those who have strayed from the truth of Christian faith and commitment. Hence the imagery of the "Damascus road," on which Saul was led to a decisive turnabout by his confrontation with Jesus.

The document was more than two years in the making, involving dozens of conferences, hundreds of participants, and thousands of signatories. It is both a proclamation of faith and a call to conversion.

1. The *roots of the conflict* go back as far as Cain and Abel, when Cain killed his brother "despite the fact that they had just offered sacrifices to the same God"(§1). There is similar conflict throughout the biblical story, which continues in Christian history as Christianity moves from being a threat to the Roman empire to becoming its official religion. When "Christian nations" started colonizing, conquest and evangelism went hand in hand; the cross blessed the sword to the advantage of the colonizers and the detriment of the colonized. The results were ugly: murder, genocide, enslavement, deculturization, racism, oppression of women and children, and exploitation of the earth. But those so abused began to rebel and in some cases defeated the colonizers. Christians were found on both sides of the struggle.

Today, therefore, colonization is more subtle; it involves economic rather than political control, and goes by the name of imperialism, featuring multinational corporations, unfair trade quotas and barriers, and military bases with nuclear weapons throughout the world, able to enforce the views of the imperialists. The result is many replicas of the "national security state." The effects of imperialism are as baleful as those of colonization, dehumanizing the majority of the world's people. But once again, movements of popular resistance to imperialism are growing, just as they did earlier against colonialism. "The movement of organized and conscious people marks the coming of age of a new historical subject" (§15).

The imperial powers, needless to say, do not take kindly to the uprisings of people who have heretofore remained pliant and docile, and the main instrument of their counterinsurgency is "low-intensity conflict" (to be treated late in this chapter) in which the great powers use mercenary troops and keep the level of killing just low enough to prevent world outcries of protest at what is nothing but murder given official sanction. The rest of the world fails to realize that what is perceived by the great powers as "low-intensity conflict" is *total war* to the victims, for they are wounded, tortured, kidnapped, murdered, and otherwise exploited by mercenaries with every kind of sophisticated military weapon short of nuclear arms (§20).

Christianity has become an important tool in this conflict, with many Christians committing themselves to the people's struggle, while other Christians support the ideology of imperialist control. "The church itself has become a site of struggle." But the issues daily become more nakedly revealed: "Never before have we been so conscious of the political implications of Christian faith" (§28). What about God's involvement in all this? If God is not on both sides, on whose side is God found?

2. The analysis of the roots of the conflict leads to a strong affirmation of *the faith of the poor*. This demands a break with the faith of the past. The God of the missionaries was far too often "a God who blessed the powerful, the conquerors, the colonizers" (§30), who demanded resignation in the face of oppression. The Jesus they learned of was "barely human," floating above history and all conflict (§31). He "condescended" to the poor rather than entering the struggle with them. But the hearers of such preaching began to raise questions: Why does God allow us to suffer so much? Why does God always side with the rich and powerful?

All this led to reading the Bible "with new eyes," and discovering that "Jesus was one of us," both poor and condemning the rich. He was "the very opposite of what we had been taught." His message of the kingdom of God was of a kingdom for the poor. It was not another world but "this world completely transformed in accordance with God's plan" (§§35-38).

Jesus invoked the wrath of the political and religious authorities, who branded him a "subversive" and killed him on that account (§39). But the poor "can now see the true face of God in the poor Jesus — persecuted and oppressed like them" (§40). So today, the poor "want no gods except the God who was in Jesus" (§31):

God is on the side of the poor, the oppressed, the persecuted. When this faith is proclaimed and lived in a situation of political conflict between the rich and the poor, and when the rich and the powerful reject this faith and condemn it as heresy, we can read the signs and discern something more than a crisis. We are faced with a *kairos*, a moment of truth, a time for decision, a time of grace, a God-given opportunity for conversion and hope [§43].

3. How does the world look from this rediscovered perspective? The signatories next discuss "Our Prophetic Mission," an extensive treatment of contemporary sins that must be exposed and condemned, all of them variants on, or consequences of, the primal sin of *idolatry*, the worship of a false God that "serves the total war being waged against the people" (§47). "In our countries, the worship of money, power, privilege, and pleasure has certainly replaced the worship of God" (§50). Such faith is anti-people, and because of that "it demands absolute submission and blind obedience" (§51). It is embodied in the national security state:

> It was for the sake of security that the people of ancient times turned to the Baals and other idols. Today, our oppressors turn to money and military power and to the so-called security forces. *But their security is our insecurity.* We experience their security as intimidation and repression, terror, rape, and murder. Those who turn to the idols for security demand our insecurity as the price that must be paid. They fear us as a threat to their security [53, italics added].

Idolatry demands a scapegoat on whom to pin the blame when things go badly. Anyone with socialist "leanings," for example, is a perfect scapegoat, and can be destroyed as a threat. This perspective justifies persecution of the church, and economic repression that leads to the starvation of children, a replica of sacrificing children to idols in Jeremiah's time. Massacres, death squads, contras—are all justified in the necessity for scapegoats.

The strongest denunciations (at least to North American ears) are launched against *heresy*, "a form of belief that selects some parts of the Christian message and rejects other parts, in such a way that those doctrines which are selected for belief become themselves distorted" (§62). Just as South Africans have declared apartheid a heresy, the signers of the Damascus Road document declare unequivocally *"We denounce all forms of right-wing Christianity as heretical"* (§63, italics added).

Eight biting paragraphs that defy succinct analysis spell out this contention in exquisite detail. The main charge is that rightwing Christianity, either consciously or unconsciously, provides "legitimation of idolatry" (§64), and insists on blind obedience to authority. It thereby "promotes authoritarianism and domination" (§67), and in trying to keep religion out of politics invokes a type of religion that supports the status quo. The political consequence is that rightwing Christianity "is fanatically anticommunist," and identifies Christianity exclusively with capitalist values. The war against communism is a holy war: "Christian values like loving your enemy, forgiving seventy times seven, compassion, solidarity, and calling the sinner to conversion are conveniently forgotten once a person or group is labelled 'communist' or 'subversive'" (§71).

This is not the worst. *Apostasy* goes a step further and "abandons the Christian faith altogether" (§72), although it pretends not to have done so. Priests, pastors, nuns, theologians, church leaders, base communities are attacked, harassed, imprisoned, tortured by apostates. Military chaplains defend policies of total war. Vicious attacks are leveled at liberation theology.

Hypocrisy is also scored. Hypocrites today follow the line of caution and "prudence." They do not want to rock the boat. They remain quiet when citizens disappear. They claim to be nonpartisans who want "balance." They favor democracy, but "do not wish the people to exercise power effectively" (§78). They employ a double standard: nonviolence by the poor, military intimidation by the state. "They are either part of the rich and powerful or afraid of them" (§77).

Idolatry is a sin against the first commandment. *Blasphemy* is a sin against the second, taking God's name in vain. "It is blasphemy to misuse the name of God in defense of imperialism" (§80), so the writers maintain, and then make specific reference to the Institute for Religion and Democracy, a rightwing religious lobby in the Untied States whose distortions of the truth are cited as modern instances of blasphemy. The same is true of priests who "provide spiritual service to leaders of death squads" (§80). Conclusion: "To invoke the name of the God of life to justify death and destruction is blasphemy" (§80).

4. In the light of this litany of evil and wrongdoing, it is not surprising that the penultimate section is entitled "The Call to Conversion." The Damascus Road experience—Saul's transformation from a defender of the status quo to Paul the participant in a movement designed to "turn the world upside down" (Acts 17:6)—indicates that change is possible for anyone. Saul was confronted with two images of God—the god on the side of the repressive political authorities and the God who sided with "one who had been crucified as a blasphemer." Everyone (including the writers and signers of the document) is in need of being "converted again from the idol of Mammon to the worship of the true God" (§87). "While we see clearly the idolatry, the heresy, the hypocrisy, and the blasphemy of others, we need to search our own hearts for remnants of the same sins" (§91).

The "Conclusion" presents the stakes as high. What is at stake is not just "morality or ethics," but a situation in which "the name of God is being blasphemously misused." To counteract this, Christians must organize just as the oppressors do:

Solidarity is not optional if we are to promote the cause of God in the world. We call on fellow Christians in the Third World, in industrial capitalist countries, and in socialist countries to build a network of exchange and cooperation [Conclusion].

Is There a "Kairos Situation" in North America?

Each *kairos* document ends with a similar plea for help; the problems are too overwhelming to be tackled alone; only united efforts by the world's oppressed will bring transformation.

Where does this leave North Americans, who are uniformly identified as part of the problem rather than part of the solution? Is there a *kairos* for us as well, a "critical time" in which decisive decisions must be made?

I believe we must answer this question in the affirmative, and that our responsibility as Christians today is to discern the shape of that answer in the light of the *kairos* documents:

1. We must first of all acknowledge *the accuracy of their analysis* of our role in their lives. They strip away the blinders of our self-deception and force us to acknowledge that the way they perceive us is not only "the way they perceive us" but the way we truly are. Our national timidity in dealing with South Africa has made us complicit in racism; our determination to manipulate Central American countries to our advantage has led to decades of carnage; our consistent support of all dictators who do our bidding has been replicated throughout the world; our national phobia about "communism" has made it possible for the right wing to jeopardize human rights at home and destroy human lives abroad.

The clearest example of our complicity has been the conscious adoption by our leaders of the policy of "low-intensity conflict" as a way to destroy peoples' uprisings for freedom. The aim of this policy is to exert sufficient pressure — military, political, economic, psychological, or any necessary combination thereof — to prevent uprisings or revolutions that would jeopardize American interests or American prestige, but not so severe as to engender significant protest or outrage at home. The reasoning goes: if we can hire mercenary troops to kill and be killed for our designs, and do so without inordinate "body counts," the public will not object. But if there are massive numbers of casualties, and particularly if the casualties were to be American boys, the policy would backfire, and we would be forced either to retreat ingloriously or to move to *high*-intensity conflict, with the risk that this would be unacceptable to the folks at home and disastrous to our "international image." The strategy is to "go public" as little as possible, and when it is necessary to do so to "go public" with the best propaganda tools in the business. What the policy fails to admit is that (as the writers of the Damascus Road document remind us) low-intensity conflict to us is total war to them. But that, the defenders of the policy tell us, is simply the price we must pay for American hegemony. What is so appalling is not that the United States incidentally does some unfortunate things in upholding its "place in the sun," but that, as Jack Nelson-Pallmeyer points out, *we are engaged in an active, all-out war against the poor of the world*, and are willing to do whatever is necessary to win that war decisively.[7]

2. When we acknowledge complicity in such policies, we are at the beginning of a Damascus Road experience of our own, a radical turnabout and a commitment to walk in another direction. This means that our decisive time will be acknowledgment that, in biblical imagery, *we are servants in the pharaoh's court* and must take steps to disengage. In the biblical story, the pharaoh was an all-powerful monarch, not unlike Julius Caesar, Adolf Hitler, or Genghis Kahn. The biblical story is important today because a handful of dissidents—the Jews—refused to "say uncle" to the pharaoh. Moses, their somewhat reluctant leader, had grown up in the court and was called by God to break with all that it represented.

There is no blueprint available—at least not yet—for doing this today. To the reformists, it may mean deciding to stay within the court and use their influence for long-range change. To others, it will mean seeking to subvert the intentions of the pharaoh, to thwart the consolidation of his policies, and to change direction as soon as possible. Whether this can be done through the ballot, or by persuasion in the public forum, or by non-violent resistance, or by disengagement from the court itself and adoption of a different lifestyle, or by joining more militant groups committed to global change, is not yet clear.[8] What *is* clear is that this is a matter for urgent attention for those whom the Central American *kairos* statement calls the "servants of Jahweh": the pharaoh's plans must be thwarted.

3. This will present *a time of testing for the churches*. How far are mainline Protestant and Catholic churches ready to go to engage in a radical challenge to the pharaoh's power? The answer is clear: not very far. (A recent attempt within the Presbyterian Church of the United States of America to explore becoming a "resistance community," was unceremoniously and decisively shot down.) In the language of the South African *kairos* document, we too need to move beyond "state theology" and "church theology," and the institutional prospects for doing so are minimal. Individual Christians committed to radical change will therefore have to fashion alternative structures within their churches (similar to the "base communities" in Latin America) through which to move closer to a "prophetic theology." This will mean a lot of denunciation of the church and the state, since both move with Neanderthal slowness when challenged to change.

On the other hand, churches are not solely the defenders of the status quo. They have another side that occasionally surfaces: standing with victims, calling the pharaoh and lesser monarchs to account, and discovering that creative resources from the heritage sometimes reappear in times of need.

There are two reasons why, no matter what else is done, the liberation struggle must continue within the churches. *First* of all, the churches themselves need a liberation message that can deliver *them* from co-optation by the pharaohs of this world. The breath of the Holy Spirit that is blowing today in Third World churches could fan new flames of ardor and commitment even in North American ecclesiastical establishments. The *second* reason for engaging in the liberation struggle within the churches is that there are no other vehicles in society with more potential for keeping the struggle alive. The recuperative power of the gospel can help even churches to avoid commitment to enticing ideologies, particularly those of the right wing, that try to co-opt liberation concerns to their own ends. Attacks on rightwing Christianity as "blasphemy" will have to be as pointed as those of the creators of the Damascus Road document.

4. How, then, do we begin an assault on the pharaoh's court? Surely by "speaking truth to power." It can be questioned whether middle-class persons have any significant influence in a world dominated by corporate structures in the control of a tiny power elite. Our illusion of power (the ballot, "shareholder resolutions," dissent in public life, and so on) may be greater than its actuality. And yet, as long as there are structures that provide access to the molding of public opinion, we are obligated to use them.

One way of "speaking truth to power" is to concentrate on the issue of power itself. In most Third World countries, for example, where the internal power of a dictator may be inordinate, the power of such countries on the international scene is virtually nil: they have no control over their own destinies, they cannot decide what crops to grow if shareholders in a multinational corporation rule otherwise, they cannot gain access to world markets save as First World nations allow, and they are saddled with debts so massive that they can never be free of immobilizing indebtedness. In such situations, the Christian message is one of liberation *from* such dependency, and liberation *for* control over their lives. They must pray and struggle for power.

In North America, however, the situation is different and the liberating message is different. If Third World nations scarcely know the taste of power, First World nations are drunk with it. If Third World nations have too little power, First World nations have too much, and with awesome consistency use it destructively. The task in *our* situation, therefore, in "speaking truth to power," is to insist that rather than seeking more power for ourselves, we must share it; and to insist that our remaining power must be used creatively rather than destructively. Stated so baldly, the insistences sound like platitudes, but the truth is that if we do not begin to share power, it will finally be taken from us, and that if we continue to use it destructively, we will reap the seeds of a whirlwind that will destroy us.

3. Joining the Company

It is not enough just to enlarge the cast and intensify the plot. We must also join the company, move from being spectators to being participants.

The comments above have initiated this process, but we must now take account of some of the difficulties this entails.

1. *On being an "oppressor."* As we have seen, Third World persons believe, and with good reason, that those of us in the First World are responsible for much of their misery, and (to drive the thrust all the way home) that white males are particularly culpable as oppressors.

Inasmuch as those who work most wholeheartedly for liberation are those who are most in need of liberation themselves, we must ask if there is any way in which those of us who are denominated "oppressors" can also claim to be among the "oppressed," and thus freed up to work for our own liberation as well as the liberation of others.

This is a suspicious-sounding argument, laden with self-serving potential, but I am persuaded by Basil Moore, writing out of the South African struggle, that it is a fruitful one to explore:

> I am prepared [he writes] to trust and stand alongside people who are fighting *for themselves* and their own freedom, if I know that their freedom is bound up with mine. I cannot wholeheartedly trust people who are fighting *for me*, for I fear that sooner or later they will tire of the struggle [in *The Challenge of Black Theology in South Africa*, p. 5, rendered in inclusive language, italics added].

All of us occupy territory on both sides of the hyphen in the "oppressor-oppressed" contrast, and Karen Lebacqz has made the point forcefully from within the feminist struggle. In *Justice in the Unjust World* (Augsburg, Minneapolis, 1987) she acknowledges that "by virtue of skin color, solvency, education, religious background, and nationality," she has advantages denied to most women. She is part of a group that rules and oppresses. She cannot experience the oppression that Jews have felt, or the desperately poor and disenfranchised, the wheelchair occupant, the black woman. And yet, she is a woman, "and even in white, solvent, well-educated Christian America, women are oppressed" (p. 14). So she can "speak both as an oppressor and as oppressed," and this posture, rather than being the basis for a cop-out, helps her "to temper my oppressor mentality by remembering my own experience of oppression and by attending to the voices of the oppressed" (p. 15).

There is also a need to identify the *source* of our own oppression. Unless we can "name" it, we will remain caught in its thrall, for we will be unaware of its hold over us. Surely our oppressor is not some group within our socio-economic system but the very socio-economic system itself. We have been conditioned by that system to accept a collection of "virtues" meant to be self-evident: the necessity of upward mobility, both personally and professionally; the willingness to compete, by fair means or foul, against those who threaten us in any way; a commitment to "look out for Number One," because no one else will; a conviction that the payoff for hard work is increasingly lavish material comfort; a willingness to put jobs ahead of families; and a belief that it is necessary to check our moral values at the entrance to the work place.⁹

We have allowed ourselves to be locked into social structures in which greed and exploitation are two sides of the same coin. We need to recognize that we have been oppressed without even knowing it, if we are to achieve liberation from such structures. In so doing, we will be contributing to the liberation of others as well, for they too are oppressed, in different ways, by those same structures.

Although I am not sanguine that "a revolution of the ruling class" will sweep through American society, I am convinced that if we are to "liberate the oppressed" today, it will come about only as we "name" our various oppressors and together challenge their sovereignty.

2. On being a "traitor to one's class." The cost of attempting this will be great. If it was our initial plight to be categorized by the left as sell-outs, it will be our increasing plight to be categorized by the right as traitors. "You have inherited a wonderful situation," we will be told, "the benefits of which are due to market capitalism, and you are not only ungracious to bite the hand that feeds you, but unpatriotic and disloyal as well." Concern for the social good will be viewed as a betrayal of the merits of "individual initiative"; concern for the poor will be linked to fomenting violence or espousing economic determinism, thus unveiling our ultimate apostasy: we are really "communists" at heart.

Such charges may not threaten us in the abstract, or when uttered by rightwing Christians (to be attacked by whom is a badge of honor), but when they are pronounced by friends, colleagues, and those who control our employment, the pressures to conform are great. Gustavo has some salient warnings for us:

> Rediscovering the other means entering [the other's] world. It also means a break with ours. . . . Solidarity with the poor means taking stock of the injustice on which this order is built, and of the countless means it employs to maintain itself. It also means understanding that one cannot be *for* the poor and oppressed if one is not *against* all that gives rise to the way people exploit one another [in Geffré, pp. 59–60, rendered in inclusive language. Italics in original].

Jürgen Moltmann and Douglas Meeks make a similar point:

> There is no solidarity with the victims of racism, sexism, and capitalism without the betrayal of their betrayers. Whoever wants genuine communion with the victims must become the enemy of their enemies. Thus if he or she comes from the ranks of the enemy, he or she will become a betrayer. To become free from the oppressive prison of

one's society means to become a "stranger among one's own people" [in *Christianity and Crisis*, December 15, 1978, p. 316].

3. *On broadening the base.* We have seen that among the indigenous liberation theologies, the initial need for separateness is gradually being replaced by a willingness to work together, not only for mutual self-enrichment, but because only in solidarity can they effect social change. There is nothing the pharaohs would like more than to have such groups absorbed with infighting.

Such groups are unlikely to be enchanted, at least yet, by the prospect of joining forces with white middle-class Americans; it is also unlikely that white middle-class Americans feel easy, as yet, among those with whom past associations have been conflictual. It is threatening to be asked to "broaden the base," and enter alliances with people coming from different backgrounds and perspectives. But doors must be set ajar now, so that later they can be entered. If the liberation struggle is to move beyond private dreams, the base must be broadened to include all persons genuinely committed to liberation, whether Christians or not. Otherwise, the Christian struggle for change will mire in ecclesiastical backwaters.

The real "broadening of the base" will not, however, entail only strategic alliances. It will entail the forging of new friendships, and to complete the full circle of our journey we must in conclusion call on Gustavo for direction. Commenting on Isaiah's statement that "the Lord God will wipe away tears from all faces, and the reproach of his people he will take away from all the earth" (Isa. 25.8), Gustavo writes:

> Woe to those whom the Lord finds dry-eyed because they could not bring themselves to solidarity with the poor and suffering of this world! If we are to receive from God the tender consolation promised by the prophet, we must make our own the needs of the oppressed; our hearts must be moved at seeing a wounded person by the wayside, be attuned to the sufferings of others, and be more sensitive to persons in conflict and confusion than to "the order of the day."
>
> Only if we know how to be silent and involve ourselves in the suffering of the poor will we be able to speak out of their hope. Only if we take seriously the suffering of the innocent and live in the mystery of the cross amid that suffering, but in the light of Easter, can we prevent our theology from being "windy arguments" (cf. Job 16:3) [*On Job*, p. 103].

On an even more personal and practical level:

> To be committed to the poor is to have friends among the poor. It is not enough to say you are committed to the poor as a culture. You must be committed to concrete persons and to living among them.

Then it is not so difficult to have friends. . . .

To share our lives with the poor, to have personal friendships, is very important. It's not enough to see the social group—class, race, culture, though that's important. It's the personal relationships that are ultimately important. If we don't have friendships with actual persons, I don't think we are really committed to the poor [interview in *The Other Side*, November 1987, p. 13].

Where, in all this, does *hope* enter? We have seen throughout our journey that hope is the precious and unexpected ingredient that the poor discover and nurture. It is not something the rest of us can create; we can only receive it. The Damascus Road document, the most specific in its denunciation of the sins that characterize the United States, nevertheless issues an urgent appeal in its final paragraph for solidarity with like-minded Christians, not only in Third World and socialist countries, but in "industrial capitalist countries" as well. In the light of our track record of destruction of the poor of the world, it is almost a miracle that those who have been our victims should hold out such an olive branch, and express an explicit desire to work with us.

This is a grace far beyond anything of which we are worthy, not to be refused or taken lightly, and it augers well for the creation of bonds of trust that can one day become cords of compassion. That we, being who we are, are invited to participate in the struggle, rather than being written off ahead of time, is the most hopeful line in the entire script.

CONCLUSION

Moving beyond Program Notes

The mediation of the historical task of the creation of a new humanity assures that liberation from sin and communion with God in solidarity with all persons — manifested in political liberation and enriched by its contributions — does not fall into idealism and evasion. But, at the same time, this mediation prevents these manifestations from becoming translated into any kind of Christian ideology of political action or a politico-religious messianism. Christian hope opens us, in an attitude of spiritual childhood, to the gift of the future promised by God. It keeps us from any confusion of the Kingdom with any one historical stage, from any idolatry toward unavoidably ambiguous human achievement, from any absolutizing of revolution.

—A Theology of Liberation, p. 139 (238)

These may be the most important words we need to hear from Gustavo in conclusion. They are important because they remind us of something about his perspective (which the critics frequently ignore), and because they point to something about our perspective (which we frequently ignore).

As far as *Gustavo's perspective* is concerned, the words remind us not only that he does not use the gospel to escape into "idealism" or "evasion," temptations that are totally out of character for him, but also that he does not use the gospel to escape into any of the following: equating the gospel message with a specific "Christian ideology of political action," identifying the gospel with a "political-religious messianism," confusing the kingdom of God with some historical stage of human development, developing idolatrous regard for ambiguous human achievements, or absolutizing revolution as the fullness of the gospel, temptations that are also totally out of character for him, despite what the critics say.

That is quite a list. It gives the lie once and for all to charges that Gustavo has "reduced" the gospel to "mere" human endeavor, or become idolatrously and uncritically committed to a single political option.

As far as *our perspective* is concerned, the words are a continous warning against complacency, and that is the warning we need most to hear. Pre-

183

cisely because the gospel cannot be reduced to the kind of equivalencies against which Gustavo warns us, there is need for vigilance of a sort that well-fed Christians would like to avoid. When so much that we have held dear is already under fire, we would like to feel that retreat from the most egregious sins of complicity is enough, and that we thereby earn the right to be left alone, holding on to whatever remaining comforts we can salvage in the process. If Gustavo is wrongly accused of trying to equate the gospel with an "absolutizing of revolution," we are rightly accused of trying to equate the gospel with an "absolutizing of the status quo," or at least opting only for cosmetic change.

These are things that Gustavo's vision will never let us do. We too need to be reminded that the struggle on earth for a just society is never over. If full justice will never be achieved simply by a revolution of the left, it will even more surely never be achieved by the domination of the right. Every advance, however secure it initially seems, is precarious, and can be neutralized not only by naked power, but by that same naked power clothing itself as good, and parading under such banners as "aid," "development," "moderation," "prudence" or (most tempting) "spiritual renewal."

One of our hymns begins, "The strife is o'er, the battle won." In heaven, perhaps; on earth, never. Never, as long as history lasts, will our program notes be enough, never will the script come to the last page, never will good emerge a permanent victor over evil, never will the resolution be achieved, never will the curtain come down to a conclusion.

There is no conclusion. The curtain stays up and the play goes on.

And we are on stage.

APPENDIX I

Writings by Gustavo

Liberation theology got underway not as a hardcover industry, but as a continuous exchange of talks, mimeographed materials (often clandestinely distributed), notes, reports on conferences, essays, and responses. After refining, many products of this process made their way into print in Spanish or Portuguese, and subsequently in English.

Gustavo's own writings are a bibliographer's nightmare. He (understandably) uses similar lecture materials on different occasions in different parts of the world; one of these will be published in a given country and then a somewhat similar, but not identical, lecture will be published in another country. English translations of both articles may subsequently appear in the United States, and sometimes different translations of the same article will be published. The disentangling of these sources makes the "synoptic problem" in New Testament scholarship seem like child's play in comparison.

Confronted once with a sizeable bibliography of his writings in many languages, Gustavo took one look and responded, "Is always the same article." The disclaimer, although containing a grain of truth, is too modest. For one who leads an "activist" life at home and a teaching-lecturing life abroad, he has created an extraordinary output.

The most accessible and fullest bibliography in English is Curt Cadorette, *From the Heart of the People,* pp. 130-38, which is also the best single volume for "situating" Gustavo in his Peruvian context. It is recommended to readers on both scores.

Books

This section describes all of Gustavo's books in English and Spanish, listed in the order of their original publication.

1. *Líneas pastorales de la Iglesia en América latina,* CEP, Lima, 1968, revised edition 1976, 75 pp.

This small book on "pastoral approaches of the church in Latin America" brings together themes Gustavo was presenting at conferences and retreats between 1964 and 1976. It is important as a reminder that pastoral rather than "political" concerns were paramount from the time of his earliest writing. The book reflects on the reality in which the church is living, and the kind of theology needed to respond to that reality.

Gustavo initially raises the question, "What is theology?" His treatment indicates some of the roots of his later formulation of theology as "critical reflexion on praxis in the light of the Word of God."

Part 1 describes four kinds of relationships to pastoral situations: the "Christendom" model, the "new Christendom" model, the new deepening and maturity in the faith, and the prophetic task in the church. Part 2 engages in a theological analysis of these four situations. The content of both parts anticipates materials treated in the early chapters of *A Theology of Liberation,* and the method used exemplifies the principle that theology is the "second act" rather than the first (see esp. pp. 10-11).

An appendix offers initial reflections on Vatican II from a Third World perspective, suggesting that it represents the passage from a church-centered to a Christ-centered ecclesiology (see p. 72).

2. *A Theology of Liberation: History, Politics, and Salvation,* Orbis, 1973, xi and 323 pp.; fifteenth anniversary edition, 1988, xlvi and 264 pp. (English translation of *Teología de la liberación: Perspectivas,* CEP, Lima, 1971).

From the moment of publication, this work received worldwide acclaim, and remains, twenty years later, the most important single treatment of liberation theology. Parts 1, 2, and 3 are a descriptive clearing of the air by examination of earlier concepts of the theological task and different responses the church has made historically ("Christendom," the "new Christendom," "the distinction of planes") along with options before the Latin American church today in moving through "developmentalism" and "dependency" into a process of "liberation."

Gustavo's creative theological contributions are contained in part 4, which comprises more than half the work. He treats "Liberation and Salvation" (chap. 9), "Encountering God in History" (chap. 10), "Eschatology and Politics" (chap. 11), "The Church: Sacrament of History" (chap. 12), and "Poverty: Solidarity and Protest" (chap. 13). An important indication of his methodology is that "The New Humanity" is treated in chapters 9-11 before turning to "The Christian Community and the New Society" in chapters 12-13. Most of the material in part 4 is presented in summary and paraphrased in various parts of the present volume.

The book went through many printings and sold over 86,000 copies in fourteen years. The fifteenth anniversary of its publication in English (1988) seemed a fitting time for a new edition, for it was also Gustavo's sixtieth birthday (1928) and the twentieth anniversary of Medellín (1968). It would be hard to find three events more worthy of simultaneous celebration. The work was reedited (with a view to inclusive language), reset, given a new cover, and presented to Gustavo at Maryknoll, home of Orbis Books, in the summer of 1988, along with the completed typescript of *The Future of*

Liberation Theology, a massive *Festschrift* honoring Gustavo; it was published the following year.

There are five kinds of changes in the anniversary edition: (1) the already voluminous notes have been updated and expanded so that they now occupy more than 80 pages, a reference resource beyond compare; (2) sexist language has been replaced, although masculine pronouns are still used for God (in citations of biblical sources), a matter that may or may not have been resolved by the time of the next anniversary edition; (3) an important page from Arguedas's *Todas las sangres* (included in the Spanish edition but omitted from the original English translation) has been restored, though not, alas, translated; (4) a 30-page introduction has been added, subtitled "Expanding the View" (also printed in Spanish as "Mirar lejos," *Páginas,* October 1988), in which Gustavo details the theological developments during the interval between the two editions; and (5) the section on "Christian Fellowship and Class Struggle" (pp. 271-79, original edition) has been replaced by a new section, "Faith and Social Conflict" (pp. 156-61, anniversary edition)—an attempt on Gustavo's part both to clear up "misunderstandings" in the original text and take advantage of new pronouncements by the magisterium that support his position. This section is analyzed in chapter 4, above.

Whenever *A Theology of Liberation* is quoted in the present text, the initial page citation refers to the 1988 edition. A second page citation locates the same passage in the 1973 edition.

3. *Liberation and Change* (with Richard Shaull), John Knox Press, Atlanta, 1977, 200 pp., edited and introduced by Ronald H. Stone.

Gustavo and Richard Shaull, one of the earliest interpreters of liberation theology to U.S. readers, collaborated to give the Schaff Lectures at Pittsburgh Theological Seminary in 1976. Gustavo lectured on "Freedom and Salvation: A Political Problem" (pp. 3-94), and responded to Shaull's lectures on "The Death and Resurrection of the American Dream" (pp. 181-84). His voluminous notes are found on pp. 185-98.

Gustavo's first lecture, "Freedom and Truth," is a historical study that traces the problem of freedom from earliest Christian experience through Thomas Aquinas, while the second lecture, "Freedom and Critical Reason," brings the discussion into modern times, with frank appraisals of the difficulty Catholicism had in coping with such themes as "freedom" and "toleration." These heavily documented chapters are the fruits of historical research Gustavo did during his earlier student days in Lyons for a master's degree in theology. The third lecture, "Freedom and Liberation," is particularly apropos to his present concerns. It includes the most important assessment he has yet made in English of the contribution of Bartolomé de Las Casas (pp. 61-69, also printed in Spanish in *Páginas,* September 1976), and a substantively important section on "Liberation and Freedom" (pp. 75-94) that draws together such meaty themes as the rising consciousness of the formerly "absent" of history, the need to do theology "from the world of oppression," the relation of the liberation of Christ to political liberation, and evangelism as "the subversion of history."

4. *El Diós de la vida,* Pontificia Universidad Católica del Peru, 1982, 96 pp. See also item # 10 below.

This small volume of Bible studies, dedicated to the memory of Archbishop Romero, contains talks given at the Lima summer institute in February 1981. They celebrate "the God of life" in a world where death is an increasing companion of Christians.

Three questions are brought to focus. The question "Who is God?" is answered by a consideration of God as Father (pp. 9-43). (Gustavo asserts in a footnote that in his culture the image of "father" is a way of speaking about God as love, but he acknowledges that in other cultural contexts this same truth can be communicated by referring to God as mother, and notes that many biblical passages speak of "the maternal love of God.") Biblical materials include treatment of such events as the exodus, the messianic promises, the God of the covenant, and God as the *gō'ēl,* the redeemer. Only such a God of love can save us from idolatry.

The question "Where is God?" is answered by discussing the kingdom of God (pp. 43-63). God is frequently "absent" from the temple, from the deliberations of religious authorities, and from religious actions done to gain divine credit. But God is "present," both in the cosmos where "the heavens declare the glory of God," and in history, where God says, "I will dwell with you," and tells us that the Word became flesh and pitched a tent in our midst.

The question "How do we speak of God?" is answered by a consideration of prophetic and contemplative speech. Here we receive an early run-through of themes developed later in the book *On Job.* The same question is posed: "How do we speak of God from the perspective of poverty and suffering?" Four ways of speaking of God are delineated: the language of popular faith (the early Job), ethical-religious language (represented by Job's friends who see poverty and infirmity as signs of God's punishment), prophetic language that can argue honestly with God (Job and Elihu), and contemplative language, which speaks *to* God rather than only *about* God (the Job of the concluding chapters).

Some of Gustavo's critics charged that his book *On Job* (1987) was a contrived attempt to clear himself of charges launched in 1984 of "horizontalism" and lack of concern for "transcendence." The above summary makes clear that the main themes of *On Job* were in place by 1980.

5. *The Power of the Poor in History: Selected Writings,* Orbis, 1983, 240 pp., Foreword by Robert McAfee Brown (English translation of *La fuerza histórica de los pobres,* CEP, Lima, 1979).

This collection of essays appeared in Spanish in 1979, soon after the Puebla Conference, but was not translated into English until 1983. It is the book most attacked by the Vatican (see chapter 6, above) and yet it contains some of Gustavo's most unassailable affirmations.

Part 1, "Biblical Overview of the Sources of Liberation Theology," consists of a single essay on "God's Revelation and Proclamation in History." As its title promises, it places liberation squarely in the context of biblical faith and celebration. This essay alone should have forestalled charges of heterodoxy by Gustavo's opponents.

Part 2, "From Medellín to Puebla," contains three essays that illustrate shifts of emphasis between the two conferences. These are revisions of Gustavo's introductions to three collections of essays, articles, and position papers described in note 13 to chapter 1, above, dealing respectively with "signs of renewal," "signs of liberation," and "signs of struggle and hope." They are among his most "political" writings, and were meticulously attacked by the Congregation for the Doctrine of the Faith.

Part 3, "Puebla," includes Gustavo's devastating attack on the European-oriented "Preliminary Document," summed up in his contention that the draft presents religion as a "tranquilizer," and a long commentary on the results of Puebla, "Liberation and the Poor: The Puebla Perspective," highlighting Puebla's achievements and calling on the church to take them seriously.

Part 4, "The Underside of History," contains two articles. The first is a feisty, profound, and massively documented historical essay drawing together many previous writings, "Theology from the Underside of History." It contrasts "Western theology" (the Enlightenment, Kant, individualism, rationalism, the modern spirit) and "theology in a world of oppression," represented by the "absent" of history, the underdogs, and "the scourged Christs of the Indies" (an image from Las Casas), concluding that in our day it must be the poor who preach the gospel. The final brief and irenic essay on Bonhoeffer notes that occasionally someone conditioned by "dominant theology" can nevertheless come to share "the view from below," and cast his lot with the victims.

6. *We Drink from Our Own Wells: The Spiritual Journey of a People,* Orbis, 1984, xxi and 181 pp. Foreword by Henri Nouwen (English translation of *Beber en su propio pozo: En el itinerario de un pueblo,* CEP, Lima, 1983). Gustavo here deals with spirituality more fully than he has done before. But the book does not represent a "new direction"; it is simply the amplification of material already present in an often overlooked section of *A Theology of Liberation* entitled "A Spirituality of Liberation" (pp. 116-20 [203-8]).

Gustavo insists that spirituality and liberation cannot be separated, and that it is a false spirituality that removes us from historical struggle rather than immersing us in it more deeply. "Liberation," he declares, "is an all-embracing process that leaves no dimension of human life untouched" (p. 2).

Part 1 describes the contextual situation in which the plaintive query is heard, "How shall we sing to the Lord in a foreign land?" It is an alien world in which "the spiritual journey of a people" must take place. The direction must be against death-dealing and toward the reign of life.

In light of the stark human situation, part 2 examines the biblical resources available for pilgrimage, especially Romans 8 and Galatians 5. As John of the Cross recognized, a time comes when supports are removed and "here there is no longer any way." The course ahead is uncharted and can be ventured upon only by faith. At this point people become "free to love," to give life, to liberate. The choice, once again, is between death and life. But the walking is not solitary; it is that of "an entire people," which in itself is a source of strength.

Part 3, the most "practical" section of the book, develops the theme "free to love," and relates it specifically to life in Latin America, though the themes are applicable anywhere. Five characteristics of a "new spirituality" are described: conversion, gratuitousness, joy, spiritual childhood, and community. A summary of these themes is offered in chapter 4, above.

7. *On Job: God-Talk and the Suffering of the Innocent,* Orbis, 1987, xix and 136 pp. (English translation of *Hablar de Dios desde el sufrimiento del inocente,* CEP, Lima, 1986).

The basic argument of the book *On Job* is summarized in the first half of chapter 4, above. As noted in item #4 above, the main substantive themes had been arrived at in *El Diós de la vida*. Here we need only note the structure of the argument.

The introduction is important not only for what is affirmed about theological method, but for the way Gustavo relates "theological method" to the everyday lives and cries of the people. The problem the book explores is not how to create a "theodicy," an intellectual defense that will reconcile the existence of God and the simultaneous existence of evil, but, in Gustavo's words, "How are we to talk about God?" More particularly: "How are we to talk about God from within a specific situation—namely, the suffering of the innocent?" (p. xviii).

Part 1 deals with "The Wager" between God and the satan, and takes Job from his abundant prosperity to the "garbage heap," where he is supposed to curse God but refuses to do so. He begins to reflect on the suffering of the innocent.

Part 2, "The Language of Prophecy," brings Job's friends onto the scene. They turn out to be "sorry comforters." Job discovers the suffering of others and the fact that to be related to God also means to be related to them. He must align himself with them even while his own perplexities remain unsolved.

Part 3, "The Language of Contemplation," leads Job from talking only *about* God to talking *to* God, and realizing that both ways of talking are not only indispensable but are finally two perspectives on talking in a single way. He begins to find how to "surrender to love" and to move "beyond justice."

The book has immense scholarship behind it (there are 27 pages of notes), but its power lies in its direct and human honesty, quite apart from whether the footnotes are explored or not. Gustavo challenges many of the conclusions of other commentators, and breaks new ground for those who have always approached Job with "Western eyes."

8. *The Truth Shall Make You Free,* Orbis, 1990 (English translation of *La verdad los hará libres: Confrontaciones,* CEP, Lima, 1986).

There must have been times during his "confrontations" with Rome when Gustavo wondered whether fidelity to the "truth" would make him "free" or lead to his downfall. The three contributions in this book demonstrate that even in the face of formidable opposition, devotion to truth can finally be vindicated. Although each contribution was occasioned by an explicit set of historical circumstances, all three stand on their own quite apart from that, and will continue to be helpful long after the occasions of their production are forgotten.

When the University of Lyons offered to examine Gustavo on the corpus of his writings, during his struggles with Rome in 1985, one stipulation was that he make a "presentation" of his position. The result, contained in the first part of the book, is a clear summary of themes central to his thought: (1) the issue of religious language and the relation of spirituality and methodology, (2) the recognition that theology must be done from "the underside of history," and some of the consequences of that decision, and (3) the centrality of the resurrection event for Christians. The "presentation" is followed by an intriguing stenographic report of the colloquy between Gustavo and his eight university examiners that resulted in Gustavo's being awarded the doctorate in theology *summa cum laude.*

The second part of the book is an essay, "Theology and the Social Sciences," printed in *Páginas* nine months earlier. It relates to criticisms that his theology is dominated by an uncritical acceptance of the social sciences, and that "Marxist analysis" had eroded his understanding of Christian revelation, particularly through his employment of the concept of "class struggle." The essay is described in more detail in chapter 4, above.

The third and major contribution is the essay, almost two hundred pages in length, from which the book gets its title, "The Truth Shall Make You Free." This is, in effect, Gustavo's magisterial reply to his accusers. In the course of affirming those things that are central to his life and faith, he disposes, one by one, of the complaints of the Sacred Congregation. Read as a rebuttal, the essay is skillful dialectics, a creative tour de force that wins a debate already receding in memory; read as a statement of faith, it is winsome and will long survive the context that occasioned it. The entire essay is described in more detail in chapter 6, above.

9. *Dios o el oro en las Indias (Siglo XVI),* Instituto Bartolomé de Las Casas-Rímac, and CEP, Lima, 1989, 177 pp.

The cover of the Spanish edition of this book is striking—a crucified Christ represented in the style of "popular" Amerindian art juxtaposed with a handful of Spanish gold coins. "God or gold in the Indies" is the way Gustavo chooses to set the stage for his massive work on Bartolomé de Las Casas, of which this is the first of four projected volumes, four chapters out of a promised seventeen.

In the initial chapter, Gustavo describes the slaughter of the Amerindians in the sixteenth century at the hands of the Spanish conquerors, particularly in La Española — today Haiti and Santo Domingo — conditions that motivated Las Casas's first protests against such treatment, consequences of "colonial" policies that made it possible to view the Amerindians as subhuman.

Las Casas not only defended the rights of the Amerindians and indicated the social and economic causes of their victimization; he went further and analyzed — with biblical acumen — the idolatry that transformed gold into a god to whom the Spaniards willingly surrendered themselves. Denunciation of this false god is found in Las Casas's earliest writings and remains central throughout his life.

In response to this challenge, the conquistadores sought to justify their greed — or their "idolatry" as Las Casas insisted on calling it in Pauline terms — theologically, enlisting various church leaders to take their part, and in the second chapter Gustavo continues a description of the historical context in which the polemics against him were carried on.

To counter the stubborn idolatry of the Christian invaders, Las Casas proposed, we learn in chapter 3, the unwelcome notion that Christ, not gold, represents the true "mediator" of salvation in the history and evangelization of the Indies. Even more inspired by the story of the last judgment (Matthew 25:31-46), he audaciously affirms that it is in the Amerindians, whom the "Christians" see as unwelcome heathen, that Christ is truly present.

The final chapter develops this theme in detail, exploring Las Casas's contention that it is the "scourged Christ of the Indies" who continues to be whipped and crucified in the unjustified deaths of the "heathen," at the hands of the Spaniards.

It is around this controversy, and this controversy alone, that Gustavo's interpretation centers. The confrontation, he believes, is between two mutually exclusive theological perspectives, two mutually exclusive ways of understanding Christ and his work. On the one hand, there is a justification for the European presence in the Indies, based on the conviction that the riches of the Indies have been providentially provided by God. On the other hand, there is a christological perspective, growing out of the gospel, that starts historically with the poor of the land, the Amerindians, identifies with them, and denounces the alternative as idolatry. From a biblical perspective, gold ("mammon") is opposed to God, and Las Casas constructs his theology on the conviction that it is not possible to serve these two masters; one must choose between them.

And, Gustavo reminds his readers in conclusion, that is still — in more subtle ways — the situation today.

10. *El Diós de la vida,* CEP, Lima, 1990.

This is a greatly expanded version of the earlier work described in item #4 above. The basic structure is retained: there are the same three questions, Who is God?, Where is God?, and How do we speak of God? But the responses are richer because the whole wealth of the biblical material can now be brought to bear on them, rather than the small number of passages that could be treated in the earlier edition.

One could play interesting textual games with the material ("Why is the sequence of topics in part 1 changed?"), but that would miss the point, which is that the intensity of concern is greater in the new edition. The title, "the God of life," was not idly chosen nor retained. It is the message of *life* that needs to be heard in 1991 even more than in 1981, for the power and presence of death has increased throughout Latin America.

So in responding to the question "Who is God?," with the answer that "God is love" (part 1), there is greater stress on "the Lord as the friend of *life*," who comes with open arms, the *living* God who comes as gō'ēl (redeemer) to do justice and save the people. This is the God of the covenant, who can be depended upon, who embodies tenderness and demand, who wants acts of worship and deeds of justice, who does battle with idolatry and death.

To the second question "Where is God?," the new text develops more fully than its predecessor the theme of "the God who *comes*," who is not only present in the cosmos but in history as well, who announces "I will dwell in the midst of you." The God who comes declares that the day of the Lord is at hand, the time is completed, the kingdom of God is already here ... so seek the kingdom and justice of God! It is a message addressed to all: all the nations, all the least (who shall be first), all the poor (who are the special objects of God's preferential love). And because the kingdom is both grace and demand, a whole "kingdom ethics" is elaborated out of that fact.

The third question is "How do we speak of God?" In the earlier edition, this question preceded a 28-page treatment of the book of Job. But in the interval Gustavo's book on Job appeared, so the rest of the material is basically new. Speech about God is linked to the presence of the Spirit, as Gustavo's treatment of the second chapter of Acts reminds us. And the Spirit, too, is *life*, just as Yahweh, the God of love (part 1), is life, and Jesus, the God of the kingdom (part 2), is life.

These are claims that must be lived out (by the power of the Spirit) amid injustice and death. The claims are neither sentimental nor escapist, because the context is always the suffering of the poor, the need for justice for the poor, and the presence of the God of life is found in the linkage of gratitude and justice.

Representative Articles

Two of Gustavo's books, *The Power of the Poor in History* and *The Truth Shall Make You Free,* are collections of articles. The following are a further sampling of articles in English that are substantive statements of his thought, arranged in roughly chronological order. For those who read Spanish, the most frequent repository of his writings is the Peruvian journal *Páginas,* Lima.

"Liberation Development," *Cross Currents,* Summer 1971, pp. 243-56.

"Liberation Movements and Theology," *Concilium* 93, Schillebeeckx, and van Iersel, eds., *Jesus Christ and Human Freedom,* Herder and Herder, New York, 1974, pp. 135-46.

"Liberation, Theology and Proclamation," *Concilium* 96, Geffré/Gutiérrez, eds., *The Mystical and Political Dimension of the Christian Faith,* Herder and Herder, New York, 1974, pp. 57-77.

"The Hope of Liberation," Anderson and Stransky, eds., *Mission Trends No. 3: Third World Theologies,* Paulist Press and Eerdmans, New York and Grand Rapids, 1976.

"Faith and Freedom," Eigo, ed., *Living with Change, Experience, and Faith,* Villanova University Press, Villanova, 1976, pp. 15-54 (also available as "Praxis of Liberation and Christian Faith," Mexican-American Cultural Center, San Antonio, 1976).

"The Poor in the Church," *Concilium* 104, Greinacher and Müller, eds., *The Poor and The Church,* Seabury Press, New York, 1977, pp. 11-16.

"Liberation Praxis and Christian Faith," Gibellini, ed., *Frontiers of Theology in Latin America,* Orbis, 1978, pp. 1-33.

"Two Theological Perspectives: Liberation Theology and Progressivist Theology," Torres and Fabella, eds., *The Emergent Gospel,* Orbis, 1978, pp. 227-55.

"The Irruption of the Poor in Latin America and the Christian Communities of the Common People," Torres and Eagleson, eds., *The Challenge of Basic Christian Communities,* Orbis, 1981, pp. 107-23.

"Significado y alcance de Medellín," Dammert et al., *Irrupción y caminar de la Iglesia de Los pobres: Presencia de Medellín*, Instituto Bartolomé de Las Casas-Rímac and CEP, Lima, 1989, pp. 23–73 (only in Spanish).

Interviews

Gustavo's clarity and humor are both communicated through interviews, which are an important resource for knowing his human side. The following are a sampling, listed chronologically, from sources relatively available:

Dow Kirkpatrick, "Liberation Theologians and Third World Demands: A Dialogue with Gustavo Gutiérrez and Javier Iguiñez," *Christian Century,* May 12, 1976, pp. 456-60.

Teófilo Cabestrero, *Faith: Conversations with Contemporary Theologians,* Orbis Books, Maryknoll, 1980, pp. 95-105.

James Brockmann, S.J., "The Prophetic Role of the Church in Latin America: A Conversation with Gustavo Gutiérrez," *Christian Century*, October 19, 1983, pp. 931-35.

Mario Campos, "Gutiérrez: 'Joy of the Poor Confounds the Powerful,' " *Latinamerica Press,* May 10, 1984, pp. 3-5.

La Republica, "Gustavo Gutiérrez: 'Criticism Will Deepen, Clarify' Liberation Theology," *Latinamerica Press,* Sept. 14, 1984 (also included in Hennelly #47).

Kathleen Hayes, "Gustavo Gutiérrez: Opting for the Poor," *The Other Side,* November 1987, pp. 10-13.

Elsa Tamez, *Against Machismo,* Meyer-Stone, Oak Park, Ill., 1987, pp. 39-48.

APPENDIX II

Writings by Others

Those who compile, or turn to, listings of books as a way to understand liberation theology need to remember Gustavo's comment (cited at the beginning of chapter 1) that "all liberation theology originates among the world's anonymous, whoever may write the books or declarations articulating it," and Hugo Assmann's warning that "it is a great mistake to attempt to understand what liberation theology is and represents by way of a consideration of authors and their writings. . . . Any attempt to analyze the theology of liberation as a movement of ideas is indicative of a failure to understand its principle dimension, which is spiritual and pastoral."

Bearing these caveats in mind, we still need pointers for further exploration. A tremendous body of literature continues to accumulate, trying to articulate liberation theology from a variety of viewpoints, and the greater our acquaintance with it, the more informed our own judgments will be.

A Way to Begin

Because liberation theology is a "people's theology," it is appropriate to begin not with professional theologians but with an example of the people's own expression of faith. A stunning example is Philip and Sally Scharper, eds., *The Gospel in Art by the Peasants of Solentiname,* Orbis, 1984. Solentiname was a lay Christian community in Nicaragua founded by Fr. Ernesto Cardenal, and destroyed by Somoza's troops before his fall, for Bible study and revolutionary activity were increasingly seen to be mutually supportive endeavors. The inhabitants of Solentiname, not highly educated, spent much of their time trying to relate the gospel story to their own situation. They did this through discussions of the Bible, and some of them, despite lack of professional training, did it through art. The book contains thirty-one paintings of events in the life of Jesus, with appropriate excerpts from the people's own discussion of the events. In all cases, the setting is the Nicaraguan countryside, with indigenous architecture, clothing, and topography, thus exemplifying a consistent theme of liberation theology that the biblical story is also a contemporary story. For those with eyes to see, the paintings provide pertinent social commentary: Herod's banquet table, on the occasion when the head of John the Baptist is displayed, features Coca Cola, an indication of where imperialist power lines up in the biblical drama, and the soldiers' uniforms, in the episode of the slaughter of the innocents, are combat fatigues courtesy of the United States Army.

The experience of engaging in Bible study on Sunday (or any other weekday) to figure out what to do on Monday (or any other weekday) is characteristic of such groups of people, developed in the base communities. The most immediate experience of the power of this sharing is found in the four volumes edited by Ernesto Cardenal, *The Gospel in Solentiname,* Orbis, 1976-1982, from which the brief excerpts in the above-cited book are taken. After organizing the lay community, Cardenal stopped preaching a homily after the reading of the gospel at Mass, and invited the people to engage in their own exegesis. The taped conversations that resulted provide the text for the four volumes, in which it becomes clear that the wisdom of the "simple" often confounds the learning of the "wise," as dimensions of the biblical story, missed by the rest of us, spring to life.

Another mode of entrance into liberation theology is biography. Liberation theology is not theory found in books but commitment expressed in lives . . . and deaths. Whenever men and women begin to live out the meaning of the gospel in oppressive situations, they are in for trouble. Of the thousands who have paid the price of martyrdom, one story that comes through with special power is that of Oscar Romero, archbishop of San Salvador. A routinely conservative priest who (probably for that reason) was made archbishop, Romero went through a conversion experience, realized that the gospel called him to side with the poor, and realized further that to side with the poor meant to side against the military junta. James Brockman, in *Romero: A Life*, Orbis, 1989, captures the flavor of Romero's life in a detailed account of events that made it a foregone conclusion that the junta would murder him. The important thing to realize is that Romero is typical of many of his generation—priests or sisters or lay persons whose conventionality is challenged by brutal abuses of power, demanding from them a new life dedicated to identifying with the poor and oppressed. What is even more important to realize is that for every Oscar Romero we know about, there are thousands who have likewise been changed and likewise destroyed, and that the powers of hell, even when embodied in cruel and inhuman dictators, will not finally be able to prevail against them.

Overall Bibliographical Help

If we approach books from a perspective like that just sketched, they can help rather than hinder deeper understanding. There are a few overall bibliographical resources that can assist the serious reader or researcher:

1. The most extensive bibliography is the annual edition of *Bibliografía Teológica Commentada del area iberoamericana,* Isedet y Aidet, Publica-

ciones El Escudo, Buenos Aires, 1973 et seq. The first three volumes total 1,201 pages. There is nothing else remotely approaching the depth and breadth of the coverage.

2. The best overall road map, in briefer form, is Pablo Richard, "The Theological Literature of Latin America," in Boff and Elizondo, eds., *Theologies of the Third World: Convergences and Differences,* T & T Clark, Edinburgh, 1988, pp. 76-79. The word "indispensable" must be used sparingly, but it applies to this compilation, which describes both the work of individual theologians and overall themes and subject matter.

3. An extraordinary compilation of notes and references can be found in Daniel Schipani, *Religious Education Encounters Liberation Theology,* Religious Education Press, Birmingham, 1988, esp. pp. 5-8, 55-67, 101-14, 143-55, 194-209, and 250-60.

4. There is an extensive bibliography in Spanish in Gotay, *El pensemiento cristiano revolucionario en América latina y el Caribe,* Ediciones Sígueme, Cordillera, 1983, pp. 371-89.

5. A number of the footnotes in the present volume present brief bibliographies of subject matter being explored in the text. See esp. chap. 1, nn. 1, 2, 13 on history; chap. 3, n. 4 on praxis; chap. 5, nn. 5, 6 on use of the Bible; chap. 5, n. 9, on base communities; chap. 7, n. 1, on EATWOT; chap. 7, n. 2, on examples of non-Latin American liberation theologies; and chap. 7, n. 8, on a variety of North American responses to the challenges of liberation theology.

North American Introductions and Assessments

The following is a baker's dozen of books looking at liberation theology from a North American perspective, or drawing on its insights for the North American scene. It should be supplemented by the material in chap. 7, n. 8:

Berryman, Philip. *Liberation Theology,* Pantheon Books, 1987.

Brueggemann, Walter, *The Prophetic Imagination,* Fortress, Philadelphia, 1978, and *Hopeful Imagination: Prophetic Voices in Exile,* Fortress, Philadelphia, 1986.

Chopp, Rebecca, *The Praxis of Suffering: An Interpretation of Liberation and Political Theologies.* Orbis, 1986.

Cleary, Edward, *Crisis and Change: The Church in Latin America Today,* Orbis, 1985.

Ellison, Marvin, *The Center Cannot Hold: The Search for a Global Economy of Justice,* University of America Press, Washington, D.C., 1983.

Ferm, Deane William, *Third World Liberation Theologies: An Introductory Survey,* Orbis, 1986.

Garcia, Ismael, *Justice in Latin American Theology of Liberation,* John Knox Press, Atlanta, 1987.

Haight, Roger, *An Alternative Vision: An Interpretation of Liberation Theology,* Paulist Press, Mahwah, N.J., 1985.

Herzog, Frederick, *God-Walk,* Orbis, 1989.

Mahan, Brian, and Richesin, L. Dale, eds., *The Challenge of Liberation Theology: A First World Response,* Orbis, 1981.

Migliore, Daniel, *Called to Freedom: Liberation Theology and the Future of Christian Doctrine,* Westminster, Philadelphia, 1980.

McCann, Dennis, *Christian Realism and Liberation Theology: Practical Theologies in Conflict,* Orbis, 1981.

Nessan, Craig. *Orthopraxis or Heresy: The North American Response to Latin American Liberation Theology,* Scholars Press, 1989.

Schipani, Daniel, ed., *Freedom and Discipleship, Liberation Theology in Anabaptist Perspective,* Orbis, 1989.

Welch, Sharon, *Communities of Resistance and Solidarity: A Feminist Theology of Liberation,* Orbis, 1985.

Representative Voices in the Latin American Struggle

It is almost invidious to select a few representative voices from Latin America, where there are scores of notable exemplars who can equally well contribute to our understanding, and thousands of "the world's anonymous" who are voiceless as far as communicating directly with North Americans is concerned. Deane Ferm, in *Profiles in Liberation Theology* (Twenty-Third Publications, Mystic, Conn., 1988) gives brief biographies of sixteen Latin American writers. His selection is helpful and I have added a few names beyond those whom he profiles. In each case, representative books have been chosen that speak a clear word to North American readers:

Assmann, Hugo, *Theology for a Nomad Church,* Orbis, 1976; "The Power of Christ in History: Conflicting Christologies and Discernment," in Gibellini, ed., *Frontiers of Theology in Latin America,* Orbis, 1979, pp. 133-50.

Bidegain, Ana María, "Women and the Theology of Liberation," in *Festschrift,* Orbis, 1988.

Bingemer, María Clara, *Mary, Mother of God, Mother of the Poor* (with Ivone Gebara), Orbis, 1989.

Boff, Clodovis, *The Bible, the Church, and the Poor* (with George Pixley), Orbis, 1989; *Feet-on-the-Ground Theology: A Brazilian Journey,* Orbis, 1987.

Boff, Leonardo, *Way of the Cross—Way of Justice,* Orbis, 1980; *Passion of Christ, Passion of the World,* Orbis, 1987.

Cardenal, Ernesto, ed., *The Gospel in Solentiname,* 4 vols., Orbis, 1976-82; *Flights of Victory/Vuelos de Victoria,* Orbis, 1985.

Comblin, José, *The Church and the National Security State,* Orbis, 1979; *Cry of the Oppressed, Cry of Jesus: Meditations on Scripture and Contemporary Struggle,* Orbis, 1988.

Couch, Beatriz, *Towards a New Humanity: Seeing the World through Bib-*

lical Eyes—A Third World Feminist Perspective, Meyer-Stone, Oak Park, Ill., 1990.

Dussel, Enrique, *A History of the Church in Latin America: Colonialism to Liberation, 1492-1979,* Eerdmans, Grand Rapids, 1981; *Ethics and Community,* Orbis, 1988.

Echegaray, Hugo, *The Practice of Jesus* (preface by Gustavo), Orbis, 1984.

Galilea, Segundo, *The Way of Living Faith: A Spirituality of Liberation,* Harper and Row, San Francisco, 1988; *Spirituality of Hope,* Orbis, 1989.

Libânio, João Batista, *Spiritual Discernment and Politics: Guidelines for Religious Communities,* Orbis, 1982.

Maduro, Otto, *Religion and Social Conflicts,* Orbis, 1982.

Mesters, Carlos, *Defenseless Flower: A New Reading of the Bible,* Orbis, 1989.

Míguez Bonino, José, *Doing Theology in a Revolutionary Situation,* Fortress, Philadelphia, 1975; *Toward a Christian Political Ethics,* Fortress, Philadelphia, 1983.

Miranda, José Porfirio, *Marx and the Bible: A Critique of the Philosophy of Oppression,* Orbis, 1974; *Marx against the Marxists: The Christian Humanism of Karl Marx,* Orbis, 1980.

Richard, Pablo, ed., *The Idols of Death and the God of Life,* Orbis, 1983; *Death of Christendoms, Birth of the Church: Historical Analysis and Theological Interpretation of the Church in Latin America,* Orbis, 1987.

Segundo, Juan Luis, *The Liberation of Theology,* Orbis, 1976; *Jesus of Nazareth: Yesterday and Today,* 5 vols. Orbis, 1984-88.

Sobrino, Jon, *Jesus in Latin America,* Orbis, 1987; *Spirituality of Liberation: Toward Political Holiness,* Orbis, 1988.

Tamez, Elsa, *Bible of the Oppressed,* Orbis, 1982; *Against Machismo,* Meyer-Stone, Oak Park, Ill., 1987; *Through Her Eyes: Women's Theology from Latin America,* Orbis, 1989.

A new publishing venture has recently been initiated, *Teología y Liberación* [Theology and liberation], projecting fifty volumes that will comprise what Pablo Richard calls "the first general synthesis of South America theology." Published originally in Portuguese, the volumes will appear subsequently in many other languages as well. The English translation is a collaboration of Orbis Books and Burns and Oates (England). The volume on Mary, noted above, by Gebara and Bingemer, is in this series, as is Leonardo Boff's *Trinity and Society,* Orbis, 1988. Other volumes will be written by such authors as Ronaldo Muñoz, José Comblin, Enrique Dussel, João Batista Libânio, Ricardo Antoncich, and Julio de Santa Ana.

Notes

Introduction: Arranging the Program Notes

1. Gustavo deals with Ayacucho particularly in *Job*. The quotation is on p. 102, and the initial italicized question is repeated in the 15th anniversary edition of *TheoLib*, p. xxxiv. The dedication is on p. v.

1. A Collective Biography of the Authors of Liberation Theology

1. The basic historical reference work is Enrique Dussel, *A History of the Church in Latin America: Colonialism to Liberation,* Eerdmans, Grand Rapids, 1981, translated by Alan Neely. It includes much detail, massive documentation, important appendices, and many of the charts and maps (pp. 346–60) for which the author is famous. Dussel has also taken briefer historical excursions over the material: *History and the Theology of Liberation*, Orbis, 1976, with a helpful bibliography, and its continuation, *Ethics and the Theology of Liberation*, Orbis, 1978.

See also H. McKennie Goodpasture, *Cross and Sword: An Eyewitness History of Christianity in Latin America*, Orbis, 1989, which tells the personal side of the history with many contemporary documents. Pablo Richard, *Death of Christendoms, Birth of the Church*, Orbis, 1987, also treats the history but with proportionately greater emphasis on recent times; extensive bibliography. McGovern offers a brief historical survey in his chapter 1, and an extensive treatment of colonialism in chapter 6. Hugo Assmann, *Theology for a Nomad Church*, Orbis, 1976, treats the history from a different perspective. For the period during and after Pope John XXIII, see Hugo Cabal, *The Revolution of the Latin American Church*, University of Oklahoma Press, 1978.

Penny Lernoux, *Cry of the People*, Doubleday, Garden City, N.Y., 1980, contains powerful material on martyrdom and the baleful role of the United States in Latin American history. Her recent *People of God*, Viking, New York, 1989, details the ongoing struggle between a hierarchical and a people-centered concept of the church. See also her essay, "In Honor of Gustavo Gutiérrez," in *Festschrift*, pp. 77–83.

2. Gustavo has been working for years on a huge treatment of Las Casas that will be the definitive work in the field. The first of four volumes has appeared in Spanish, *Dios o el oro in las Indias (Siglo XVI)*, Instituto Bartolomé de Las Casas-Rimac, and CEP, Lima, 1989. The book is briefly described in Appendix I. Gustavo's three major treatments of Las Casas in English are in *LibChange*, pp. 60–68, *Emergent*, pp. 141–45, and *PP*, pp. 194–97. The summary of Las Casas's themes in the text is drawn from these sources.

A volume of Las Casas's own writings is available in English, *The Devastation of the Indies: A Brief Account*, Seabury, New York, 1974, a documentation of atrocities committed against the Amerindians by the conquistadores.

Two of the most accessible books on Las Casas are Juan Friede and Benjamin Keen, eds., *Bartolomé de las Casas in History*, Northern Illinois University Press, De Kalb, 1971, treating Las Casas's life, ideology, experience of the New World, and heritage, with a bibliography of 106 items; and Lewis Hanke, *Aristotle and the American Indians*, Indiana University Press, Bloomington, 1959, a treatment of the debates in Spain between Las Casas and Sepúlveda.

3. Documentation on the use of the Bible will be found in chapter 5, note 5.

4. A full account of the history of papal social teaching is Donal Dorr, *Option for the Poor: A Hundred Years of Vatican Social Teaching*, Orbis, 1983. See also Ricardo Antoncich, *Christians in the Face of Injustice: A Latin American Reading of Catholic Social Teaching*, Orbis, 1987, and Christine Gudorf, *Catholic Social Teaching on Liberation Themes*, University Press of America, Lanham, Md., 1980. The major documents on Catholic social teaching can be found in Joseph Gremillion, ed., *The Gospel of Peace and Justice: Catholic Social Teaching since Pope John*, Orbis, 1976, and David O'Brien and Thomas Shannon, eds., *Renewing the Earth: Catholic Documents on Peace, Justice, and Liberation*, Image Books, Garden City, N.Y., 1977. I have provided a shorter summary of this history in *Theology in a New Key*, Westminster, Philadelphia, 1978.

5. All the documents of Vatican II, along with commentaries, are available in Walter Abbott, ed., *The Documents of Vatican II*, America Press, New York, 1966.

6. The clearest setting forth of the doctrine of "national security," to which the summary in the text is indebted, is José Comblin, *The Church and the National Security State*, Orbis, 1979, esp. chaps. 4–6. See further material in chapter 5, below.

7. The basic report of the Medellín Conference, including initial addresses, position papers, the full texts of the final documents, and the papal allocution, is Second General Conference of Latin American Bishops, *The Church in the Present-Day Transformation of Latin America in the Light of the Council*, vol. 1, Position Papers; vol. 2, Conclusions; General Secretariat of CELAM, Bogotá, 1970.

On the twentieth anniversary of Medellín, Gustavo wrote a long and appreciative appraisal of its significance and scope, available in Dammert et al, *Irrupción y caminar de la Iglesia de los pobres: Presencia de Medellín*, Instituto Bartolomé de Las Casas-Rimac and CEP, Lima, 1989, pp. 23–73, "Significado y alcance de Medellín." Published too late to be used in the present work, it will repay careful study.

Hennelly includes the texts of the most important documents—"Justice," "Peace," and "Poverty in the Church"— as document #10.

Medellín's location in the sweep of Latin American church history is focused in Dussel, *History*, esp., pp. 137–48. The story of developments between Medellín and Puebla is found on pp. 149–231, and Puebla itself is described on pp. 231–39.

For the inner workings of CELAM between Medellín and Puebla, and attempts to derail liberation theology, see François Houtart, "Theoretical and Institutional Bases of the Opposition to Liberation Theology," in *Festschrift*, pp. 261–71. Theological developments before, during, and after Medellín are described in fascinating detail in Roberto Oliveros, *Liberación y teología; génesis y crecimiento de una reflexión*, CEP, Lima, 1971, available only in Spanish, a book that also provides an overview of Gustavo's theology.

8. López Trujillo, *Liberation or Revolution?*, Our Sunday Visitor, Huntington,

Ind., 1977. All the quotations are from this book. Hennelly includes chapter 2 as document #16.

9. Gustavo did a long dissection of the "Preliminary Document," a condensed version of which is in *Christianity and Crisis*, September 18, 1978, an issue devoted to Puebla. The material is available in longer form in *PP*, chap. 5. The document itself, which has a certain archival interest, is "La evangelización en el presente y en el futuro de América Latina," Consejo Episcopal Latinoamericano, 214 pp.

10. The best single source on Puebla is Eagleson and Scharper, eds., *Puebla and Beyond*, Orbis, 1979, which contains the full text of the final document (pp. 122–285), along with essays on the historical background and the conference itself (Lernoux, Sandoval), texts and commentary on the pope's speeches in Mexico (Elizondo), interpretive essays on the final document (McGrath, Sobrino, Gremillion, Brown), and a detailed topical index. Hennelly includes excerpts as document #22.

Levine, ed., *Churches and Politics in Latin America*, Sage Publications, Beverly Hills, 1980, contains essays by Poblete (pp. 41–54) and Berryman (pp. 55–86) that provide, respectively, further historical background and a spirited description of the conference itself. Berryman's notes and references (pp. 82–86) are very helpful.

For Gustavo's estimate of Puebla, see *PP*, chap. 6, "Liberation and the Poor: The Puebla Perspective" and citation in n. 7 above.

11. For primary source material on Nicaragua, see Rosset and Vandemeer, *Nicaragua: Unfinished Revolution*, Grove Press, New York, 1986. The fullest interpretive history is Gutman, *Banana Diplomacy: The Making of American Foreign Policy in Nicaragua, 1981–1987*, Simon and Schuster, New York, 1988. For an overview of issues created by the U.S. pressure on Nicaragua, see Dickey, *With the Contras*, Simon and Schuster, New York, 1985. For documented accounts of contra atrocities, see Cabestrero, *Blood of the Innocent*, Orbis, 1985, and Brody, ed., *Contra Terror in Nicaragua*, South End Press, Boston, 1985.

For a careful theological statement of the relation of Christianity and Marxism in the Nicaraguan struggle, see the important study by Giulio Girardi, *Faith and Revolution in Nicaragua: Convergence and Contradictions*, Orbis, 1989, a translation of the second half of *Sandinismo, Marxismo, Cristianismo: La Confluencia*, Valdivieso Center, Managua, 1987. Personal testimonies dealing with the issue are contained in Margaret Randall, *Christians in the Nicaraguan Revolution*, New Star Books, Vancouver, 1983, and Teófilo Cabestrero, *Revolutionaries for the Gospel: Testimonies of Fifteen Christians in the Nicaraguan Government*, Orbis, 1986.

On the position taken by Frs. d'Escoto, Fernando Cardenal, and Ernesto Cardenal, see Cabestrero, ed., *Ministers of God, Ministers of the People: Testimonies of Faith from Nicaragua*, Orbis, 1983, foreword by Robert McAfee Brown, which consists of interviews with the three priests. Hennelly includes the moving letter of Fernando Cardenal, written to his friends after the Vatican disciplined him, as document #36.

McGovern describes the Nicaraguan situation in chapter 9. See also the sympathetic essay by César Jerez, "Gustavo Gutiérrez: A Friend of Nicaragua," in *Festschrift*, pp. 59–64.

12. For details of the Boff story, see the full account by Harvey Cox, *The Silencing of Leonardo Boff*, Meyer-Stone Books, Oak Park, Ill., 1988. McGovern devotes considerable space to the controversy in chapter 11, and Hennelly includes texts of the charges against Boff and his reply as documents #48–49.

13. Another way to trace the story of the years from the close of the Vatican

Council to the present, and Gustavo's role in them, is to read five volumes, published by CEP, Lima, that gather together documents from individuals, groups, church meetings and conferences all over Latin America, to illustrate what was happening to *the people*. Only the first of these (*Between Honesty and Hope*, Maryknoll Documentation Series, 1970) has appeared in English. The sequence of the titles provides a helpful clue to changing moods within each period:

Signos de renovación [Signs of renewal], 1966–1969
Signos de liberación [Signs of liberation], 1969–1973
Signos de lucha y esperanza [Signs of struggle and hope], 1973–1978
Signos de vida y fidelidad [Signs of life and faithfulness], 1978–1982
Signos de nueva evangelización [Signs of a new evangelization], 1983–1987

Gustavo contributes an introductory essay to each volume, summing up his own assessment of the events of the period. The first three of these are available in English in *PP*, as chaps. 2, 3, and 4, respectively. The introduction to *Signos de liberación*, "Liberation Praxis and Christian Faith," is also in Gibellini, *Frontiers*, pp. 1–32.

2. An Individual Biography of One Author of Liberation Theology

1. Material in this section is derived from an interview in *Latinamerica Press*, May 10, 1984, pp. 3–6, 8, and personal conversations with Gustavo and François Houtart. See also Frei Betto's engaging essay, "Gustavo Gutiérrez: A Friendly Profile," in *Festschrift*, pp. 31–37, and Sergio Torres, "Gustavo Gutiérrez: A Historical Sketch," in ibid., pp. 95–101.

2. The comments on both Mariátegui and Arguedas are indebted in large part to the excellent book by Curt Cadorette. See also the comments of Stephen Judd about both Mariátegui and Arguedas, "Gustavo Gutiérrez and the Originality of the Peruvian Experience," in *Festschrift*, pp. 68–76. The essay by Michael Candaleria is "José Carlos Mariátegui: Forgotten Forerunner of Liberation Theology," *Christian Century*, October 14, 1987, pp. 885–87. One of Mariátegui's books is available in English, *Seven Interpretive Essays on Peruvian Reality*, University of Texas Press, Austin, 1988.

3. On Arguedas, see Cadorette, pp. 67–75, and his essay, "Peru and the Mystery of Liberation," in *Festschrift*, pp. 49–58. See also Greider, "Crossing Deep Rivers: The Narrative Poetics of José María Arguedas in Light of Liberation Theology," doctoral dissertation, Graduate Theological Union, Berkeley, California. Gustavo's essay on Arguedas, "Entre las calandrias," is in Trigo, *Arguedas: mito, historia y religión*, CEP, Lima, 1982. The only novel of Arguedas in English is *Deep Rivers*, University of Texas Press, Austin, 1978, which will repay (and require) careful reading.

The following are only a sampling of explicit references to Arguedas in Gustavo's books: *TheoLib*, pp. vi, vii, 111 (195), 154 (269), 176, n.6; *LibChange*, p. 93; *PP*, pp. 19, 21, 204; *Wells*, pp. 21, 139, 152; *Job*, xi, xv–xvii, 105, 106.

4. In the published version of this talk, the autobiographical dimension is not retained (cf. *Fe cristiana y cambio social in América latina*, Ediciones Sigueme, Salamanca, 1973, pp. 231–45; esp. pp. 232–35), but José Míguez Bonino, a Protestant theologian who was at the meetings, took notes, and between his brief reconstruction (in Torres and Eagleson, eds., *Theology in the Americas*, Orbis, 1976, p.

278) and the published text itself we can recapture the personal thrust of Gustavo's comments. Portions of the address are also available in English in "Praxis of Liberation and Christian Faith," Mexican-American Cultural Center, San Antonio, 1976, and as "The Hope of Liberation," in Anderson and Stransky, eds., *Mission Trends No. 3*, Paulist/Eerdmans, New York and Grand Rapids, 1976, pp. 64–69.

5. Material in this section is taken from Broderick, *Camilo Torres: A Biography of the Priest-Guerillero*, Doubleday, Garden City, N.Y., 1985, pp. 150, 157–58; Guzman, *Camilo Torres*, Sheed and Ward, New York, 1969; and conversations with Gustavo.

6. Oliveros, *Liberación y teología*, CEP, Lima, 1977, includes an account of the meeting at Petrópolis, and reports that Gustavo's presentation was "the most substantive of the conference." His report of the meetings is available in English in Hennelly as Document #4.

7. Surprisingly, this watershed speech had never been translated or appeared in print, until Hennelly incorporated it as document #7—an important gift to the theological world.

8. An excelleñt account of the background documents, the maneuvers leading up to the conference, the major addresses, and the Final Document itself (pp. 160–75), is John Eagleson, ed., *Christians and Socialism: Documentation of the Christians for Socialism Movement in Latin America*, Orbis, 1975. Assmann et al., *Cristianos por el Socialismo: Exigencias de una opción*, Iglesia y Sociedad, Montevideo, 1973, is a series of appraisals in Spanish. Hennelly includes the Final Document as Document #14.

9. On Puebla, see chapter 1, notes 9 and 10.

10. The best and fullest treatment of Romero is James Brockman, *The Word Remains: A Life of Oscar Romero*, Orbis, 1982, recently expanded and republished as *Romero: A Life*, Orbis, 1989. A briefer account is Plácido Erdozaín, *Archbishop Romero: Martyr of Salvador*, Orbis, 1981, with an interpretive Foreword by Jorge Lara-Braud. Brockman has also edited a beautiful collection of excerpts from Romero's letters, interviews, sermons, and articles, *The Violence of Love: The Pastoral Wisdom of Archbishop Oscar Romero*, Harper and Row, New York, 1988. Hennelly includes material about Romero in documents #27, 28, and 30. An indispensable collection of Romero's public statements, together with his four major pastoral letters (whose importance far transcends the immediate circumstances of their creation) is Romero, *Voice of the Voiceless*, Orbis, 1985.

For the overall context of Romero's ministry, see Berrymañ, *The Religious Roots of Rebellion: Christians in Central American Revolutions*, Orbis, 1984, esp. pp. 91–161, and 271–72.

11. Material on the return visit to Lyons is taken from the first part of *Truth*.

3. Act One: Commitment to the Poor

1. Data is available from many sources. The figures cited here are chiefly drawn from the *New York Times*, March 29, 1988, section 4, p. 1, citing information released by the Worldwatch Institute; Cadorette; McGovern, *Marxism: An American Christian Perspective*, Orbis, 1980; and Berryman, *The Religious Roots of Rebellion*, Orbis, 1984. The McCoy article cited is "Popular Religion in Latin America," *America*, December 31, 1988, pp. 533–36.

2. See *TheoLib*, chap. 13, "Poverty, Solidarity, and Protest," pp. 162–73 (287–306). See also the section on "The Meaning of Poverty," in Gustavo's analysis of the "Preliminary Document" for Puebla, *PP*, pp. 114–15.

3. Some analyses make views of development go hand in hand with "dependency theory," a tool of social analysis initially used by liberation theologians but now virtually ignored. See further the discussion in chapter 4 on "Theology and the Social Sciences."

4. Because *praxis* is such a central — and misunderstood — concept, a brief bibliography follows:

Casalis, Georges, *Correct Ideas Don't Fall From the Skies*, Orbis, 1984.
   A series of independent essays arguing for the emergence of "correct ideas" from the social sciences.
Freire, Paulo, *Pedagogy of the Oppressed*, Herder and Herder, New York, 1972.
   The most important single work. Difficult reading, and must be absorbed slowly, but essential; *The Politicals of Education*, Bergin and Garvey, South Hadley, Mass., 1985. Independent essays that illumine various aspects of praxis.
Gramsci, Antonio, *Letters from Prison*, ed. Lawner, Harper Colophon, New York, 1973.
   Reflections on "the philosophy of praxis" and the relation of thought to action, by one who was an important influence on Gustavo.
Holland, Joe, and Henriot, Peter, *Social Analysis: Linking Faith and Justice*, Orbis, 1983.
   The best single treatment of relating praxis to the United States social scene.
Hoffman, John, *Marxism and the Theory of Praxis*, International Publishers, New York, 1975.
   An introduction by an orthodox Marxist. See esp. chaps. 1, 2, 8–10.
Lamb, Matthew, *Solidarity with Victims: Toward a Theology of Social Transformation*, Crossroad, New York, 1982.
   Difficult but important reading on the relation of theory and practice in contemporary theology.
Metz, Johann Baptist, *Faith in History and Society: Toward a Practical Fundamental Theology*, Seabury, New York, 1980.
   Reflections on praxis by one of the few German theologians to take liberation theology seriously. See esp. pp. 44–88.
Tracy, David, *Blessed Rage for Order*, Seabury, New York, 1975; *The Analogical Imagination*, Crossroad, New York, 1981; *Plurality and Ambiguity*, Harper and Row, New York, 1987.
   Up-to-date reflections on praxis by a North American Roman Catholic theologian.

5. It is significant that Gustavo requested that the first study by the Bartolomé de Las Casas Institute deal with women in the culture. The result was Carmen Lora, *Woman: Victim of Oppression, Bearer of Tradition*. It is also significant that of the substantive contributions to the *Festschrift* for Gustavo, a third are by women. See particularly the contributions of Bidegain, "Women and the Theology of Liberation," pp. 105–20; Schüssler Fiorenza, "The Politics of Otherness," pp. 311–25; Heyward, "Doing Theology in a Counterrevolutionary Situation," pp. 397–409; Isasi-Díaz, "*Mujeristas*: A Name of Our Own," pp. 410–19; Mananzan, "Theological Perspectives of a Religious Woman Today," pp. 420–32; and particularly Bingemer, "Women in the Future of the Theology of Liberation," pp. 473–90.

Tamez, *Against Machismo*, Meyer-Stone Books, Oak Park, Ill., 1987, is a series of interviews with male theologians in Latin America on how they perceive the role of women. See also the report in chap. 11 of the women's conference sponsored by EATWOT. Tamez has edited a volume of essays by Latin American women, *Through Her Eyes: Women's Theology from Latin America*, Orbis, 1989.

6. See West, Guidote, Coakley, eds., *Theology in the Americas: Detroit II Conference Papers*, Orbis Probe edition, 1982, pp. 80–84.

4. Act Two, Scene One: Theology as Critical Reflection on Praxis

1. While the portions of *Job* we are about to examine are Gustavo's most sustained treatment of "God-talk," several earlier writings are also important. In *El Diós de la vida*, talks originally given in Lima in 1981, he has already arrived *in nuce* at many of the themes developed more fully in *Job*. See especially chap. 3, "Desde la Práctica y la Contemplación," pp. 63–93. He also explored the same theme at the EATWOT Conference in New Delhi in 1981, in "Reflections from a Latin American Perspective: Finding Our Way to Talk About God," Fabella and Torres, eds., *Irruption of the Third World: Challenge to Theology*, Orbis, 1983, pp. 222–34. The same basic approach to God-talk governs his essay "Theology and the Social Sciences," in *Truth*. An extensively expanded version of *El Diós de la vida*, to be published in Spanish in 1990, carries the implications of this starting point into many areas not touched upon in the earlier version.

See Haight, "The Logic of the Christian Response to Social Suffering," in *Festschrift*, pp. 139–53, for an extended commentary on material in *Job*.

2. Gustavo frequently deals with the theme of "the two interlocutors." The fullest treatment is in "Theology from the Underside of History," *PP*, chap. 7, pp. 169–221, along with the final chapter, "The Limitations of Modern Theology: On a Letter of Dietrich Bonhoeffer," ibid., pp. 222–34, an appreciative account of what Bonhoeffer was trying to do in his own situation. Much of the material in "Theology from the Underside of History" is included in *LibChange*, pp. 60–94, and in "Liberation Theology and Proclamation," Geffré, pp. 57–77.

See also "Two Theological Perspectives: Liberation Theology and Progressivist Theology," in *Emergent*, pp. 227–55, and "The Historical Power of the Poor," the introduction to *Signos de lucha y esperanza*, available in English in *PP*, pp. 75–107.

3. See the materials cited in note 2, above, with special emphasis on "Theology from the Underside of History," originally published as a separate pamphlet ("Teología desde el reverso de la historia," CEP, Lima, 1977), a full and magnificently documented account of tendencies, trends, strengths, and weaknesses of the various attempts of "dominant theology" over four centuries to adjust to new currents of thought and action that characterized the First World theological scene.

4. Gustavo's chief analyses of Metz are in *TheoLib*, pp. 126–30 (220–25); *LibChange*, pp. 57–59; and *PP*, 182–83. In addition to the responses cited in the text, Metz has recently continued his dialogue with liberation theology in "Theology in the Struggle for History and Society," *Festschrift*, pp. 165–71. A similar exchange has been conducted by Jürgen Moltmann and José Míguez Bonino; see Hennelly, document #19.

5. The essay "Theology and the Social Sciences" was originally published in *Páginas*, September 1984, pp. 4–15. It draws on writings that date back to a con-

ference in 1974 — a full decade earlier — and thus represents a matured theological position rather than an eleventh-hour attempt to placate the Sacred Congregation, as some critics have charged. See *Liberación: diálogos en al CELAM*, Bogotá, 1974, esp. pp. 68–85, 87–92, 157–59, and 228–29. The essay is now available in English as the second part of *Truth*.

6. Some critics have made the presumed reliance of liberation theologians on "dependency theory" the main prong of their attack. But they have tried to reduce this solely to a matter of economics, and have failed to discern the degree to which, quite apart from economics, Latin Americans *are* victims of psychic, political, and military "dependency." The matter is extensively discussed in McGovern, chaps. 6 and 8, and he has provided a helpful summary of the issues in "Dependency Theory, Marxist Analysis, and Liberation Theology," in *Festschrift*, pp. 272–86. Note also the careful way Gustavo relates individual instances of social analysis to an overall methodology that critically uses many contributions from the social sciences.

7. This is a point Gustavo had already emphasized on the first page of *TheoLib*, p. xiii, and at the 1974 CELAM meetings noted above.

5. Act Two, Scene Two: Theology in the Light of the Word of God

1. See *TheoLib*, anniversary edition, pp. xvii–xliv. The phrase "expanding the view" comes from one of the last utterances of Pope John XXIII: "It is not that the gospel has changed; it is that we have begun to understand it better. ... The moment has come to discern the signs of the times, to seize the opportunity and to *expand the view*" (pp. xlv–xlvi).

2. The point is important enough for Gustavo to insist on it on three separate occasions in *TheoLib*: pp. 23–25 (36–37), 103–4 (176–77), and 137 (235). There is also a more lengthy treatment of the theme in *Truth* that will be summarized in chapter 6.

3. As we have already seen, this theme is not an "add-on" to Gustavo's agenda, inserted late in the day to forestall the critics, but has been there from the first. The section "A Spirituality of Liberation" in the first edition of *TheoLib*, pp. 203–8, is only one example.

4. The best summation of Gustavo's theological position is, of course, *TheoLib*, but there are also a number of shorter essays that furnish summaries of his theology as a whole. See Appendix I for examples.

5. I have traced this process in more detail in "How Vatican II Discovered the Bible," *National Catholic Reporter*, October 21, 1988, pp. 12, 14, in which I argue that Gustavo's strong biblical orientation makes him one of the most faithful inheritors of the outlook of Vatican II.

One of liberation theology's most enduring contributions will be the way it has forced all Christians to read the Bible in a new way. Out of an immense literature, the following at least must be noted and commended for further study:

Carlos Mesters, *Defenseless Flower: A New Reading of the Bible*, Orbis, 1989, is a firsthand description of the effect of the Bible in the base communities. José Miranda, *Marx and the Bible*, Orbis, 1974, was a ground-breaking work relating the biblical message to issues of social justice. Norman Gottwald, ed., *The Bible and Liberation: Political and Social Hermeneutics*, Orbis, 1983, is an important collection of essays applying the methods of sociological interpretation to the Bible, the relation of the Bible to Marxist thought, etc. George Pixley, *The Exodus: A Liberation Perspective*, Orbis, 1987, is a careful study of the full text of a book that has been central to liberation concerns. Thomas Hanks, *God So Loved the Third World; The Bible, the Reformation, and Liberation Theologies*, Orbis, 1983, deals with the theme of oppression throughout the Bible, and then relates Isaiah to the contemporary world. Elsa Tamez, *Bible of the Oppressed*, Orbis, 1982, is a thorough exegetical study of oppression and the "good news of liberation." Of a more technical nature are Severino Croatto, *Exodus: A Hermeneutic of Freedom*, Orbis, 1981, and *Biblical Hermeneutics*, Orbis, 1987.

The clearest example of using liberation perspectives for interpreting the Bible on the North American scene is Ched Myers's massive *Binding the Strong Man: A Political Reading of Mark's Story of Jesus*, Orbis, 1988.

6. For examples of Gustavo's use of scripture, see the indices of *TheoLib*, pp. 257–60 (309–12), and *Job*, pp. 133–66. See also his detailed exegesis of such themes in *TheoLib* as: the relation of creation and salvation (pp. 86–91 [150–60]), eschatology (pp. 91–97 [160–68]), humanity as the "temple of God" (pp. 106–110 [190–96]), Jesus' parable of the last judgment (pp. 112–16 [196–203]), poverty (pp. 165–73 [291–99]), and, of course, the detailed textual exegesis throughout Job. The expanded edition of *El Diós de la vida*, not yet available in English, contains exegetical treatments of many biblical passages. See Appendix I.

McGovern provides an extended treatment of Gustavo's use of the Bible in chapter 4. Material in the rest of the present section on the Bible is from *PP*, chap. 1.

7. See further "The Irruption of the Poor in Latin America and the Christian Communities of the Common People" in Torres and Eagleson, eds., *The Challenge of Basic Christian Communities*, Orbis, 1981, pp. 107–23. On the theme of idolatry and false gods from a Latin American perspective, see Richard et al., *The Idols of Death and the God of Life*, Orbis, 1983, with an all-star cast of contributors.

8. See "God's Revelation and Proclamation in History," in *PP*, pp. 12–16.

9. Because the base communities are one of the most distinctive features of liberation theology, a more extended bibliography is offered here:

Overall works: Barreiro, *Basic Ecclesial Communities: The Evangelization of the Poor*, Orbis, 1982, is particularly good on biblical foundations. Cook, *The Expectation of the Poor: Latin American Basic Ecclesial Communities in Protestant Perspective*, Orbis, 1985, is the fullest study yet made. Mesters, *Defenseless Flower* (see note 5, above) indicates the role of the Bible in the base communities. Pastoral Team of Bambamarca, *Vamos Caminando: A Peruvian Catechism*, Orbis, 1977, is an example of the kinds of teaching materials that emerge in the life of a base community. Torres and Eagleson, eds., *The Challenge of Basic Christian Communities*, Orbis, 1981, offers reflections from one of the EATWOT conferences, dealing with base communities throughout the Third World.

Works on wider topics that put the base communities in context: Phillip Berryman, *Liberation Theology: Essential Facts about the Revolutionary Movement in Latin America and Beyond*, Pantheon Books, New York, 1987, is especially valuable because it *begins* with the direct experience of the poor and the emergence of the base communities. Berryman follows the same procedure in his much larger *The Religious Roots of Rebellion*. Leonardo Boff, *Church: Charism and Power: Liberation Theology and the Institutional Church*, Crossroad, New York, 1985, contains several essays about the base communities (which got him into trouble with Rome), esp.

chaps. 7–10. Bruneau, "Basic Christian Communities in Latin America," in Levine, *Churches and Politics in Latin America*, Sage, Beverly Hills, 1980, is an overall survey concentrating on Brazil. Schipani, *Religious Education Encounters Liberation Theology*, Religious Education Press, Birmingham, 1988, deals with the base communities in chapter 5. Richard Shaull, *Heralds of a New Reformation: The Poor of South and North America*, Orbis, 1984, one of the most important books of overall interpretation, deals with base communities in chap. 8. McGovern devotes the whole of chapter 10 to the base communities, under the intriguing title, "A New Way of Being Church." A valuable pamphlet in Spanish by Frei Betto, "¿Que es la comunidad ecclesial de base?," Centro Ecuménico Antonio Valdivieso, Managua, n.d., offers a description of the Brazilian experience "from within."

10. Berryman, *The Religious Roots of Rebellion*, pp. 10ff., has a fascinating series of parallels between biblical stories and contemporary stories. I have developed the theme of "Reading the Bible with Third World Eyes" in *Unexpected News*, Westminster, Philadelphia, 1984.

11. For stylistic convenience we will use the term "base communities," although the more accurate descriptive rendering might be "Christian base communities" or "ecclesial base communities." The usual descriptive Spanish term is "comunidades ecclesiales de base," and the resultant ancronym CEB.

The term "base" is, of course, susceptible to a variety of meanings. Here it means "basic," in the sense of dealing with fundamentals, and "base" in the sense of the base of a pyramid—i.e., the bottom, which is where most of the people of the communities are located in a stratified society. Opponents of the base communities no doubt employ a third, and pejorative, meaning of the term.

12. The balance of the chapter just summarized deals with "Faith and Social Conflict," and pursues such controversial themes as "class struggle" in the life of the church, material we have previously explored.

13. In *TheoLib* Gustavo treats the topics of this section *before* developing his theology of the church, in order to start with the human situation to which the church must then respond. I have reversed the sequence here to stress the intimate connection between the base communities and the church as a whole.

14. See *TheoLib*, p. 82 (146). The importance of these chapters is further underlined by the centrality they give to the themes of the book's subtitle: "History, Politics, and Salvation."

15. The balance of the chapter deals with "A Spirituality of Liberation," which we have already explored.

6. The Plot Thickens: Some Unscripted Entrances, or Gustavo under Attack

1. The article by Lefever is "Liberation Theology as a Utopian Heresy," *Face to Face, an Interreligious Bulletin,* Winter 1987, pp. 18–20. McCann's review is in *Commonweal,* November 4, 1988. Novak's comments are in *Will It Liberate?,* Paulist Press, Mahwah, N.J., 1986. The excerpts from the Santa Fe Document are cited in Nouwen, *¡Gracias!,* Harper and Row, New York, 1983. The Neuhaus quotation is in Schall, ed., *Liberation Theology in Latin America,* Ignatius Press, San Francisco, 1982, p. 395, italics added. Gustavo's comments on "domestication" are in Gibellini, *Frontiers of Theology in Latin America,* Orbis, 1979, pp. 33 and 23, respectively. The image in this quotation is also found in *PP,* p. 64, and *LibChange,* p. 86.

McGovern deals with critics of liberation theology throughout his book, but gives special attention in chapter 5 to three groups: Latin Americans (López Trujillo and Roger Vekemans), Europeans (the Vatican International Theological Commission and Cardinal Ratzinger), and North Americans (Thomas Sanders, Dennis McCann, Richard Neuhaus, and Schubert Ogden). See also the discussion in Ferm, *Third World Liberation Theologies: An Introductory Survey*, Orbis, 1986, chap. 5, "Liberation Theology and Its Critics," for a useful survey of the conventional attacks.

2. The full text is in Hennelly, document #37.

3. Conservative criticism of Gustavo in Peru has been relentless. Oliveros, *Liberación y teologia: génesis y crecimiento de una reflexión 1966–1977*, CEP, Lima, 1977, gives an account of both Latin American and European attacks in part 3. A sampling of individual critiques, in addition to that of López Trujillo, cited in chapter 1, note 8, includes Juan Gutiérrez Gonzalez, *Teología de la Liberación, Evaporación de la Teología*, Editorial La Cruz, Mexico, 1975, and Ricardo Durand Flores, S.J., *Observaciones a Teología de la Liberación*, Obispada del Callao, Callao, Peru, 1985. The last title is particularly important since Durand is successor to Cardinal Landázuri as head of the Peruvian episcopal conference and thus has great power. A corporate attack is the "Declaration of Los Andes," issued in July 1985 at the height of the controversy with Rome, available in English in Hennelly, document #51. A spirited defense of Gustavo in response to the "Declaration" was made by Ronaldo Muñoz, available in Hennelly, document #52.

4. As far as I know, the document was never published. I received a copy through a source I have no intention of revealing.

5. The text of the *Concilium* statement is in Hennelly, document #44, and Rahner's letter is document #38. The statement from the faculty of the Pacific School of Religion is in the author's files.

6. The full text of the "Instruction" is in Hennelly, document #45. See the response in Juan Luis Segundo, *Theology and the Church: A Response to Cardinal Ratzinger and a Warning to the Whole Church*, Winston, Minneapolis, 1985.

7. The text is available in *Páginas*, November/December 1984. Frei Betto, a friend of Gustavo, queries whimsically, "Who can swear that the final text, more favorable to him than the initial draft, was not formulated by Gustavo's own pen?" (*Festschrift*, p. 33).

8. The full text is in Hennelly, document #53.

9. The text comprises well over half of the collection *Truth*.

10. McGovern, chaps. 6–8, and also his earlier *Marxism: An American Christian Perspective*, are the clearest and fairest treatments of the relation of Marxism to liberation theology, and should be consulted. From a Latin American perspective, see also Míguez Bonino, *Christians and Marxists: The Mutual Challenge to Revolution*, Eerdmans, Grand Rapids, 1976.

In light of the inordinate fear that Marxism evokes among U.S. readers, the following brief comments are offered:

(1) If a descriptive category (like "class struggle") describes what is happening in the world, it must be taken seriously even if Karl Marx said it; if a descriptive category (like "human perfectibility") does not accurately describe what is happening in the world, it need not be taken seriously, even if a theologian said it.

(2) The presence of an idea in the Bible (like "liberty for the oppressed") is not invalidated because Karl Marx affirmed it 1800 years later.

(3) Certain parts of Marxist analysis can be affirmed without affirming the whole

Marxist philosophy. (This is perhaps the biggest single difference between liberation theologians and the Sacred Congregation.)

(4) "A social mortgage has been placed on all private property," was not said by Karl Marx but by Pope John Paul II.

In response to claims of the Sacred Congregation that violence is an inevitable consequence of Marxist social analysis, the following comments are offered:

(1) The issue of violence in relation to liberation theology is usually imposed by thinkers from outside. It is not the center of Latin American debate, for it is not a realistic option for most oppressed (and unarmed) people.

(2) The human situation is *already* violent, not only because of repression and terrorism, but because of injustice, unemployment, malnutrition, and starvation — all of them "violent" realities.

(3) Gustavo distinguishes three kinds of violence: (a) the *institutionalized violence* of the present order, (b) the *repressive violence* that defends institutionalized violence, and (c) the *counterviolence* to which Christians may sometimes feel forced in the face of massive injustice.

(4) Appeals to counterviolence are morally appropriate only when all other means to bring about social change have failed.

(See further on these themes, Brown, *Religion and Violence,* second edition, Westminster, Philadelphia, 1987.)

7. Act Three: Some Scripted Entrances, or What Liberation Theology Means for Us

1. Torres recounts the origins of EATWOT in "Dar-es-Salaam 1976" in Boff and Elizondo, eds., *Theologies of the Third World: Convergences and Differences,* T & T Clark, Edinburgh, 1988 (*Concilium* #199), pp. 107–15. Bingemer describes the ten-year General Assembly at Oaxtepec, Mexico, in 1986, in "Third World Theologies: Conversion to Others," in ibid., pp. 116–23. Gibellini, in *The Liberation Theology Debate,* Orbis, 1988, traces the history of EATWOT in chapter 4, "Doing Theology in a Divided World."

Full reports of the EATWOT conferences, described briefly in the text, are contained in the following:

Torres and Fabella, eds., *The Emergent Gospel: Theology from the Underside of History,* Orbis, 1978.

A report on the Dar-es-Salaam conference, August 5–12, 1970. Gustavo's contribution is "Two Theological Perspectives: Liberation Theology and Progressivist Theology," pp. 227–55.

Appiah-Kubi and Torres, eds., *African Theology en Route,* Orbis, 1979.

A report on the Accra conference, December 17–23, 1977.

Fabella, ed., *Asia's Struggle for Full Humanity: Toward a Relevant Theology,* Orbis, 1980.

A report on the Asian Theological Conference, jointly sponsored with EATWOT, Sri Lanka, January 7–12, 1979.

Torres and Eagleson, eds., *The Challenge of the Basic Christian Communities,* Orbis, 1981.

A report on the conference in São Paulo, Brazil, February 20–March 2, 1980. Gustavo's contribution is "The Irruption of the Poor in Latin America and the Christian Communities of the Common People," pp. 107–23.

Fabella and Torres, eds., *Irruption of the Third World: Challenge to Theology,* Orbis, 1983.

A report on the New Delhi conference, August 17–29, 1981. Gustavo's contribution is "Reflections from a Latin American Perspective," pp. 222–34.

Fabella and Torres, eds., *Doing Theology in a Divided World,* Orbis, 1985.

A report on the Geneva conference, January 5–13, 1983, which also included First World theologians. (See Kirby, "Worlds in Dialogue," *Commonweal,* March 11, 1983, pp. 134–36).

Fabella and Oduyoye, eds., *With Passion and Compassion: Third World Women Doing Theology,* Orbis, 1988.

A selection of essays originating from regional meetings of women theologians from Africa, Asia, and Latin America.

The above listing suggests two conclusions: (1) EATWOT would never have made it without Virginia Fabella, and (2) many PhD theses are going to be ground out of all this material.

2. It is impossible to present an adequate bibliography for these various movements. The following are simply pointers:

For a "theology of struggle," emanating from the Philippines, see Cariño et al., *Theology, Politics, and Struggle,* National Council of Churches, Manila, 1986; Ed de la Torre, *Touching Ground, Taking Root; Theological and Political Reflections on the Philippine Struggle,* Socio-Pastoral Institute, Quezon City, 1986; Asedillo and Williams, eds., *Rice in the Storm: Faith and Struggle in the Philippines,* Friendship Press, New York, 1989.

Examples of Asian liberation theology are two books by Aloysius Pieris, a Sri Lankan, *Love Meets Wisdom,* Orbis, 1989, and *An Asian Theology of Liberation,* Orbis, 1988. Two writers coming from an Asian perspective who communicate particularly well to U.S. readers are C. S. Song, *Theology from the Womb of Asia,* Orbis, 1986, and Kosuke Koyama, *Mount Fuji and Mount Sinai: A Critique of Idols,* Orbis, 1985. See further the massive bibliography in Anderson, ed., *Asian Voices in Christian Theology,* Orbis, 1976, pp. 260–321.

For Minjung theology in Korea, see Christian Conference of Asia, *Minjung Theology: People as the Subjects of History,* Orbis, 1983, and Jung Young Lee, ed., *An Emerging Theology in World Perspective: Commentary on Korean Minjung Theology,* Twenty-Third Publications, Mystic, Conn., 1988.

For a Jewish theology of liberation, see Marc Ellis, *Toward a Jewish Theology of Liberation,* second edition, Orbis, 1989, a book that is opening new doors, and a Palestinian counterpart, Naim Ateek, *Justice and Only Justice: A Palestinian Theology of Liberation,* Orbis, 1989.

3. For black theology, see especially James Cone, *For My People: Black Theology and the Black Church,* Orbis, 1984; Gayraud Wilmore, *Black Religion and Black Radicalism,* second edition, Orbis, 1983; Cornel West, *Prophesy Deliverance!,* Westminster, Philadelphia, 1982; Wilmore and Cone, eds., *Black Theology: Key Documents and Shorter Writings, 1966–1979,* Orbis, 1979.

For feminist theology, see Rosemary Ruether, *Sexism and God-Talk,* Beacon Press, Boston, 1983; Carter Heyward, *The Redemption of God,* University of America Press, Washington, D.C., 1982; Letty Russell, *Household of Freedom: Authority in Feminist Theology,* Westminster, Philadelphia, 1987; Denise Carmody, *Feminism and Christianity: A Two-Way Reflection,* Abingdon, Nashville, 1982; Elisabeth Schüssler Fiorenza, *In Memory of Her: A Feminist Reconstruction of Christian Origins,*

Crossroad, New York, 1983. An important Asian contribution to feminist theology has been Marianne Katoppo, *Compassionate and Free: An Asian Woman's Theology,* Orbis, 1980. See also chapter 3, note 5, for feminist perspectives on liberation theology in *Festschrift.*

For Amerindian theology, see Vine Deloria, *God is Red,* Delta, New York, 1973, and interpretive material in Reist, *Theology in Red, White, and Black,* Westminster, Philadelphia, 1975. An appreciation of Amerindian spirituality can be gained from such writings as Neihardt, ed., *Black Elk Speaks,* University of Nebraska Press, Lincoln, 1988.

For gay and lesbian concerns, see Edwards, *Gay Liberation: A Biblical Perspective,* Pilgrim Press, Boston, 1984; Scroggs, *The New Testament and Homosexuality,* Fortress, Philadelphia, 1983. For a moving account of being refused ordination because of sexual orientation, see Glaser, *Uncommon Calling,* Harper and Row, San Francisco, 1988.

For a sense of the people behind the above theologies, see Ferm, *Profiles in Liberation; 36 Portraits of Third World Theologians,* Twenty-Third Publications, Mystic, Conn., 1988.

4. See *The Kairos Document: Challenge to the Church,* Eerdmans, Grand Rapids, 1986 (page references are to this edition). The text is also included in Logan, ed., *The Kairos Covenant: Standing with South African Christians,* Friendship Press, New York, and Meyer-Stone, Oak Park, Ill., 1988, with papers from a conference on the Kairos Document in Chicago, Illinois, in November 1986. For background on the situation in the churches in South Africa that produced the statement, see, among many others, Alan Boesak, *Black and Reformed,* Orbis, 1984, and *Comfort and Protest,* Westminster, Philadelphia, 1987; Charles Villa-Vicencio, *Trapped in Apartheid,* Orbis, 1988; Albert Nolan, *God in South Africa,* Eerdmans, Grand Rapids, 1988, and "Theology in a Prophetic Mode," in *Festschrift,* pp. 433–40; Frank Chikane, *No Life of My Own,* Orbis, 1989; and a detailed treatment of the relationship between South African and North American black theology: Dwight Hopkins, *Black Theology U.S.A. and South Africa: Politics, Culture, and Consciousness,* Orbis, 1989.

For the overall African scene, see Justin Ukpong, "Theological Literature from Africa," in Boff and Elizondo, eds., *Theologies of the Third World, Concilium,* T & T Clark, Edinburgh, 1988, pp. 67–75, and Ferm, *Third World Liberation Theologies,* Orbis, 1986, chapter 3.

5. *Kairos: Central America, A Challenge to the Churches of the World,* unpaged, is available from the New York Circus, Inc., P.O. Box 37, Times Square Station, New York, N.Y. 10108. A useful study guide to the document is available from The Inter-Religious Task Force on Central America, 475 Riverside Drive, Room 563, New York, N.Y. 10015.

6. The *Kairos* statement from the seven countries, "The Road to Damascus," is available from the Center of Concern, 3700 13th Street N.E., Washington, D.C. 20017.

7. See his *War against the Poor: Low-Intensity Conflict and Christian Faith,* Orbis, 1989. If it were possible to choose only one book to describe and document the sins of U.S. foreign policy, this would be the book.

8. This sentence cries out to be expanded, suggesting a variety of options in working for change. The most that can be done here is to suggest some of the literature that has been most challenging to the author in struggling with these issues:

In addition to the book by Nelson-Pallmeyer cited in note 7, above, his other writings pose serious issues for North American Christians, *Hunger for Justice: The Politics of Food and Faith,* Orbis, 1980, and *The Politics of Compassion: Hunger, The Arms Race, and U.S. Policy in Central America,* Orbis, 1986. Both books combine passion with well-documented evidence that must bring any sincere reader to new perceptions.

Four examples, out of many, that further document the folly of U.S. foreign policy, are Bonner, *Weakness and Deceit: U.S. Policy in El Salvador,* Times Books, New York, 1984; Bonner, *Waltzing with a Dictator: The Marcoses and the Making of American Policy,* Vintage Books, New York, 1988; Cockburn, *Out of Control,* Atlantic Monthly Press, New York, 1987, "the story of the Reagan administration's secret war in Nicaragua, the illegal arms pipeline, and the contra drug connection"; and LaFeber, *Inevitable Revolutions: The United States in Central America,* Norton, New York, expanded edition, 1984, in which the effects of American foreign policy in Central America over the last century are portrayed with consummate skill. For those who wonder why the United States is not loved by Central Americans, LaFeber's review of the dreary history of imperialistic diplomacy will put their perplexity to rest. The need for liberation from such oppression is painfully clear after reading his sobering and responsible chronicle.

Tabb, ed., *Churches in Struggle: Liberation Theologies and Social Change in North America,* Monthly Review Press, New York, 1986, contains essays and responses suggesting how individuals and churches can work for change. Among the most practical and direct books are Marie Augusta Neal, *A Socio-Theology of Letting Go: The Role of a First World Church Facing Third World Peoples,* Paulist Press, New York, 1977, and *The Just Demands of the Poor: Essays in Socio-Theology,* Paulist Press, New York, 1987, both developing the theme that relinquishment is the message of the gospel for North Americans. Among the most challenging books are Richard Shaull, *Heralds of a New Reformation,* Orbis, 1984, and *Naming the Idols: Biblical Alternatives for U.S. Foreign Policy,* Meyer-Stone, Oak Park, Ill., 1988. Shaull combines biblical exploration with contemporary demands for justice in ways that are initially disquieting but ultimately liberating. Chapter 10 in the latter work, "Exposing and Overcoming Idolatry," should be required reading for all inhabitants of the twentieth century.

Wheaton and Shank, *Empire and the Word: Prophetic Parallels between the Exilic Experience and Central America's Crisis,* EPICA Task Force, Washington, 1988, is a radically disconcerting combination of biblical exegesis and social analysis. An account of one attempt by North American churches to break with demonic principalities and powers and side with the victims is Golden and McConnell, *Sanctuary: The New Underground Railroad,* Orbis, 1986.

Another approach, less radical but no less important, has been that of the U.S. Roman Catholic bishops, whose two pastoral letters on nuclear weapons and the economy have stirred widespread discussion and created some existential discomfort in high places. A splendid review of the history and substance of these documents is Phillip Berryman, *Our Unfinished Business: The U.S. Catholic Bishops' Letters on Peace and the Economy,* Pantheon Books, New York, 1989. The texts of the two letters are available from the U.S. Catholic Conference, in Washington, D.C. An appraisal of these and other statements on social justice issues by religious bodies (Protestant, Catholic, and Jewish) is Brown and Brown, eds., *A Cry for Justice: The Churches and Synagogues Speak,* Paulist Press, Mahwah, N.J., 1989.

Evans, Evans, and Kennedy, *Pedagogies for the Non-Poor,* Orbis, 1987, explores the challenge of transformative education for the non-poor that would break down "the ideology of privilege." Holland and Henriot, *Social Analysis,* Orbis, 1983, delivers important insights for fulfilling the concerns of the subtitle, *Linking Faith and Justice.* King, Maynard, and Woodyard, *Risking Liberation,* John Knox Press, Atlanta, 1988, deliberately addresses itself to middle-class concerns and possibilities from the perspectives of economics, sociology, anthropology, and theology.

Emerging from all of these writings is a realization that North Americans still have to take more seriously than they have the radical thrust of such articles as Dorothee Sölle, "Resistance: Toward a First World Theology," *Christianity and Crisis,* July 23, 1979, pp. 178–81.

9. A theologically responsible challenge to capitalism, is Ulrich Duchrow, *Global Economy: A Confessional Issue for the Churches?,* World Council of Churches, Geneva, 1987. Arguing that the churches are already breaking ranks with apartheid and nuclear weapons, he indicates that the same logic must force a showdown between Christianity and capitalism. I have reviewed the book in "Global Realities, Local Theologies," *Christianity and Crisis,* February 15, 1988, pp. 45–46.

Index of Concepts and Titles

Index of Names